AF801826

VIEWERS IN DISTRESS

VIEWERS IN DISTRESS

Race, Gender, Religion, and Avant-Garde Performance at the Turn of the Twenty-First Century

Stefka G. Mihaylova

University of Michigan Press
Ann Arbor

Published in the United States of America by the
University of Michigan Press
Manufactured in the United States of America
Printed on acid-free paper
First published July 2023

A CIP catalog record for this book is available from the British Library.

Library of Congress Cataloging-in-Publication data has been applied for.

ISBN 978-0-472-07632-1 (hardcover : alk. paper)
ISBN 978-0-472-05632-3 (paper : alk. paper)
ISBN 978-0-472-90370-2 (open access ebook)

DOI: https://doi.org/10.3998/mpub.11504996

The University of Michigan Press's open access publishing program is made possible thanks to additional funding from the University of Michigan Office of the Provost and the generous support of contributing libraries.

FOR LUKE

Acknowledgments

In writing this book, I have relied on the generosity of many people. I want to begin by acknowledging the work of the anonymous readers for the University of Michigan Press who read the book with immense care, providing extensive and constructive comments. One of them thoroughly annotated the entire manuscript. Because of their efforts this book is much better than it would have been without them. I am also grateful to the University of Michigan Press's editor LeAnn Fields, who supported me through every stage of the publishing process.

The conception of this book emerged when Odai Johnson suggested that I develop a graduate seminar about the historical avant-garde in my first year as faculty at the University of Washington's School of Drama. Teaching this seminar led me to rethink my dissertation—about the politics of gender and race in contemporary performance—in terms of the histories and theories of the avant-gardes. Conversations with colleagues from various departments, who I met through the Center for Performance Studies and the Simpson Center for the Humanities, sustained me with rigorous questions. Equally significant have been conversations with colleagues from other institutions. My fellow members of the Feminist Research Group at the International Federation for Theatre Research offered valuable feedback to early articulations of what became book chapters, as did colleagues at the conferences of the American Society for Theatre Research, including, crucially, Elin Diamond, Julia A. Walker, and Mike Sell, among others.

At the School of Drama, my home department, I had many fruitful informal conversations with Deborah Trout, a professor of costume design, and Jeffrey Fracé, a professor of acting, who talked to me about the ways in which the avant-gardes have inspired their artistic practices. Lynn Thomas, a historian who served as an interim chair of the School of Drama, and our divisional dean, performance scholar Catherine Cole, offered mentorship and support at a crucial moment of this book's development, as did Scott Magelssen, my colleague from the PhD program at the School of Drama, and our current chair, Geoff Korf. Thank you, also, to my graduate students Catherine Heiner, who helped prepare the manuscript for submission to the press, and Amna Farooqi, who helped obtain permissions for the illustrations.

Though this book has traveled far from my dissertation, I remain indebted to my dissertation committee at Northwestern University—Tracy C. Davis, Susan Manning, Christopher Lane, and Jennifer Brody—who encouraged my curiosity about contemporary performance and my comparatist tendencies and tried to cultivate analytical rigor in my work.

Following graduation, I have continued to rely on Tracy C. Davis, my former dissertation chair, for intellectual inspiration. Her high criteria have guided me in working on this book, however imperfect the result may be. I am equally grateful to my friend and colleague Ann Folino White, who was part of my cohort in graduate school. Throughout our friendship, Ann and I have gone together through many academic rites of passage, including qualifying exams and dissertation defense. She continued standing by me as I worked on this book. Tracy and Ann's faith in the worthiness of this project carried me through when my own faith was lacking.

I am also very grateful to Kornelia Slavova, a professor and translator of American drama at Sofia University and my MA thesis advisor, for introducing me to American drama. To this day, whenever Kornelia speaks about American drama, I wonder why anyone would do anything else but write, stage, translate, or study it.

Finally, thank you to my partner Luke Haddock for standing by me throughout this process. Though he is not a scholar, Luke, more than any scholar I know, believes in the ability of theater scholarship to enrich life. This book is for him.

Work on this book was supported by a Society of Scholars Research Fellowship from the Simpson Center for the Humanities and a Royalty Research Fund Fellowship at the University of Washington.

Contents

Digital materials related to this title can be found on the Fulcrum platform via the following citable URL: https://doi.org/10.3998/mpub.11504996

Illustrations

Introduction

"CAN WE ALL GET ALONG?"

THE ARGUMENT

In May 1992, amid the unrest that shook Los Angeles following the acquittal of four police officers who had brutally beaten him during his arrest, Rodney King appeared on television asking for an end to the violent protests. "Can we all get along?" he pleaded. His question became one of the most quoted lines associated with the Los Angeles riots.

Thirty years later, King's words resonate with the paradoxes of the 1990s. The last decade of the twentieth century began optimistically. In November 1989, the fall of the Berlin Wall marked the end of the Cold War that had defined international politics for several decades. The Western liberal democratic model seemed to have prevailed over its Soviet counterpart, and politicians envisioned a "new world order" under which the most powerful political players in the world would work together to bring security and economic prosperity to the largest number of people possible. Emboldened by the dissolution of the Eastern Bloc, political scientist Francis Fukuyama declared the end of history. He believed that liberal democracy—a system based on the constitutional protection of individual rights, the rule of law, and active self-government—had proven its superiority to alternative political models and would eventually gain more and more ground even if it suffered setbacks in the short term. Even if we interpret Fukuyama's words generously, the Los Angeles riots were a major example of a setback. Likewise, the armed ethnic conflict in Bosnia and Herzegovina, which had already begun by the time the Los Angeles riots erupted, indicated that history still weighed heavily on people's lives and aspirations. And yet, King's words retain the hopefulness of that time; he seems convinced that if we tried hard enough, we could get along.

The beginning of the new century was equally defined by hopefulness and disillusionment. Polemical postracial utopias, such as Paul Gilroy theorized in *Against Race* (2000), marked the end of the millennium, urging readers to imagine a world in which a transformation of consciousness had enabled humans to overcome the seductive power of racial and ethnic divisions.[1] But the terrorists acts of 9/11 and the 7/7 London attacks, carried out by Islamic fundamentalists, revealed the immensity of the gap between those utopian visions and the political reality. Rather than converge around the ideals of Western liberalism, as Fukuyama had hoped, the world seemed to be regrouping along a new line of division, between religious fundamentalism and secular pluralism. And with secularism perceived as inherent to Western liberalism, and Islam, broadly if incorrectly thought of as foreign to the West, the new realignment evoked the legacies of colonialism and racism.

Those legacies would further become the focus of public attention during the global recession that began with the subprime mortgage crisis in 2008 and disproportionately affected the economic well-being of Black Americans and ethnic Britons.[2] Nonetheless, when Barack Obama became the first Black president of the United States in 2008, some wishfully declared that the postracial American society had finally been achieved, only to be disillusioned by a series of killings of unarmed Black people by vigilantes and police officers. And when in May 2016, London celebrated its first Muslim mayor, Sadiq Khan, the historic election was overshadowed by the right-wing populist wave that peaked with the Brexit referendum and Donald Trump's victory in the US presidential campaign later that year. In the increasingly polarized British and American societies, racial, ethnic, class, gender, and religious differences were becoming overwhelmingly important to the political process. For Fukuyama, this was a troubling development. Liberal democracy would not survive without narratives and values that individuals could hold in common, across specific social identities.[3] Under those circumstances, a new progressivism emerged on American and British university campuses and beyond, finding political expression in the Black Lives Matter and #MeToo movements. That progressivism was defined by the hope that new performative practices, including public condemnations of racism, and speech free from social bias, would get us to a promised land where, finally, we could all get along.

Throughout this tumultuous period, theater artists engaged with their audiences' struggles and aspirations, conveying their faith that theater could help not only figure out how we could get along, but also why we were not getting along; why history still mattered in violent ways, and how it could matter differently. In 1994, Anna Deavere Smith's play *Twilight: Los Angeles, 1992* premiered at the Mark Taper Forum, grappling with these questions. As in her earlier play, *Fires in the Mirror* (1992), about the Crown Heights riot in New York, she interviewed hundreds of people affected by the LA riots and enacted their stories in a solo performance, as a series of monologues. Her interviews with members of the African American and the Korean American communities, who had clashed during the unrest, revealed their disaffection with the liberal project, from which they felt left out. The American dream—a powerful depiction of the liberal concept of "the good life," a life spent not just struggling but thriving—seemed out of reach in a racially biased society. Smith's response to their disaffection was at once familiar and innovative: a performance of a range of viewpoints by a Black woman who, without claiming impartiality, was trying to bear witness to the hardships endured by her informants; it was a postmodern take on the classic liberal practice of *sympathy*, embodied by a minoritized subject.

At the same time, on the other side of the Atlantic, British playwright Sarah Kane was grappling with similar questions, provoked by the Bosnian crisis. How could she, a British playwright, bear witness to the loss, grief, and terror endured by the civilians trapped into the conflict? Her response—the formally daring play *Blasted*, which opened in 1995 at the Royal Court Theatre Upstairs in London (and which I analyze in chapter 1)—entailed placing white British characters in a war as brutal as that in Bosnia but fought in Britain. In doing so, Kane, like Smith in *Twilight*, was practicing sympathy: imaginatively placing oneself in the circumstances of another individual (or individuals), typically one who suffers.

For Adam Smith, the Enlightenment philosopher who theorized sympathy in his study *The Theory of Moral Sentiments* (1759), sympathy is the affect that binds modern individuals together, enabling harmony in a society of equals. Without sympathy—i.e., without the will of trying to see oneself in the other's shoes and, hence, trying to understand what the world may look like from the other's perspective, however imperfect that attempt may be—the liberal project could fail. Importantly, sympathy is not to be confused with *empathy*, a concept that, according to performance historian Gay Gibson Cima, did not emerge before the nineteenth century. In practicing sympathy, the individual remains aware that no matter how vivid their imagination and how good their intentions, they will never be able to fully inhabit the suffering (or joyful) person's circumstances and, hence, affectively merge with that person. In contrast, empathy entertains the possibility of such merging, threatening to "appropriate the other's pain as if one has mastered it fully, and [to] subject the other to that mastery and voyeurism."[4]

But because of the inevitable gap between the sympathizing individual and the object of their sympathy, the ideal sympathetic relationship that Smith described transpires only between white, propertied men. Bound by their privileged position, they can imaginatively swap places more easily than, for instance, a man and a woman could. Thus, from its inception, the sympathetic relationship was gendered and racially marked, just as the classic liberal social contract was a "racial contract," according to the Black philosopher Charles W. Mills.[5] Nonetheless, throughout the history of Western modernity, social activists—from abolitionists to animal rights activists—have tried to nurture sympathy between privileged and disadvantaged subjects, arguing for the expansion of liberal rights across social strata and identity groups. Often, such activists tried to do so from the theatrical stage, following Smith's observation of the similarities between a theatrical spectator feeling for a character and a person feeling for a suffering or joyful fellow human.

Indeed, preoccupation with sympathy, as an affective practice inherent to liberalism, has shaped theater making from melodrama through Stanislavsky's system and beyond, as theater makers drew on theories of sympathy as sources of verisimilitude and sometimes strove to recreate sympathy as a more inclusive practice. Abolitionist melodramas, including the numerous stage adaptations of Harriet Beecher Stowe's novel *Uncle Tom's Cabin* (1851), argued for the moral equality of enslaved Black people—and, as white people's moral equals, for their right to freedom—by emphasizing Black people's capacity for suffering in tear-inducing scenes. The hope was that if the sentimental play (or novel) managed to move the spectator (or reader), they would then act to alleviate the suffering of those afflicted by social ills.[6] But the task of nurturing sympathy for the enslaved, already challenging because of the inherent gap between the sympathetic observer and the subject of their sympathy, was further complicated when the observer was white and the suffering individual Black. To resolve that complication, sentimental representation tended to reimagine Black people as "white inside," affirming the moral superiority of whiteness.

Additionally, the ability to make spectators weep for the downtrodden was taken as proof of sentimentalism's verisimilitude. If an effectively enacted scene of suffering could make spectators weep, then the scene must be lifelike and therefore truthful, the logic went. In turn, that truthfulness, activists believed, would move spectators from tears to action. This belief compelled some activists to purposefully grapple with the racial dynamics of sympathy and sentimentalism. Thus, the radical Black and white abolitionists, who fought in town halls, churches, and public squares for the emancipation of slaves, experimented with new social and aesthetic practices of extending fellow-feeling to people different from themselves, openly acknowledging the racial bias of classic liberal thought.[7]

Like sentimental actors and activists, the Russian theater maker Konstantin Stanislavsky was drawn to sympathy as a tool for achieving verisimilitude on stage, albeit under a different aesthetic contract: that of theatrical naturalism. As he worked to transform sympathy into a foundational principle for creating a role, he, too, quite unexpectedly (as I explain in chapter 2) found himself confronted by sympathy's racial politics. Stanislavsky conceived of realist characters as individuals whose uniqueness is defined by their specific thought patterns and psychological processes. Those patterns and processes become apparent by the way characters act within the given circumstances of a play. Therefore, to enact a character realistically, an actor had to try to imaginatively inhabit that character's given circumstances to the best of their ability, while staying away from social stereotypes. But how could a Russian actor bridge the gap between their own life experiences and the circumstances of the Black Moor Othello?

And so, in trying to bear witness to the experiences of minoritized subjects, Anna Deavere Smith and Sarah Kane aligned themselves with the long performance history of trying to extend sympathy to one's social other. Even the controversies their works provoked resonated with the experiences of earlier theater makers as they confronted the difficulties of sympathizing across racial, gender, and class divides. In *Twilight*, Smith's acting technique, which has been described as Brechtian, highlighted the distinction between herself, the Black female performer, and the diverse individuals caught in the LA riots whose stories she told from the stage. In this way, she tried to emphasize that her retelling of those stories was by no means impartial. But despite her efforts, Smith was critiqued for appropriating her informants' stories and for reinforcing racial stereotypes. Kane, too, sought to avoid stereotyping the fighting Serbs and Bosnians as mired in uncivilized, "Balkan" clannishness, by creating a white, educated, and cruelly biased English character who enacts unspeakable atrocities. But Kane was panned for her allegedly gratuitous representation of violence that, critics said, did nothing to illuminate the Bosnian conflict.[8] Importantly, the controversial reception of Smith's and Kane's plays also revealed spectators' own reflective practices, as spectators too considered the difficulties of getting along with others by going to the theater.

This book is about theater artists, spectators, and protesters who, like Smith and Kane, tackled the question of how to get along with others at the turn of this century, in the British and American societies still bound by liberal ideals and haunted (*pace* Marvin Carlson) by the biases inherent in classic liberal theory and in the theatrical aesthetics that engaged with those ideals. Like earlier activists and performers, those artists, spectators, and protesters—including artists Suzan-Lori Parks, Sarah Kane, Gurpreet Kaur Bhatti, Forced Entertainment, and Young Jean Lee's Theater Company, as well as the British Sikh protesters who marched against Bhatti's play *Behzti (Dishonour)* in 2004 and the Yale students who protested a professor's opinions about regulating students' choices of Halloween costumes in 2015—understood that liberalism entails specific social and aesthetic practices, including practices of theater making and spectatorship. This understanding led them to revise or altogether reject established representational conventions and habits of social engagement, including those of sentimentalism and realism, as well as liberal decorum. Their acts of revision and rejection were often audaciously experimental and, by liberal standards, sometimes politically extreme. This is why I describe them as avant-garde.

In asking from the stage what it means to extend sympathy across race and ethnicity and under what aesthetic contract such sympathy may occur, those artists sometimes stretched the established connections between sympathy and realism, and sympathy and sentimentalism, to a breaking point. Meanwhile, the students at Yale, who called for administrative regulation of Halloween costumes to avoid racially offensive choices, and the Sikhs who protested Bhatti's satire of the corruption in the British Sikh community, while still framing their demands as liberal, went beyond that breaking point, assuming antiliberal stances and militant "choreographies of protest."[9] In a visually arresting demonstration, the Sikh protesters recalled the political and symbolic history of Sikh warriors, while insisting that in an ethnically diverse society, theater artists' expressive freedom must be limited in the name of equality and justice. Likewise, in rebuffing the offers of sympathy and the reasoned arguments of their liberal opponents, the protesting students at Yale recalled the antiliberal philosophy and radical aesthetic of the Black Power Movement. But even as they questioned fundamental liberal rights, those protests remained inspired by the liberal democratic promise of dignity for all. In that, they followed a pattern described by Mills, who notes that throughout modern history, efforts to extend liberal rights to minoritized groups have produced radical modes of liberalism, reframing classic liberalism's foundational concepts and principles.[10]

• • •

As anyone who has studied the avant-garde will have noticed, I have already used the term *avant-garde* in two ways: broadly, as bold artistic and social experimentation; and, more narrowly, as an antiliberal trend that puts aesthetic innovation to utopian social and political ends. The broader definition includes postmodernism as one of the post–World War II Western avant-gardes. Scholars who adopt this definition draw on Jean-Francois Lyotard's defense of postmodernism in *The Postmodern Condition* (1986), against critics who see postmodern art as futile experimentation, packaged for the market and unable to challenge power structures. For Lyotard, this mistaken perception derives from conservative critics' demand that art should help post–World War II Western subjects articulate their lived experiences as a coherent "totality." But Lyotard worries about the untheorized politics of that totality. He suggests that by insisting that art should make the disparate experiences of those people "transparent and communicable," such critics are in fact arguing for a totalizing and totalitarian concept of life.[11] Conversely, he sees the value of postmodern art precisely in questioning the politics of seemingly coherent totalities and in its efforts to make manifest alternative modes of being. Through these efforts, he claims, postmodernism aligns itself with older avant-gardes.[12] The rhetoric of his defense resonates with avant-garde affect: "Let us wage a war on totality; let us be witnesses to the unpresentable; let us activate the differences and save the honor of the name [*postmodernism*]."[13] And thus ironic playfulness gives way to militant assertion. Even postmodernism, for all its definitional disregard for social, moral, and aesthetic hierarchies, appears to be drawn to a code of honor. It is at this moment, the moment when postmodernism demands that its worthiness be acknowledged, that it becomes avant-garde, a point to which I will return shortly.

But historians of the Western avant-gardes have questioned Lyotard's view. They have argued that while opposing the totalities of "bourgeois," i.e., liberal, institutions and principles, avant-garde movements, such as Russian Constructivism and Italian Futurism, envisioned totalizing social utopias and tried to bring them forth by forging alliances with totalitarian political elites.[14] Even when the avant-garde promises freedom, it "enforces it in doctrinaire fashion," notes Hans Magnus Enzensberger in a well-known essay.[15] Taking this history into account, Mike Sell describes the avant-garde as "by definition and for better *and* worse, an antiliberal, antiparliamentary trend [. . .] rooted in the military tendencies of extreme ideological positions [. . .] that tend to be lumped crudely together in terms of 'Left' and 'Right.'"[16] In other words, while postmodernism has been deeply suspicious of totalities, including, famously, the grand narrative of modernity's unstoppable progress toward more perfect societies, the avant-gardes have striven to articulate their own grand narratives of progress. While postmodernism—an offspring of philosophical skepticism—deconstructs, the avant-garde—a positivist mindset—tries to produce performative speech acts. "I now pronounce this urinal a sculpture by signing my name on it," Marcel Duchamp declared in 1917, although he did not actually utter those words and did not sign the urinal with his own name. Indeed, more than a century later *The Fountain* is a paradigmatic example of avant-garde provocation.

Such a broad contrast is, of course, easily challenged. *The Fountain* is as much a performative speech act asserting the artfulness of everyday things—their worthiness as objects of artistic contemplation—as a deconstruction of the concept of high art defined by the practices of the bourgeois museum. As Sell notes, an act or an object is not avant-garde (or, for that matter, postmodern) because of its formal features; instead, it becomes avant-garde (or postmodern) in a specific discursive situation.[17] Or as Paul Mann, on whom Sell draws, contends, "art is always already bound up in discursive contexts," i.e., in complex, interrelated conversations about culture, economics, and politics, and what distinguishes the avant-garde as a movement is its "reflexive awareness of the fundamentally discursive character of art."[18] Again, this discursive awareness is equally true of postmodernism, but postmodernism and the avant-garde situate themselves differently within the same discursive context. Avant-garde art requires a critic, critics, or an entire audience (the more the better) to be astounded and converted into a new way of perceiving, thinking, and living. Better still if that critic is at first self-righteously upset by the avant-garde's provocation, but later professes belief in the avant-garde's social and artistic message. So desperate is the avant-garde's need for the indignant philistine critic—a "proof" of the avant-garde's power to shock and, hence, transform—that in the absence of such a person, the avant-garde artist will invent them.[19] In contrast, the postmodern artist is as happy to provoke as to indulge, and certainly wants to sell their art. Thus, they equally address the philistine and the discerning intellectual, insisting that the distinction between them is contingent. In turn, this attitude has gained postmodernism a reputation for opportunistic relativism, political passivity, and unprincipled peddling.[20]

Finally, the same aversion to moral stringency and categorical rigor informs postmodernism's approach to the past. As historians have pointed out, behind the well-known cliché of the avant-garde's break with history (i.e., the past as narrated by bourgeois historians) is a more complex reality. Rather than break with the past, avant-garde activists reframe it as inexorably moving toward the utopian futures that justify their political projects. Thus, in Vladimir Lenin's Russia, history had always already followed an unchangeable course toward communism, and in Benito Mussolini's Italy, toward fascism. Lenin and Mussolini, their propagandists claimed, merely made this course apparent.[21] In contrast, postmodernism is willing to revisit the past, while insisting that such returns are never innocent. Thus, for postmodernism the past becomes "a dialogic space of [possible] understanding and self-understanding."[22]

Here, the case of neo-avant-garde art, as art conscious of its own history, again complicates distinctions between the avant-garde and postmodernism. Art critic Hal Foster, for instance, describes the (neo-)avant-garde of the 1950s and 1960s, as art that performs a radical return to the avant-garde of the 1910s and 1920s with "a critical consciousness of both artistic conventions and historical conditions."[23] For Foster, however, this return does not collapse the difference between the avant-garde and postmodernism, because the neo-avant-garde intends to create in the present its own version of a utopian future, conducting its own attack on art institutions, including the canonization of the historical avant-garde.[24]

In this book, I use the terms *postmodern* and *avant-garde* to describe the dynamic that occurred between artists and spectators, as they found themselves in a novel discursive situation: one in which a spectator who manages to position themselves as a victim of social oppression acquires a seemingly inordinate power to radicalize a piece of art (or a piece of representation more generally) that was not intended to be perceived as radical. (To be clear, those spectators' claims that they had been victimized, directly or indirectly, as members of minoritized groups, were by no means illegitimate. But what is at stake here are the specific ways in which such spectators embodied their victimization in public.) The plays and performances that make up my case studies, even when deliberately experimental and critical of sexism and racism, did not intend to antagonize their spectators. One of those plays, Gurpreet Kaur Bhatti's *Behzti* (2004), appeared formally conventional and, to a liberal critic's eye, not politically risky. And yet it provoked a violent protest by Sikh spectators who felt that their religion was hurtfully disrespected, stirring a fierce debate about theater artists' ethical responsibility to a diverse audience. Conversely, *The Shipment* (2009), a critique of race relations in Obama's America, by Young Jean Lee, who has described her work as intentionally trying to unsettle her audience, caused complaints from white spectators who felt they were not made uncomfortable enough and, hence, did not get enlightened.

Typically, such a mismatch between artistic intentions and spectators' responses is no news to critics; most believe that at least some degree of mismatch is inevitable. But the spectators I write about challenged this truism. They held the artists accountable for the impact their art had produced, claiming that the artists had created hurtful representations that were either acutely insensitive to the lived experiences of specific minoritized groups or gratuitously violent. Such claims were made even when the artists in question and their audience belonged to the same minoritized group. The apparent paradox here is that artists and spectators were both concerned about the effects of racism and sexism and committed to exposing and redressing them. At the heart of their misunderstanding was the appropriate aesthetic of exposure and redress.

This seeming paradox first attracted me to their works, and this study is an attempt to understand it. I argue that these discrepancies between artistic intention and spectators' reception exemplify a larger discursive shift: a moment in which certain core values that had long organized debates about art and representation, and hence were perceived as self-evident and commonly shared, were challenged by social participants who saw them as contributing to social oppression. Those values included support for the artist's expressive freedom as an absolute good, particularly when the artist represents a minoritized group, and belief in the power of aesthetic innovation to illuminate social wrongs. Or as the French theorist Jacques Rancière may have put it, in the period I discuss, there took place a significant redistribution of *the sensible*—"the system of self-evident facts of sense perception that simultaneously discloses the existence of something in common and the delimitations that define the respective parts and positions within it."[25] As a result, works that would not have previously been understood as radical or avant-garde were seen as trying to achieve radical and avant-garde objectives. The artists involved in these productions were perceived as aggressively contesting key social arrangements, ostensibly in the name of equality and justice, but through an aesthetic that some spectators found disturbing and offensive. In response, those spectators staged their own radical acts.

I further argue that this shift is tied to the emergence of a new discursive subject: a *feeling subject* constituted through historical trauma, a subject who, moreover, conceives of history *as* trauma and demands that artists and their supporters acknowledge the feeling subject's pain by adopting a rigorous code of representational transparency. If any part of a play could offend a minoritized group, whether or not the offence was intended, the logic goes, that play may cause individuals within that group to relive the trauma of their past or continuing oppression. This cannot be tolerated. The feeling subject's militant displays of sympathy for victims of systemic oppression, and above all, that subject's utopian belief that proper speech can succeed in righting wrongs that have defied legal measures, are the clearest expressions of that subject's avant-garde character, as well as of their political progressivism.[26] Like earlier avant-garde artists, the feeling subject upholds a theory of representation whereby words and images shape bodies and minds in more immediate ways than the liberal individual is capable of conceiving. This is why the insistence on proper speech or, more generally, on "correct" representation is integral to the feeling subject's progressivism.

Both that theory and the larger discursive shift to which it belongs have important implications for theater scholarship. As groups of spectators take issue not only with individual artists' works but also with the mainstream standards for critical conversation about performance, informed by liberal thought, critics may find that established definitions of mainstream or radical art no longer serve us. A modernist reliance on the formal qualities of an artwork, long critiqued by feminist, postcolonial, and Marxist critics as limited, becomes strikingly inadequate. Instead, if we need to describe a work as conventional, avant-garde, postmodern, or otherwise, it may be both more accurate and more productive to do so on the basis of the work's reception at a particular moment.

This is not a novel idea. Theater scholars have long understood practices of spectatorship (including those of reviewing, patronage, and subscription, among others) to be constitutive of the significance of both individual performances and larger performance movements. Additionally, as a target for recruitment to avant-garde projects and sometimes as the very material from which avant-garde art is made (in genres such as the happening), spectators have been of immense importance to avant-garde artists and theorists alike. Thus, in Peter Bürger's inescapable *Theory of the Avant-Garde*, spectators' participation in avant-garde performances is not simply an aesthetic experience; instead, it becomes part "of a liberating life praxis."[27] Likewise, for Paul Mann, spectatorship is integral to the discursive economy in which the avant-garde is immersed.[28]

And yet, in the cultural moment that this book explores, the spectator has risen in status. For Bürger, the avant-garde spectator's role is secondary to that of the avant-garde artist. Spectators' responses, no matter how forceful they can be, "remain reactions, responses to a preceding provocation. Producer and recipient remain clearly distinct."[29] In the case studies I describe, this hierarchy is turned upside down, and the spectator rather than the artist leads the "attack on the status of art" in turn-of-the-century Britain and America, thus fulfilling the avant-garde's proper function (as Bürger sees it).[30] Spectators behold the arguably offensive transgression in the artists' works and, in doing so, suggest that the artists, for all their good intentions, may be more complicit with the liberal status quo than they wish to admit.

According to Rancière, aesthetics involves the perception of art forms as simultaneously "forms of art *and* [. . .] forms that inscribe a sense of community. [. . .] These forms define the way in which works of art or performances are 'involved in politics.'"[31] In other words, he suggests that artistic representation does not just reflect larger discursive shifts, but actively shapes them. Following his lead, I view the theater disputes I analyze as integral to the larger contestation of Western liberalism, evident in widely circulated controversies, such as the publication of caricatures of religious figures by the Danish daily the *Jyllands-Posten* in 2005 and the protest over Halloween costume politics at Yale in 2015. Therefore, understanding how reception transformed mainstream theater productions into avant-garde acts helps illuminate the challenge to liberalism inherent in such nontheatrical conflicts.

• • •

Several interrelated factors inform the performance disputes that I analyze as examples of that challenge to liberalism. One of them is the growing diversity of US and British audiences and publics. According to the Pew Research Center, between 1990 and 2015, the foreign-born population of the United States more than doubled, accounting for one-third of the population increase in that period.[32] Likewise, the foreign-born population of the United Kingdom has grown steadily since the end of World War II, when large numbers of immigrants from former British colonies began relocating to regions with strong economies, but especially since 1997 when the government made it easier to bring foreign spouses into the country.[33] This increased diversity enriched the two countries' cultures and economies, but it also produced frictions that were aggravated by persistent inequalities and long-held prejudice. In the meantime, due in no small part to the success of the feminist and antiracist critical projects of the second half of the twentieth century, the repertoire of mainstream performance venues began diversifying too, however slowly, and so did their audiences. That meant that groups of spectators within the same auditorium, on the same night, could be making sense of a show not just in terms of different values, but in terms of different systems of signification.

Accounting for the need for new social and critical habits that this increasing diversity made apparent, the artists whose works I examine avidly explored gender, racial, and religious topics. Meeting or clashing with spectators' perceptions of when such explorations are appropriate and when insulting, their shows became part of the renewed debate about the limits of freedom of expression. At different points in time, censorships laws in Britain have made exceptions to this fundamental democratic principle, banning blasphemy and racist insults among other offensive speech acts. The United States, too, despite its reputation for extremely strong free-speech protections, restricts certain kinds of speech considered obscene or denigrating. But the Islamic terrorist acts of the early 2000s—including the assassination of Dutch filmmaker Theo van Gogh in 2004, in retaliation for his critique of sexism in Islamic societies—and the ongoing pressure to counteract racist speech made artists' freedom of expression newly topical. While artists and their supporters worried about the detrimental effects of self-censorship that those developments had provoked, progressive spectators felt that free-speech protections gave too much leeway to insensitive depictions of gender and race. As Shannon Jackson has pointed out, in the United States, performance that explicitly engages with race tends to disrupt the commonly shared distinctions between reality and theatrical illusion. American spectators, she observes, have been inclined to perceive negative stage representations of race as the artists' actual negative opinions toward racial minorities.[34] Likewise, playwright David Edgar complained in a 2006 essay that British spectators had been increasingly conflating the representation of racism and sexism with the promotion of racism and sexism.[35] Such spectators' push for more sensitive, hence, arguably more empowering representations of minoritized individuals and communities has been a major force in what I describe as the radicalization-through-reception of mainstream stages. But spectators would probably never have gained such power without the growing influence of neoliberalism on the economy and culture that enabled theatergoers to position themselves as interested stakeholders.

Economic geographer David Harvey defines neoliberalism as "in the first instance a theory of political economic practices that proposes that human well-being can best be advanced by liberating individual entrepreneurial freedoms and skills within an institutional framework characterized by strong private property rights, free markets, and free trade."[36] Developed by a group of economists at the University of Chicago, neoliberal doctrines were first tried out in the 1970s in Chile, under Augusto Pinochet's dictatorship. But over the next two decades, neoliberal practices spread globally when the International Monetary Fund restructured the economies of the Global South, and along with other institutions, such as the World Trade Organization and the World Bank, began regulating global finance and global trade.[37] As a result, social inequality deepened despite overall economic growth, and neoliberal economic theory became a dominant ideology. As political theorist Wendy Brown put it, by the beginning of the twenty-first century neoliberalism had become "a peculiar form of reason that configures all aspects of existence in economic terms," including "principles of justice, political cultures, habits of citizenship, practices of rule, and above all, democratic imaginaries."[38] In the United States, the beginning of neoliberalism is associated with Ronald Reagan's tax reforms that, according to his critics, benefited the wealthy with the dubious promise of "trickle-down" gains for the middle classes and the poor. At the same time in Britain, Margaret Thatcher's government's cuts in spending and closures of struggling industries remade the structure of society, dramatically reducing the political power of the working class. At that time, too, British theatergoers were encouraged to think of themselves as art investors entitled to a return of their investment. In chapter 3, I show how this reimagining of the spectator's role informed the Sikh protest against the Birmingham Repertory Theatre's production of *Behzti*.

Neoliberalism also contributed immensely to the emergence of the feeling subject, through its specific re-interpretation of identity politics:

the idea, emerging from the progressive social movements of the 1960s and 1970s, that to accomplish liberalism's promise of equality, liberal publics and governments need to address the specific systemic ways in which minoritized groups have been disadvantaged in liberal democratic societies. As neoliberalism spread, it discredited Marxist approaches to social politics and, through its focus on individual entrepreneurship, undermined class-based political collaborations across ethnic groups. Consequently, identity politics not only became the sole acceptable way to address social disparity, but it was appropriated by conservative political groups to advance the interests of economically privileged people.[39] Being a wealthy white person was no longer an embodiment of privilege, but a specific identity, whose opinions on social and political issues now had to be seriously considered, in a public sphere dedicated to honoring cultural diversity.[40] Failing to do so would amount to discrimination, arguably in the same way that invalidating the perspective of impoverished Black Americans would be considered an instance of systemic racism. This apparent paradox relies on a radical redefinition of social identity: one based not on the economic and political history of a specific group, but on that group's sense of inner worthiness that must be respected under any circumstances and publicly recognized.[41] Political alliances across identity groups are still possible and, as I show in my analysis of the *Behzti* controversy, forging such alliances entails positioning the allies as having "equally" endured the larger liberal public's lack of recognition. Recalling Lyotard's surprising call to honor at the end of his defense of postmodernism, the imperative to recognize one's worthiness, anyone's worthiness, is a central trope of a new vanguard that proposes a radical vision of social relations.

In this new political dynamic, the progressive feeling subject's signature contribution is to reconfigure histories of oppression as histories of trauma. It is by honoring a minoritized individual or group's trauma that the feeling subject recognizes their inner worthiness. And since trauma cannot be accounted for by the reasoned discourse of liberalism, the feeling subject eschews liberal debate for a public practice of emotional care. This practice entails honing the traditional liberal's awareness of representation's power to retraumatize and, crucially, disabusing that liberal of the notion that they can even begin to inhabit the circumstances of the traumatized other. Instead of showing sympathy, which the feeling subject conflates with empathy and rejects as privileging the sympathetic individual over the object of their sympathy, the feeling subject affirms the other's suffering by never questioning it. This affirmation has developed into a distinct genre of public performance that I describe in chapter 4.

Finally, the shift from a liberal culture to a culture of sensitivity that I am describing would be unthinkable without the development of new digital technologies in the last three decades. The feeling subject would not have taken shape outside of the new digital social media platforms any more than the liberal individual would have taken shape in the absence of print journalism and the coffeehouses that Jürgen Habermas celebrated in his theory of the liberal public sphere. The democratization of reporting, which informs the sensibility of the progressive feeling subject, was already an important factor in the Los Angeles riots in 1992, triggered by an amateur video recording of Rodney King's brutal treatment by the police. But social media platforms contributed two new aspects to the feeling subject's sensibility: the ability to quantify public responses to amateur reporting and the creation of echo chambers that speeded up the fragmentation of public debate, which had already begun with the proliferation of cable television networks in the 1990s.[42] In turn, that fragmentation informed the reconfiguring of identity politics from a corrective to liberal democracy to a neoliberal assertion of worthiness. But the new digital technologies also enabled the emergence of decentralized protest movements, such as the Black Lives Matter movement, that are now reviving and revising the liberal concept of sympathy. I write about this ongoing revision in the conclusion to this book.

THE METHODOLOGY

Twentieth-century histories have overwhelmingly described the avant-garde as the art of intention. Even when they avoid the clichéd narrative of the visionary artists whose bold imaginings of better societies remain misunderstood by most of their contemporary recipients—and most narratives that we still consider relevant today do avoid it—they focus on artists' innovations, eschewing serious consideration of how and why spectators engage with specific art works, shaping their significance. In fact, Bürger's *Theory of the Avant-Garde* remains relevant precisely because he refused to take for granted the stereotype of the complacent bourgeois spectator. Rather than accept this alleged complacency as somehow essential to the bourgeois public, he viewed it as an act of political resistance. If the bourgeois spectator were to abandon their own understanding of art as apolitical and accept the avant-garde's idea of art as social and political praxis (note Bürger's use of the Marxist term *praxis*), the bourgeois spectator may have to question the legitimacy of the worldview that rationalized their privileged social status as meritocratically acquired. In this book, I too conceive of spectatorship as praxis: a discursive practice whereby (*pace* Rancière) spectators, no less than the artists, assert their views of aesthetic forms as forms that inscribe (or fail to inscribe) a sense of their community's worthiness. Spectators' self-perception as coauthors of art's artistic and social significance is key to understanding the radicalism of the performances that I analyze.

Most of those performances, even when readily recognizable as experimental, took place in mainstream performance venues. For Bürger, this alone would have preempted any possibility of radicalism. But twentieth-first-century scholarship has questioned this truism. In their books, Mike Sell and James M. Harding have challenged definitions of the avant-garde in terms of venue (nonmainstream), aesthetics (experimental), and politics (anticapitalist). Instead, they have proposed that a performance becomes radical or avant-garde because of the dynamics between the participants in a performance encounter.[43] This methodological shift allows us to consider as avant-garde productions in mainstream venues that are not immediately identifiable as experimental and acts of spectatorship that cannot be easily qualified as leftist or anticapitalist. Harding and Sell choose not to go in this direction. Instead, their studies offer new perspectives on artists and movements that are already part of radical or avant-garde performance narratives, including Valerie Solanas, Carolee Schneemann, Fluxus, and the Black Arts Movement, among others. Sell has also analyzed as avant-garde nontheatrical performances, such as acts of Islamic terrorism.[44] Following the methodological implications of their scholarship, this book applies their situational approach to productions in mainstream venues, giving primacy to the spectator's role in the performance encounter.

Equally relevant to this book are Harding and Sell's analyses of the gender and racial politics of the Western avant-gardes. Earlier scholars did not entirely ignore those politics. In their narratives, male avant-garde celebrities tend to be accompanied by supportive women who, just like those celebrities, found bourgeois decorum and bourgeois art restrictive and unexciting. (Alfred Jarry's friend, playwright Madame Rachilde, comes to mind, as does Vsevolod Meyerhold's collaborator, sculptor Lyubov Popova.) And in his *Theory of the Avant-Garde* (1962), Renato Poggioli highlights the influence of the fascist preoccupation with racial degeneration on criticism of the avant-garde.[45] But several decades of feminist, postcolonial, and critical-race conversations about the politics of art have made race and gender central to Harding's and Sell's thinking. Thus, in *Cutting Performances* (2012), Harding argues that the antipatriarchal critique by feminist artists such as Carolee Schneemann and Yoko Ono is key, rather than additional, to the anticapitalist critique undertaken by the 1960s avant-gardes, uncovering the gendered blind spots in their radicalism. Equally convincingly, Sell has argued that race has been integral to the avant-garde's presentation of itself as authentic and spontaneous, in contrast to the bourgeoisie's restrictive, artificial decorum. He has written about how the early European avant-garde developed a public aesthetic of self-presentation by modelling its fashion and lifestyle on those of the nomadic Roma and the cultural stereotypes associated with them.[46] Sell calls this racial borrowing an assertion of "theatrical authenticity," drawing attention to such artists' willful self-definition as a racialized minority. In turn, by thus presenting themselves as authentic, those artists tried to assert their legitimacy.

Likewise, in the performances that I describe, the gendered body becomes central to the artists' rethinking of sympathy and liberalism, just as an identity based on racial trauma gets mobilized to legitimize the protesting audiences' demands. Thus, in their protest against *Behzti*, the offended Sikhs claimed that the production was not just denigrating their religion, but also racist. And the protesting students at Yale asserted the authenticity of their suffering by presenting themselves as crucially shaped by the historical trauma inflicted by racism. As they saw it, this trauma fully justified their antiliberal stance on freedom of speech. And though such trauma cannot be shared empathetically, given the specificity of each racialized group's oppression, the Sikhs' Catholic allies claimed that nonetheless, as a people of faith in a secular state, they were able to feel the Sikhs' racial injury. While their feeling of the Sikh's racial injury was not identical, it was, they argued, just as intensely experienced. Drawing on Sell, I describe the Catholics' strategic use of race in the controversy as an example of theatricalized credibility.

As I write in the coda, the feeling subject's critique of liberalism has been largely successful. Under the feeling subject's pressure, the liberal individual—once a paragon of socially neutral impartiality (should one take them at their word)—has been reduced, so to speak, to a situated, postmodern subject whose opinions are limited by the racial and gendered histories of liberalism. Additionally, the feeling subject has successfully imposed new rules of decorum in liberal settings, including an expectation for race- and gender-sensitive language (for instance, through warnings about potentially upsetting content) and recognition of liberalism's history of exclusion (for instance, through the acknowledgement of the Native American tribes on whose lands universities have been built). In other words, by changing the aesthetic of everyday social interactions, the feeling subject's radicalism has proven its performative power.

To explain that power, I draw on Martin Puchner's analysis of the avant-garde's performative power—its ability to gain support for its aesthetic and social vision—in his book *Poetry of the Revolution* (2006). Puchner argues that in distinction from J. L. Austin's speech act theory, where certain utterances draw performative power from institutionalized tradition, avant-garde aesthetic acts draw legitimacy from the futuristic utopias they envision. Put differently, the alluring depictions of the future that the avant-gardes imagine give them the authority to reshape the present. The contemporary avant-garde that I describe draws its performative power differently than either of those two models. Like Austinian performativity, it looks back to tradition: the principles of liberalism institutionalized in legal texts and in repertoires of public and private behavior. This tradition, contemporary progressives claim, produces enduring trauma. The imperative to stop this trauma from recurring in the present, along with a social consensus (in liberal settings) about the racial and gender bias in classic liberalism, authorizes their antiliberal practices. In other words, the progressive avant-garde legitimizes its radical demands by evoking a history that it considers both failed (because it did not fulfil its objectives) and hurtful. But even as this avant-garde rejects liberalism as producing trauma, it also affirms liberalism's promise of equality and justice for all. Yet, crucially, this avant-garde interprets equality and justice as the acknowledgment of minoritized subject's intrinsic worthiness. Only if this worthiness is publicly recognized *on the minoritized subject's own terms* can liberalism's promise be fulfilled. Paradoxically, then, liberalism's promise can only be accomplished through antiliberal means.

The feeling subject's demand that their worthiness be publicly recognized and their insistence that this recognition entails an aesthetic solution motivates my turn to affect theory: the inquiry into how narratives, by evoking specific feelings, shape social values, including gender and racial ideals, that facilitate both social cohesion and marginalization. Admittedly, this is a narrow definition of affect theory, as used specifically in literary studies, which I borrow from literary scholar Suzanne Keen.[47] In a book that is very much about the contestation of an ideology—that of liberalism—and its practices, I am especially interested in the emotions and conduct that liberalism considers "proper" to public life, i.e., sympathy and composure in the face of hardship. I am also interested in how those "proper" emotions, as well as "improper" ones, have been gendered and racialized. The negative stereotype of "the angry young Black woman," the abject edge of reasoned liberal conduct, is a strong example of such gendering and racialization. In other words, I examine how different affects circulate as liberalism is negotiated, affirmed, and contested in specific performance encounters.

For Sara Ahmed, on whose work I heavily draw, the emotions involved in processes of social cohesion or marginalization attach differently to different bodies through the public circulation of signs, especially textual signs. Thus, the liberal male subject becomes associated with dignified composure, at the same time as arguably undignified, unreasonable anger attaches to protesting Black women. Consequently, as she strives to have the legitimacy of her protest acknowledged, the Black woman needs to negotiate those enduring associations: a negotiation I analyze in chapter 4. As Ahmed points out, those affects and the representations to which they attach acquire the power to bring groups together and to marginalize because they rely on already well-established discourses of nation, race, and migration.

Additionally, I draw on Catherine Chaput's account of how the circulation of affects complicates the communicative model of semiotics, which assumes that the participants in an encounter share the same communication conventions. Only when we consider how affects attach to specific topic can we understand why people who do share the same conventions make entirely different meanings from the same encounter, or why people who do not share such conventions are able to achieve a kind of consensus based on feeling rather than on shared cultural knowledge. Chaput calls such encounters, complicated by affect, trans-situational. Her insights are particularly useful to understanding the *Behzti* controversy, where Sikh spectators split over their interpretation of the play despite their common cultural background, while Catholics claimed they understood and shared the protesting Sikhs' response, despite their differences.

Finally, I am also indebted to Saba Mahmood's theory of mimetic signification in her reflection on the controversy over the *Jyllands-Posten*'s caricature of Mohammed.[48] Muslims felt injured by that caricature, she explains, because they interpreted the satirized image according to a significative logic that posits embodied continuity between the prophet and his representations, as well as between him and his followers. According to this logic, the caricature was not just an expression of the cartoonists' opinion of Islamic fundamentalism. Instead, it hurt the prophet and his followers alike; it caused harm that they could feel in their bodies. This logic clashes with the Western liberal understanding of rational deliberation, predicated on a semiotic distinction between the sign and its referents. Drawing on Mahmood's analysis, I uncover a similarly mimetic logic of representation in the Sikh protest, as well as in the progressive avant-garde's insistence on cultural sensitivity. In both these cases, we see affect radically shorten the distance between signs, their referents, and the readers or spectators interpreting those signs.

CHAPTERS

The first two chapters analyze three returns to earlier radical and avant-garde performance, as the artists involved tried to envision better ways of getting along with social others. In chapter 1, "The Radical Formalism of Suzan-Lori Parks and Sarah Kane," I explore how in their plays *Venus* (1996) and *Blasted* (1995), Parks and Kane tried to undo the racial and gendered politics of looking in order to reimagine blackness and whiteness beyond the histories of racism and colonialism that produced them. I propose that the playwrights' attempts to overcome these histories recall the Russian formalists' imperative to estrange habitual perceptions so that life may be truly lived. In doing so, their plays become radical acts of sympathy undoing the gendered and racial hierarchies of Adam Smith's theory and reinventing sympathy as a more equitable practice. I demonstrate how in the negative critical responses to the plays' first productions we see the precursors of the spectator as a feeling subject, who eventually emerges two decades later out of the communicative and affective practices enabled by social media platforms. But in the responses to the first productions of *Blasted* and *Venus*, we already see spectators probing aesthetic forms, such as realism, for their capacity (or lack thereof) to confer worthiness on minoritized subjects. This chapter is a significantly revised version of an essay first published as a journal article in *Theatre Survey* in 2015.

Chapter 2, "A Spectator Prepares: Forced Entertainment's Theater of Critical Feeling," examines how the British company Forced Entertainment creatively returns to the happenings and to Stanislavsky's System to demonstrate, in the course of the performance encounter, how emotions inform our perceptions of ourselves and our social others. In their show *First Night* (2001), which is the chapter's case study, the actors explore the political work of emotions in the context of the Oldham race riots in 2001. This exploration is tied to the larger question of ethical spectatorship that the group has pursued since its founding in 1984. That question aligns their theatrical experiments with those of Parks and Kane, discussed in chapter 1. As in Parks's and Kane's works, in *First Night*, the actors' inquiry into the racial and gendered politics of spectatorship illuminates the aesthetic of the liberal social contract.

Chapter 3, "The *Behzti* Riot as a Contemporary Avant-Garde," examines the violent protest against the 2004 production of *Behzti (Dishonour)*, by Gurpreet Kaur Bhatti, at the Birmingham Repertory Theatre. I analyze how the riot used antiracist rhetoric to challenge the status of religion in Britain. Whereas in secular societies religion is protected as a *private* issue, the rioters argued that religious concerns should be allowed to bear on *public* representations, such as theatrical performance. I further demonstrate how the riot refashioned the seemingly conventional *Behzti* into a radical performance: a refashioning that raises questions about how riots have been used as proof of radicalism in histories of the Western avant-gardes. A key aspect of the protest was the Birmingham Catholics' (and eventually Anglicans') support for the Sikh agenda. I argue that the Sikh-Catholic alliance transformed the protest into an avant-garde act, challenging the limits of the freedom of expression in an unprecedented way.

Chapter 4, "Feeling Bad about Being White: Young Jean Lee's Theater and the Progressive Avant-Garde," begins with an analysis of Young Jean Lee's play *The Shipment* (2009) to describe the short life of the "postracial" optimism that briefly dominated the American conversation about race following Barack Obama's election. Lee and her actors expressed their skepticism toward postracial claims, urging white spectators to show their antiracist credentials by (as one character suggests) "walking on eggshells around Black people." I discuss how this suggestion becomes an imperative in the new social contract devised by avant-garde progressives. Central to this contract is the subject of feeling, predicated on a neoliberal interpretation of 1990s constructivist theories. I show how this subject tried to impose a new social ethic in the course of the Halloween-costume controversy at Yale in 2015.

Finally, the coda returns to the liberal individual, now refashioned as a postmodern figure, but still committed to a promise of shared humanity despite seemingly increasing social polarization. The coda accounts for that individual's changed position in the discourse of rights and justice at the end of the second decade of the twenty-first century and their continuing attempts to reach across the signification and affective gaps that divide us.

1

The Radical Formalism of Suzan-Lori Parks and Sarah Kane

When Sarah Kane's *Blasted* (1995) and Suzan-Lori Park's *Venus* (1996) premiered a year apart at the Royal Court Theatre in London and at the Public Theater in New York, no critic would have suggested any connection between them. Indeed, there is no obvious similarity between Kane's story about a dysfunctional couple whose violent relationship transports them from their expensive hotel room into a war zone and Parks's play about the transformation of the Khoikhoi woman Saartjie Baartman into the racist stereotype of the Hottentot Venus. But despite the distinctiveness of their themes, the two productions received strikingly similar receptions. To their critics, the graphic sexual violence in *Blasted* and the explicit humiliation of Baartman in *Venus* appeared extreme and gratuitous. The reason for this, they speculated amid anger and frustration, was Parks's and Kane's failure to provide "corrective context" within which the disturbing imagery of their plays could be properly understood.

This overlap in critical opinion may have attracted Parks's attention, because about ten years later she wrote a short piece titled *A Play for Sarah Kane and the Royal Court Theatre* (2006). (Meanwhile, Kane had died of suicidal depression in 1999.) In the play, Kane is shown lying on a chaise longue while another woman, "slightly older," watches her.

STAGE MANAGER: Places, Miss Kane. Places.

Miss Kane puts something that looks like a rope around her neck.

OTHER WOMAN: Yr not going on tonight.

KANE: I dunno.

OTHER WOMAN: Youve put your rope on.

KANE: Have I?

OTHER WOMAN: If you had it to do all over again, would you?

KANE

KANE

(Rest)

[. . .]

OTHER WOMAN: How are you these days?

KANE: Better. Worse. Yr troubles follow you.

OTHER WOMAN: Yeah?

KANE: No matter where you go. Yr troubles know. Yr address.

OTHER WOMAN: Yes.

[. . .]

KANE: Fan me, huh?

The Other Woman fans her.

OTHER WOMAN: No sweat, kid. God bless you and no sweat.[1]

The rope that Kane puts around her neck, seemingly without noticing, is a blunt metonym for the playwright's mental illness that, for some critics, provided the ultimate explanation for her notoriously violent drama.[2] And just as Kane's illness limited interpretations of her work, at least early on, in the 1990s Parks felt pressured to conform to critical expectations based on her being a Black playwright. Those expectations, just like Kane's "troubles," have followed Parks for a long time.

But *A Play for Sarah Kane* is above all about sympathy, a theme to which Parks continually returns. For Parks, sympathy—and given her interest in classic liberalism, *sympathy*, rather than *empathy*, is the correct word—is a relation of looking and being looked at. That relation, her plays suggest—as do the works of W. E. B. DuBois, bell hooks, and others—is heavily inflected by gender and race. In *A Play for Sarah Kane*, the Other Woman—possibly a stand-in for Parks herself—extends sympathy to the young woman by noticing her and watching her with care. This act of noticing restores to Kane the human complexity that the rope around her neck refutes. But the play is also about withholding sympathy. An older couple is sitting at a table close to the Other Woman and Kane, enjoying their wine and giving no sign that they have seen the arresting sight of the young woman with a rope around her neck. In Parks's work, such ostensible blindness is a performative act of marginalization.

This chapter analyzes acts of looking as acts of othering in the works of Parks and Kane and how each playwright tried to expose and undo the dynamic of looking in order to re-envision blackness and whiteness. This chapter is also about critics' acts of looking, which according to art historian Hal Foster exemplify criticism's preoccupation with "correct distance." In modern criticism, Foster explains, the question of correct distance emerges around Western critics' interest in the relationship between the Western self and its others. The term, which appears in Claud Lévi-Strauss's anthropological research, describes the critical perspective that a Western anthropologist needs to adopt toward a non-Western culture so that they do not misrepresent it. Extreme distancing—as evidenced in the Nazi exhibition of "Degenerate Art" in 1937 Berlin—is fascistic because it renders the cultural other unimportant and inhuman. But overidentifying with the other, by depicting them as a more "authentic" version of humanity that has been lost to the civilized West—as the surrealists did by calling themselves "primitives"—can be just as violent.[3] At stake are the aesthetic conventions that frame the encounter between the cultural other and the Western public.

Like numerous radical artists and thinkers before them, Kane and Parks try to renegotiate that racialized distance. Parks's reimagining of blackness in *Venus* was prompted by Nelson Mandela's request to France in 1994 to return Baartman's remains to South Africa so she could be properly buried, a process that would take the French state eight years and the passing of a special act of parliament.[4] And Kane tried to reimagine whiteness in the context of the Bosnian war that, she felt, raised questions about white people's capacity for violence and sympathy. In reimagining blackness and whiteness, the two playwrights adopt strategies that I call formalist because of their affinity with the critical strategies, if not the politics, developed by the Russian formalists and the American new critics during the first half of the twentieth century. In her scripts and essays, Parks dares her readers to imagine blackness "in itself": a wondrous new identity extricated from its limiting relationship to whiteness. And in *Blasted*, Kane shows a white masculinity unmoored from liberal personhood and divested of its claim to universalism.

When *Venus* and *Blasted* were first produced, the plays' formalism was manifested in the critics' demands for corrective context. Indeed, formalism famously redirects the meaning of an artwork, away from the social context in which it was produced and away from readers,' viewers,' and listeners' interpretations, to the artwork itself. The formalists did this because they resented the notion of art as a mere symptom of the artists' biography or of their readers' cultural milieu. Art, they insisted, has meaning beyond the contexts of its production and reception. (In turn, this assertion allowed them to talk of art in terms of "*an* artwork," a stable entity independent of readers' interpretations.) But in the practices of American new criticism, bracketing context off legitimized a literary and dramatic canon made entirely of works by white men. If all that mattered were the merits of the artwork itself, then work by female artists and artists of color could be dismissed seemingly objectively, as having no intrinsic merit.[5] This history has understandably made feminist and postcolonial critics suspicious of formalist-like practices.[6] But while I acknowledge the validity of their suspicion, I suggest that Parks's and Kane's formalism was both deliberate and innovative. Their refusal to provide "corrective context" for the violence on stage was a gesture of self-authorization whereby they abandoned familiar conventions (and spectators' need for comfort) in the name of staging forth alternative racial and gender identities. For each playwright, this idealistic objective entailed a formalist turn to the expressive means of the theater, which in *Venus* also entailed a critical return to the radical aesthetics of the Black Arts Movement and Bertolt Brecht's analysis of the theatrical apparatus.

But what did critics really want as they demanded corrective context? And what is the larger critical history within which their demand is to be understood?

BLACKNESS IN ITSELF

When *Venus* opened at the Public Theater in 1996, under the direction of Richard Foreman, who also designed the set, the outrage that it provoked by suggesting that its central, Black character may have been complicit in her plight, raised yet again one of the most inspiring and frustrating questions in modern US theater history: how to stage the racial other.[7] In a padded costume evoking Baartman's large buttocks (a distinctive feature of the Khoikhoi tribe), African American actress Adina Porter licked chocolates that fairgoers threw into her cage, let them poke and grope her, and laughed raucously and inappropriately.[8] Even the most sympathetic responses to the play revealed the difficulty of assuming a critical stance toward the racially marked body, especially the Black female body, affectively fixed into a symbol of martyrdom and victimization.[9] In fact, Shannon Jackson has proposed that the racially marked body's resistance to being reduced to a critical sign, free from affect, may be definitive of race as a social phenomenon.[10] As US

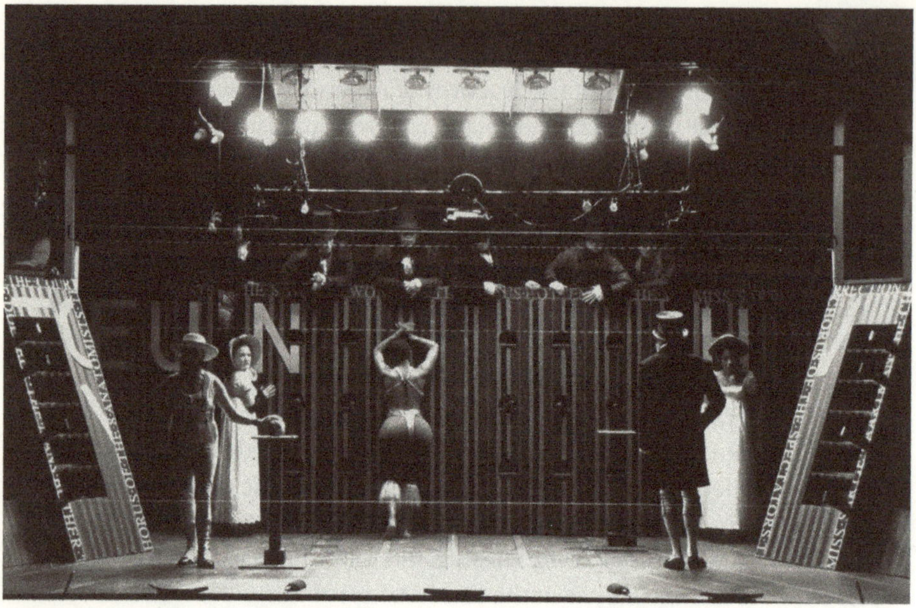

Figure 1. The Venus Hottentot, the Chorus of the Anatomists, and the Chorus of the Spectators. Scene from *Venus*, by Suzan-Lori Parks, directed by Richard Foreman. Photo by T. Charles Erickson, 1996. Reproduced by permission from T. Charles Erickson.

theater history demonstrates, on stage this resistance is highly productive of controversy, much of it focused around the question of what representational contracts may best convey the experiences of racially marked people. In this sense, art critic Abiola Sinclair's reading of Parks's experimental aesthetic as a traitorous concession to a white theatrical tradition was unexceptional, a reminder of African American artists' historical efforts to create distinctly Black art.[11]

Justified as these efforts are, they have encouraged some critics to downplay the mutual influences between Black art and white experimental movements, which in turn may have occluded the transnational framework within which Parks has placed her work. Indeed, from the early-twentieth-century New Negro Movement, through the radical Black art of the 1960s and beyond, Black artists wrote, performed, were judged, and judged themselves transnationally, exploring foreign influences and influencing foreign artists. Contemplating the future of African American theater, Alain Locke characterized the popularity of Meyerhold's biomechanics as a validation of an "essential" artistic body language that experimental European artists had just begun rediscovering, but that African American actors used effortlessly.[12] The popularity of African American jazz in Paris, Italy, and elsewhere in Europe during the early twentieth century has prompted scholars to describe the experimental art of that period as "Afromodernisms."[13] And the many sources on which female playwrights of the Black Arts Movement drew included Brecht's theater, which they resignified as a non-Western aesthetic practice.[14] For her part, Parks has referenced this history of aesthetic exchange in her scripts. For instance, the script of *Venus* includes a quote from the film *Masculin Féminin* (1966) by French director Jean-Luc Godard, in which Godard cites Amiri Baraka's emblematic play *Dutchman* (1964), a reference that I will discuss shortly. The rewards that each approach brings—Sinclair's insistence on "uncontaminated" Black art and Parks's strategic transnationalism—become obvious when we consider the scene of Venus's humiliation first through her critics' perspectives and then through Parks's own.

"The exploitation of Saartje Baartman currently going on at the Public Theater is almost as bad as the exploitation she received in real life. [. . .] Did they mean to insult us?" asked Abiola Sinclair in the *New York Amsterdam News*, a newspaper with a large African American readership.

> Foreman gave us glaring lights shining in our eyes. I could barely see some of the scenes because I had to shield my eyes from the glare. The purpose? The man who seduced Venus from South Africa was played by a woman [Sandra Shipley]. The purpose? [. . .] When given [chocolates], rather than put the pieces into her mouth she wets her fingers and circles the chocolates, putting what's collected on her fingers into her mouth. [. . .] A monkey could easily handle such a task. [. . .] And the so-called love affair with the Baron Doctor is perhaps coming from the dreams of Suzan L. Parks, rather than history.

Baartman's representation as "a full-blown accomplice in what was being done to her," Sinclair concluded, could only be "some stupid invention of a white director and a sellout playwright."[15]

Two things are notable about Sinclair's review. One is her implicit assumption that if Parks had been faithful to history, she would never have suggested anything as offensive as a love affair between the Venus and the anatomist who ended up dissecting her. The other is her discomfort with nontraditional casting, a practice most commonly used in nonrealist performance. Her two complaints could even be related; we are prone to think of history—as a story of things that happened—in realist terms, i.e., as a representation of events as they could have happened in (so-called) real life. But even critics who tied the play's experimental aesthetic to a critique of spectatorship and praised Parks and Foreman for showing "how the onlookers' fantasies" construct racial stereotypes noted that "without the corrective reality" of historical knowledge about Baartman, reading Parks's complex characters "becomes a frustrating task."[16]

Such reviews suggest that as soon as their authors identified racism as a major theme in the play, they expected a clear social commentary on it. In US (as well as British) theater criticism, such commentary is often associated with social-realist and Brechtian conventions, and for at least some critics the chorus of spectators and the nontraditional casting would have evoked Brecht's *Verfremdungseffekt*. Additionally, both realism and Brechtian aesthetics stage a conflict between an inaccurate worldview and a truthful one (a "corrective context") where the truthful worldview becomes a path to justice and redress. This association is obvious in Jean Young's review of *Venus*, who, like Sinclair, was extremely displeased that an African American actor (Peter Francis James) performed as the white character of the Baron Docteur. This casting choice, Young argued, suggested that "black men are the primary exploiters of black women."[17]

Black playwrights have long been attracted to realism's promise to reveal the intriguing internal workings of seemingly uninteresting or stereotyped people. They have also been drawn to Brecht's attempts to bring insight into social hierarchies. Director and critic Carl Weber has called Anna Deavere Smith, whose work I discussed in the introduction, the most faithful interpreter of Brecht's concept of performance, with the possible exception of Brecht's wife, actress Helene Weigel.[18] Parks's work, too, has been compared to Brecht's. For instance, critic Jonathan Kalb has argued that in *Venus*, "Parks took a new role, [. . .], something more akin to Brecht's idea of a writer who gives the audience pleasure through teaching."[19] But pleasure doesn't seem to have been part of those first spectators' experiences. Even the critics who found the casting choices and the character of the Venus acceptable noted that the critical-distancing strategies in the production were not always effective. Commenting on the chorus of spectators who groped, poked, and kicked the Venus, Alexis Greene wrote, "Though your brain tells you that this [the actress's buttocks] is padding, albeit of an artful sort, the effect is disturbing, to say the least. You cannot help but imagine the humiliation of such forced exposure and display in the flesh."[20] Harry Elam and Alice Rayner similarly remarked that "the butt clearly did not belong to the actress, but it nonetheless gave the effect of total exposure."[21] Hence, even if Parks and Foreman had intended to prompt insights into racism through a Brecht-like approach, the image of the exposed Venus made Brechtian distancing difficult.

In interviews following the end of the production's run, Parks would clarify that not providing the kind of historical account of Baartman's life that those critics expected and abstaining from realism had been deliberate choices, consistent with her larger thinking about history.[22] In the published script of *Venus*, this thinking is indicated in the two epigraphs that precede the prologue. The first, "Le travail humain / Ressuscite les choses / D'entre les mortes" (Human labor raises things from the dead), is a quote from Godard's 1966 film *Masculin Féminin*; the second, "'You don't believe in history,' said William" is from Virginia Woolf's novel *Between the Acts* (1941).

The quote from *Masculin Féminin*—Godard's critique of the reduction of Marxism to a social brand—is a paraphrase of a sentence from Marx's *Das Kapital* (1867). In English translation, the complete sentence reads as follows: "Living labor must seize upon these things [i.e., unused raw materials] and rouse them from their death-sleep."[23] Godard uses the phrase ironically. The young men and women, whose lives he narrates in the movie, loudly profess their Marxist values, but when they witness violence and injustice, they fail to interfere. In one episode, Paul, the movie's central character, is riding on the subway with a friend, when he witnesses a conflict between an attractive blond woman and two Black immigrants (presumably from a former French colony). Despite the addition of a second Black character, the episode closely follows Amiri Baraka's *Dutchman* (1964), possibly the most well-known drama from the Black Arts Movement. One of the Black characters in Godard's movie has just finished telling the blond passenger how white people do not understand the songs of Bessie Smith (in a monologue taken almost verbatim from *Dutchman*), and then, as in Baraka's play, the blond woman kills him. Most of the passengers in the subway car look away. Paul remarks on the murder but does not do anything about it; the murder doesn't seem to affect his life in any way.

Parks's reference to Marx and Baraka via Godard suggests that one way to read *Venus* is as a critical-race critique of Marx's theory of labor. In *Das Kapital*, Marx describes as "death-sleep" the condition of products and raw materials that are not being used in the process of production. Parks's use of "death[-sleep]" is at once more literal and more sinister: a strikingly accurate description of Baartman's fate. Presumed to be a "thing" because of her blackness, Baartman was transformed into a product for white people's entertainment. Even after she died, the display of her remains continued to affirm the perceived inferiority of Black people for the visitors of the Musée de l'homme (the museum of natural history in Paris), where her skeleton and a cast of her buttocks were exhibited until the mid-1970s.[24] In the words of C. Riley Snorton, Parks's reference to Marx via Godard signals the "fungibility" of the Black body—its extreme malleability and marketability—as raw material that could acquire a range of use-values depending on the industry in which it was used: cotton production, medical research, entertainment, and political theory, where the Black body can be varyingly gendered or ungendered, humanized or dehumanized, according to a white thinker's needs.[25] As suggested in Parks's use of Godard, the difference between the Black person's fungibility and the white unskilled worker's loss of humanity (or *alienation*) in the capitalist process of production derives from the degree of humanity with which each was endowed in the first place. In the Western colonial imagination, the Black person's humanity, if granted at all, was extremely precarious; hence, the Black person had little or no humanity to lose.

The disturbing scene in which the chorus of spectators gropes the Venus stages this very fungibility, as does Godard's adaptation of *Dutchman*'s ending, and ties it to a liberal politics of looking. Because the Black person is fungible, the white Frenchman Paul can see a Black person getting murdered and do nothing. Put in another way, because a person is Black, a white person can afford to look on them without sympathy. In Parks's work being the object of an unsympathetic look is the very definition of being racially marked. This becomes clearer when we revisit the significance of sympathy in classic liberalism.

As I explained in the introduction, sympathy, as Adam Smith conceived it, is the affective practice that provides social cohesion in liberal societies. Moreover, through extending sympathy for the pain or joy of another, the sympathetic observer *becomes* a liberal individual and at the same time confers dignity on the object of their sympathy. Importantly, Smith's insistence that the sympathetic observer cannot fully experience the sufferer's pain but can only imaginatively inhabit the circumstances that have brought about it preserves the sufferer's autonomy. In other words, by extending sympathy to another, the sympathetic observer at once acknowledges the latter's distinctiveness from themselves and the equality between them.[26] Thus, in the sympathetic relationship, we see the classic liberal version of Hal Foster's analytic *correct distance*. That distance is made possible by a crucial third party to the sympathetic relationship: an imagined impartial judge, "a fair and impartial spectator," who determines whether the sympathizing individual and the object of his sympathy are displaying their sympathy and suffering (or joy) appropriately.[27] Placing themselves under this judge's scrutiny shapes the behaviors of both parties. And as analysts of Smith's theory have pointed out, the way the sympathizing observer conceives of this judge's judgements defines the racial, class, and gendered limits of the sympathetic relationship, and hence of liberal personhood. These limits become apparent in artistic examinations of liberalism, especially melodrama and the sentimental novel, which, according to literary historian Margaret Cohen, were key to the formation of nineteenth-century liberal publics.[28]

Consider, for instance, the 1927 silent film *Uncle Tom's Cabin*, based on the eponymous novel by Harriet Beecher Stowe. The film opens with the wedding of the mixed-raced slaves Eliza and George on the Kentucky plantation of the Shelbys, Eliza's owners. But despite having been performed by a minister, the marriage is illegal by the laws of the pre-Emancipation South. The injustice of this situation is made palpable shortly after, as we see Eliza and George enjoy their first private moment as a family. Just as Eliza sings and plays the mandolin for her new husband, sitting in a tree under the indispensable moonlight, George's master, a slave owner on a neighboring plantation, arrives to claim his property. Framed as a conflict between two liberal rights—the newlyweds' right to privacy and George's master's right to property—the scene receives full sentimental treatment by the presence of Mr. and Mrs. Shelby, who guide the spectators' emotional response into aligning with the right victims, the newlyweds: "Please, Mr. Harris," Mrs. Shelby entreats, "Can't you respect their love?" The slippage from love to rights in her plea is a well-established sentimental tactic. In the scene, there is not really a legal conflict of rights: by law, George and Eliza are property, not a family entitled to privacy. By asking George's master to respect the couple's love, a feeling arguably common to all humans, Mrs. Shelby suggests that their love entitles them to privacy and marriage regardless of what the law may say. Likewise, by urging spectators to feel for the enslaved couple, she is urging that they treat them as free individuals because of their shared capacity for feeling: love and the pain of not being free to be with a partner of one's own choosing.

Sentimental authors were fully aware that not every reader or spectator had the capacity and will for sympathy across racial and class divides. Not incidentally did Stowe choose a light-skinned, educated couple to solicit her white readers' kindness toward the enslaved, and the 1927 film adaptation honors her choice.[29] To further ensure identification, the film director, Harry A. Pollard, also has Mrs. Shelby teach George's master (along with other unconvinced spectators) how to extend sympathy to slaves. If such spectators couldn't accept George and Eliza as their equals in feeling, at least they could identify with Mrs. Shelby; at least they could imagine themselves judged by her as their equal. Sentimental authors, in other words, were uncertain about whether the impartial judge, as imagined by the reader or spectator, could stay impartial in a scenario in which the observer is white, but the object of their sympathy is not.[30] Hence, sentimental authors made sure to provide a specifically embodied judge, such as the white, rich, and pious Mrs. Shelby, a character meant to be seen as "one of us," the target viewers.[31] This push to establish racial or class affinity as the basis of sympathy, evidenced in the popular trope of the "tragic mulatto"—the Black character who deserves white readers' or spectators' sympathy because he or she is "almost" white (George and Eliza both fit the type)—is a major reason why sentimentalism has been critiqued as assimilative by later generations of social critics.

This assimilative effect is also why Brecht tried to hinder sympathetic identification between spectator and character in his theater. In "Theatre for Pleasure or Theatre for Instruction?" he writes, "I laugh when they [the characters] weep; I weep when they laugh," prescribing a critical attitude to his ideal audience, i.e., an attitude whereby sympathy is suspended in a situation that seems to call for it.[32] He worried that sympathetic identification would discourage spectators from analyzing the systemic factors that bring about suffering, such as, in the example above, slavery itself. (If the Shelbys believe that their slave Eliza should have the same right to marriage and privacy that she would if she were free, why don't they set her free?) But Parks does not share Brecht's worries. Rather, like Baraka and Godard before her, she dramatizes white people's failure to extend sympathy to a Black sufferer, leaving them suspended between personhood and objecthood. This failure might well summarize the limited application of Brecht's Marxist method to theatrical critiques of racial inequality.

In *Venus*, Parks poignantly illuminates this failure in the play-within-the-play, *For the Love of Venus*. In this melodrama, a young white woman tries to seduce her fiancé, who is so absorbed in his dream of exploring Africa—an adventure that he sees as a rite of passage to true manliness—that he neglects her. He tells his father and his uncle that before he gets married, he wants to "love something wild," and they conspire to organize an encounter between him and the Hottentot Venus once her show comes to town. But when the young man finally meets the woman who he thinks is the Venus, she reveals herself as the Bride-to-be in disguise. This revelation is the play's happy ending.

The young woman wins her fiancé over by successfully performing for him exotic blackness in private, while remaining white in public, as his social standing requires. The Baron Docteur, the Venus's lover-dissector, is the single spectator of the melodrama, and as he watches, she watches him watch. Later, she tries to seduce him, talking to him in the words of the Bride-to-be. But, predictably, her performance of whiteness, i.e., personhood, fails, and she quickly transforms from a lover to a corpse that the doctor can dissect and analyze with all the impartiality appropriate to a true scientist.

In the short melodrama and in the Venus's attempt to repeat the performance of the Bride-to-be for her white lover, we see the Brechtian fable refracted through Parks's postcolonial lens. Or, in Parks's own terms, we are given a "repetition and revision" of the Brechtian fable, in which the stubborn intertwining of the affective and economic aspects of the colonial encounter is laid bare. To own the Black other, the melodrama suggests, is to own them emotionally, as well as economically, in a way that the Black other may misrecognize as intimate. For the white nineteenth-century man, however, the ability to maintain critical distance, to remain coolly aware that he loves "*something* wild" and not "*someone* wild," becomes a test of white masculinity, one that the Baron Docteur, just like the Young Man, passes with honors. At the same time, white Victorian femininity is shown as predicated on white (upper-class) women's successful blackface performance, a minstrel show for a single, ideal spectator. In either case, the ability to withhold sympathy from the Black other becomes a prerequisite for whiteness.

This withholding of sympathy is also dramatized in the scene of the Venus's exposure to the chorus of leering spectators. That the actual spectators of the Public Theater's production were able to sympathize with Baartman's fate, while observing the humiliated Venus, was a testimony to a changed perception of blackness, a reason for hope, and perhaps even Parks's and Foreman's intention. Those actual spectators' responses were also Brecht-like, though inflected by the same concerns with racial politics that inform the play: "I sympathize when they [the characters] withdraw their sympathy." Witnessing the chorus's cheery heartlessness, those spectators felt for Baartman across (and with the help of) the trappings of costume and dramatic character that were deliberately designed to discourage easy identification. Critical closeness, rather than critical distancing, may be the phrase to describe their response.

Parks, however, is not just interested in staging marginalized persons as possible objects of spectators' sympathy. Had this been her objective, mainstream aesthetic modes, such as realism, could have sufficed. Rather, her interest in the interracial sympathetic relation (and its limits) is tied to a radical revision of blackness. "Can a Black person be on stage and be other than oppressed?" she asks in "An Equation for Black People on Stage." "Does Black life consist of issues other than Black issues?"[33] Rethinking blackness beyond victimhood and oppression, she argues, demands that the history of blackness be theatrically revised. In turn, this revision takes Parks into avant-garde territory.

Parks's project resonates with Kristin Stile's definition of the avant-garde as a "determined act of observation" that "reconstructs the ways in which events, objects, and the relationship between them may be interpreted and lived."[34] Indeed, for Parks, staging blackness in novel ways would be just such an act of observation whereby blackness may be seen and (therefore) lived differently. The connection that she draws between blackness and theater also recalls Mike Sell's commentary on the "theatricalized authenticity" of the early French avant-garde. The Bohemians accomplished their arguably authentic lifestyle, he writes, by donning the fashions of the nomadic Roma and appropriating some of their daily practices.[35] A symbolic parallelism between the "rootless" Roma and the uprooted Africans brought to the New World as slaves is easy to draw. In both cases, their presumed lack of roots has been tied to a stereotype of their inherent dishonesty coupled with an aptitude for performing, which Parks has dramatized in her fables of Black Abraham Lincoln impersonators: *The America Play* (1994) and *Topdog/Underdog* (2001).[36] And just as the Bohemians appropriated elements of Roma culture, white blackface minstrels profited from African American music and dance, marking their racist representations as "authentically" Black.

The primal scene of Black Americans' uprooting through enslavement, and the subsequent use of that uprooting as justification for cultural appropriation, makes a clean, avant-garde "break with history" especially problematic for Black artists. Just as the captive Black worker could not lose her humanity in the same way that the white worker loses his in Marx's theory of alienation, the African American avant-garde artist cannot make a clean break with history. Parks writes in one of her essays that having been radically displaced, Black Americans grapple with the loss of their African history, and at the same time, with the surplus history of racism in America that continues to inform their present lives. In her own words, Black Americans are caught between a history "that has not yet been divined"[37] and a "time that won't quit."[38] This peculiar sense of the past—at once not enough and too much to bear—shapes Black American identity in such a way that a realist dramatic character cannot adequately express it. Hence, Parks conceives of her dramatic personae as "figures."

Figures, she explains in her essay "Possessions," are not characters. To call them so "could be an injustice. They are *figures*, *figments*, *ghosts*, *roles*, *lovers* maybe, *speakers* maybe, *shadows*, *slips*, *players* maybe, maybe *someone else's pulse*." Also, they "almost always take up residence in a corner."[39] Her description recalls Paul Gilroy's definition of blackness as constitutively decentered, having no viable myths of national origin (a shared history in a shared territory)[40]—the myths that create the "core" of white personhood, which white people (paradoxically) must be able to transcend to become truly white, i.e., "universally" human. Moreover, Parks continues, her dramatic personae are figures also because "theatre is the place [where she] *figure*[s] the world out." And doing so puts both "the history of Literature" and "the history of History" in question.[41]

On the printed page, the difference between Parks's figures and dramatic characters is signaled through her mystifying "spells" and "rests" represented by the dramatic personae's names followed by no dialogue:

The Chorus of the Court
The Venus
The Chorus of the Court.[42]

She defines the rests and spells in temporal terms:

(Rest)
Take a little time, a pause, a breather; make a transition

> A Spell
>
> An elongated and heightened *(Rest)*. [. . .] This is a place where the figures experience their pure true simple state. While no action or stage business is necessary, directors should fill this moment as they best see fit.[43]

The spells and rests, then, are the places where blackness, as an identity predicated at once on loss of origins and on a surplus of oppressive time, could become visible, if directors and actors managed to give it shape. Thus, in the spells and rests, blackness emerges as a riddle to be solved. Because of this, these devices are the most obvious marks of Parks's formalist leanings.

According to the Russian formalist critic Viktor Shklovsky, the purpose of art is to make the familiar strange through deliberate experimentation. As familiar things become new, their true essence can be grasped for the first time. Never has a stone been truly stony until an artist made it strange, he claims in his essay "Art as Technique" (1916). Failing to practice art, i.e., failing to defamiliarize, not only keeps us from grasping the true essence of things, it also allows habitual perception to destroy life. "And so life is reckoned as nothing. Habitualization devours work, clothes, furniture, one's wife, and the fear of war. [. . .] And art exists that one may recover the sensation of life; it exists to make one feel things; it exists to make the stone stony."[44] The stakes are high, as befits an avant-garde statement. Shklovsky's admonition to make the habitual strange, lest we never live, is a moving paraphrase of the avant-garde mandate that art should serve as a model for life rather than hold up a mirror to it. This admonition becomes particularly poignant when (counter to what formalism counsels) we consider it in its context: Shklovsky was a volunteer in the Russian Army in World War I at the time he wrote that essay. Thus, counter to Bürger, who sees Shklovsky's formalism as preempting a discussion of art's social function, Shklovky's defamiliarization is a life praxis that aims, in part, to mobilize against war by revealing its horrific essence.[45]

Parks's project of making blackness strange, by revealing the historical complicity of the white-dominated stage with the oppression of Black Americans, is similarly poignant. Only when blackness becomes novel can its "essence" be truly grasped; only then can blackness be lived beyond the familiarity of grieving for what could have been (had the African past not been lost) and of enduring and overcoming what is. And like other radical artists and thinkers before her, she finds realism antithetical to this project. Theater, she insists in her essay "Elements of Style," should not be primarily a means of social commentary, but "an examination of the human condition."[46] Realism, she further argues, can no longer contribute to this examination, because playwrights have been taking it for granted, rather than experimenting with it. As a result, realist drama has been reduced to bad journalism: "the play-as-wrapping-paper-version-of-hot-newspaper-headline."[47] Only when playwrights experiment with theatrical expression, she asserts, can theater do what is appropriate to it as an artform: illuminate the human condition by contemplating "the marvel of live bodies on stage."[48]

For Parks, as for Shklovsky, letting the familiar emerge as marvelous entails slowing down perception and making it difficult. This is precisely the purpose of the spells and rests ("a pause," "a breather"), and the purpose of the red lights shining in spectators' eyes in the Public Theater's production may have been similar. Even as the Venus was utterly exposed, she was also made difficult to stare at. While acknowledging the spectacular display of the Black body during colonialism and slavery, the production also resisted it. And while Sinclair saw the red lights as a white avant-garde technique, concealing the Black body from the white gaze in this manner has precedents in the theater of the Black Arts Movement. In Ed Bullin's *The Theme Is Blackness* (1966), a short piece intended "to be given before predominantly white audiences," a Speaker announces that "the theme of our drama tonight will be Blackness," and the auditorium is plunged into darkness. Twenty minutes later, the lights are back on, and the Speaker says:

> Will Blackness please step out and take a curtain call?
> BLACKNESS.[49]

In this happening, Bullins had a Black actor (the Speaker) *refuse* to embody blackness for a white audience so that spectators may become aware of how the white gaze performatively produces blackness-as-we-know-it as its effect. Likewise, by telling us that in the spells, her figures "experience their pure true simple state" and yet never prescribing how this true state is to be staged, Parks shows blackness as performative in the sense that Judith Butler describes gender. The formalist "essence" of blackness, as Parks defines it, is thus an essence that needs to be continually rediscovered.[50] Moreover, in giving both Black and white characters "spells," i.e., in treating both as figures, Parks suggests that blackness, as a question that can never be fully answered, describes all identity. Hence, in the spells, blackness (rather than whiteness) comes to stand for "the human condition."

But even as they lack a determinist core, Parks's Black figures are stubbornly fleshy. As postcolonial theorists have pointed out, whiteness entails the ability to transcend the fleshy body. The classic liberal individual accomplishes that by drawing a firm distinction between the unruly body and the reasonable mind and then bracketing off the body. The white avant-garde subject transcends the flesh by shaping it into a machinelike instrument that performs its strictly prescribed function in the futuristic technological utopia. Think of Meyerhold's biomechanical actor inspired, in part, by Taylorism, the factory management system aimed at increasing efficiency by breaking every part of manufacturing into specialized repetitive tasks. Think also of Marinetti's body, efficiently fused with his automobile. Although it has been continuously objectified, never has the Black body been instrumentalized in a similarly futuristic manner. Reflecting this difference, Parks's Black figures cannot shed their flesh even when they die. Before she dramatized this unrelenting fleshiness in *Venus*, Parks had already portrayed it in *The America Play*, where we are told the story of Little Bram Price Junior, a Black figure who returns to his house ten days after his burial, "sits down tuh dinner and eats up everybodys food just like he did when he was livin."[51] These fleshy figures, who cannot be reduced to dust, spirit, or other Western versions of immateriality, or made machinelike in a white avant-garde fashion, embody the limit of liberal as well as Western avant-garde personhood in Parks's plays, and at the same time, are integral to the radical blackness she strives to articulate.[52]

While Parks does not directly engage with Adam Smith, in her published plays she has signaled her ongoing interest in classic liberalism's impact on how Black personhood has been imagined, theorized, and performed. *The America Play* begins with a well-known quote from John Locke's *Two Treatises of Government* (1689): "In the beginning, all the world was *America*."[53] According to Scott Venters, Locke's view of America as an uncultivated wasteland is one of several influential articulations of classic liberal utopias that envisioned the perfect society as one comprised of free farmers. By reimaging the lands inhabited by indigenous peoples as a wasteland, such utopias at once erased the history of indigenous peoples and legitimized English settlers' right to property. Those settlers, Locke argued, deserved to own this land because they would "improve" it, adding value to it through their free labor.[54] In *The America Play* (1990), Parks reimagines the Lockian wasteland as "the Great Hole of History," a dystopian place where the enslaved people who cultivated the formerly indigenous lands fruitlessly dig for their past, trying to make sense of their place in the world.

Likewise, the script of *Topdog/Underdog* (2001) begins with a quote from Ralph Waldo Emerson's essay "Circles"—"I am God in Nature; / I am a weed by the wall"—in which, along with other essays of his so-called first series,[55] Emerson develops his philosophy of radical individualism.[56] This philosophy entails living a life that is "for itself and not for a spectacle"[57] and seeking for the truth "with no Past on [one's] back."[58] According to Robert Weisbusch, by elevating the experience of the private American individual against the history of the Old World (i.e., the past that burdens one's back), Emerson confronted the idea that American culture was only an imitation of the original European intellectual accomplishments.[59] Emerson's radical individual is thus predicated on the modern hierarchies of copy versus original and of privacy versus spectacle, informed by the antitheatrical discourse of eighteenth-century Puritan America. These hierarchies, Parks suggests, are also constitutive of racial difference. In *Topdog* and in *The America Play*, a Black figure, lacking a "Past on [his]back" that he could shed, is condemned to impersonate white heroes, such as Abraham Lincoln. As a result, these Black figures live lives of spectacle that exclude them from the category of liberal personhood.

In *Venus*, too, Parks revisits the relationship between history and personhood, by prefacing the script with the quote from Woolf's *Between the Acts*: "'You don't believe in history,' said William."[60] In saying so, William rebuffs the naïve idealism of another character in the novel, Lucy Swithin, who, at the threshold of World War II, still believes that unity among people is possible. In this exchange, William appears to conceive of history as "time that won't quit," a burden that discourages a utopian imagination. The novel also contrasts how owning one's history or, alternatively, being deprived of an enlivening narrative of one's past, informs (white middle-class) men's and women's sense of meaningful existence. For the patriarch Mr. Oliver, the books in his "country gentleman's library" signify "the treasured lifeblood of immortal spirits."[61] But his daughter-in-law Isa, trapped in domesticity, can find no "remedy" in Keats, Shelley, Yeats, or Donne.[62] Her inability to see herself inscribed in mainstream history (a "gentleman's library") feels like "a tooth ache."[63] As in Parks's plays, the unfulfilled need for a history that can endow the present with significance manifests as being mired in one's fleshiness.

The inability to transcend their fleshiness circumscribes Parks's figures' attempts to make utopian gestures, such as extending sympathy across race. Scene 19 of *Venus*, entitled "*A Scene of Love (?)*," consists entirely of spells:

> **The Venus**
> **The Baron Docteur**
> **The Venus**
> **The Baron Docteur**
> **The Venus [. . .]**[64]

The question mark in the scene's title suggests uncertainty about what a scene of love between a privileged individual and a minoritized subject may entail. Could they ever become equals through an act of sympathy? In the Public Theater's production, Foreman's design gestured to the ideological complications preventing such an equitable relation from taking place by enclosing the Venus in a wire cage—the same cage that was her fair booth in an earlier scene—from which she stretched out her arms to the Baron Docteur while he stood looking at her longingly.[65] Parks offers a more optimistic resolution in *A Play for Sarah Kane*, where the two women do establish a sympathetic relationship by recognizing each other as "marvelous." In that moment, they assert a mode of humanity that does not require that flesh be transcended. Instead, the fungibility of their nonnormative selves—one Black, the other disabled—becomes the constitutive condition of a different way of being with others, an enactment of radical sympathy. Perhaps this alternative mode of being with others is the figure's "pure true simple state."

WHITENESS UNDONE

Sarah Kane's *Blasted* seems to have emerged from a similarly strong impulse for sympathy, which compelled her, much like Parks in *Venus*, to probe the possibilities of theatrical expression in a formalist-like fashion. This is how she described the inception of the play in an interview:

> I switched on the television. Srebrenica was under siege. An old woman was looking into the camera, crying. She said, 'Please, please, somebody help us.' Somebody do something.' [. . .] Slowly, it occurred to me that the play I was writing was about this. It was about violence, about rape, and it was about

> these things happening between people who know each other and ostensibly love each other. [. . .] I asked myself: 'What could possibly be the connection between a common rape in a Leeds hotel room and what's happening in Bosnia? And then suddenly this penny dropped and I thought: 'Of course, it's obvious. One is the seed, and the other is the tree.' And I do think that the seeds of full-scale war can always be found in peace-time civilization and I think the wall between so-called civilization and what happened in central Europe is very, very thin and it can get torn down at any time.[66]

Kane's response to the old woman from Srebrenica recalls Gay Gibson Cima's description of radical white female abolitionists' sympathetic practices. As they campaigned against slavery and assisted fugitives along the Underground Railroad, they imagined their efforts to be judged not by an impartial spectator, as in Smith's theory, but by a "partisan" spectator: an enslaved person "passing judgement on them." The purpose of that strategy was to keep those women aware of how difficult it may be to find a connection to someone with such a low social status relative to their own, and to alert them to misconceptions about "proper moral actions" toward a person who is so extremely disadvantaged.[67]

In the excerpt above, we see Kane feeling judged by the woman from Srebrenica and finding herself failing to respond appropriately to the conflict in Bosnia. Consequently, she decides to try to transform the play she has already begun writing into a "proper moral action." This interpretation is also supported by an interview that Kane gave two years after the first production: "While the corpse of Yugoslavia was rotting on our doorstep," she said, "the press chose to get angry, not about the corpse, but about the cultural event [i.e., the opening of *Blasted*] that drew attention to it. [. . .] *Of course, the press wish to deny that what happened in Central Europe has anything to do with us.*"[68] In other words, in *Blasted* she tried to show an essential connection between the seemingly unbridgeable circumstances of peaceful Britain and war-torn Bosnia. That connection was the Britons' and the Bosnians' shared capacity for violence. If she managed to show it, the play would become "a proper moral action."

But the first production failed to make this connection clear, eventually suggesting to Kane and director James Macdonald that enabling British spectators to recognize their own capacity for extreme violence would entail an aesthetic contract that made apparent the contingency of their (presumed) self-perception as civilized people. Such an aesthetic contract was implied in the script, but it failed to take shape in the production, creating much confusion. What was the play about? The Bosnian war? British soccer violence? Many felt that because the production did not provide a framework for understanding the play's violent imagery, that imagery became gratuitous.[69] I begin with the script.

Blasted opens as a realist play in which a middle-aged, bigoted tabloid journalist rapes his much younger, intellectually disabled girlfriend. The stage directions specify that Ian is forty-five and Welsh-born, but he speaks with a Leeds accent because he has lived in Leeds for a long time. Cate is twenty-one, speaks with a lower-class South London accent, and stutters when under pressure.[70] In the interview where she talked about the inception of the play, Kane insisted that the casting should realistically represent the age difference between the two characters.[71] The script also says that the first scenes take place in a hotel in Leeds, "but so expensive that it could be anywhere in the world."[72] This ambiguous description anticipates the story's departure from realism to an allegory larger than life that occurs in the middle of the play. But the characters' conversation about a soccer match between Manchester United and Liverpool locates the beginning of the play in Britain, while Ian's racist use of terms including "Pakis," "wags," and "n——r" establishes his and Cate's whiteness. There is no doubt, then, that the sexual violence that the first two scenes portray, culminating in Ian's rape of an unconscious Cate during one of her seizures, is set in Britain. Yet at the end of scene 2, the realist contract established up to that point is suddenly suspended as an explosion destroys the hotel room and all semblance to familiar reality. Cate runs away from Ian, leaving through the bathroom window, and a soldier searching for food breaks into the room. In a disconcerting exchange, the soldier alternately eats, threatens Ian, and tells him about his girlfriend who has been raped, blinded, and killed by the enemy, before raping and blinding Ian in turn. The room is then destroyed by a bomb explosion, and the characters, stuck in an extreme situation—represented by Ian getting literally stuck in the floor of the former hotel room—are left to figure out who they are without the help of the props and trappings of their former, peaceful lives.

With the soldier's arrival, Kane also makes a significant move in characterization. Unlike Cate's and Ian's, the soldier's identity is unspecified. The script prescribes no accent or nationality for him, and all we learn about his personal history is that he has lost his girlfriend in the war. This loss, Kane suggest, is what the soldier tries to make sense of by raping Ian. As he does so, the soldier is crying his eyes out, and once he is done, he kills himself. Paradoxically, at this moment we see the only attempt in the play to represent violence in conventionally sympathetic terms: by normalizing it as a twisted act of grieving. With the exception of this scene, Kane's approach to sympathy is much more radical, as indicated by the difference between Ian and Cates' and the soldier's characterization.

In an early draft, Kane explicitly ties the soldier to the ethnic conflict in the former Yugoslavia. The soldier, who is called Vladek (a Slavic name), asks Ian: "English shit. Why did you recognize Croatia? [. . .] This is a Serbian town now."[73] If the final version had retained this reference to the Bosnian crisis, the violence the soldier commits may have been easier to contextualize, but this would also have helped reinforce the negative stereotypes about the Serbs that circulated in the mid-1990s. Conversely, making the soldier generically foreign represents violence as a human predicament not limited to a specific class, ethnicity, or gender. Indeed, Kane says as much in an interview she gave after *Blasted* was first produced: "The problems I'm addressing are the ones we have as human beings. An over-emphasis on sexual politics (or racial or class politics) is a diversion from our main problem. Class, gender, and racial divisions are symptomatic of societies based on violence or the threat of violence, not the cause."[74] In other words, violence not only produces social divisions, it may also be producing the identity categories within which we make sense of ourselves, while losing sight of what we have in common. Striking as it may sound, this hypothesis is a variation on Michel Foucault's and Judith Butler's now widely accepted understanding of identity as performative. In fact, Kane takes to an extreme the Foucauldian insight that social identities, though seemingly chosen by individual subjects, are subtly coerced upon them.

Kane's inquiry into the formative link between violence and identity continues in her play *Cleansed* (1998), which is set in a blend of two of Foucault's favorite *institutions*, a university and a clinic. Tinker, a drug dealer and self-appointed doctor, forcibly mangles his patients'/clients' bodies into crude female or male shapes. Nineteen-year-old Robin is made feminine by having Grace's clothes forced on him, while Grace receives a mastectomy and has a penis crudely sewn onto her own genitalia. While the "surgery" is ostensibly done following Grace's wish to become as similar as possible to her deceased brother Graham so she may merge with him, Tinker interprets her request with sadistic literalism. Indeed, Kane's plays and her interviews suggest that, like Foucault, she was preoccupied with the notion of normalization, including the power of realism to normalize violence by trivializing it: making "a rape in Leeds" appear "common."

In *Blasted*, Kane also ties realism's power to normalize violence to a critique of journalism as an ostensibly objective—hence, realist—discourse: Ian, the cruel, racist male character of the play is a journalist. When the soldier learns about Ian's occupation, he asks him to write about the atrocities that he (the soldier) has committed. "At home, I am clean," the soldier says. "Like it never happened. Tell them you saw me." But to Ian the soldier's story is not newsworthy.

> IAN I do other stuff. Shootings and rapes and kids getting fiddled by queer priests and schoolteachers. Not soldiers screwing each other for a patch of land. It has to be . . . [original ellipsis] personal. Your girlfriend, she is a story. Soft and clean. Not you. Filthy like the wogs. [. . .] Why bring you to light?[75]

The soldier than rapes Ian and blinds him in retaliation for Ian's refusal to testify to the atrocities that he has perpetrated. The scene is also a metaphor, however visceral, about the selective blindness inherent in realism that, like journalism, picks and chooses what to include in its allegedly objective representations. Only when realism gets suspended, Kane seems to suggest, can we see violence for what it is: a capacity shared by all humans.

In the play's final version, realism is precarious even before the explosion in scene 3. Stage time flows in realist and nonrealist ways at once. Scene 2 begins "very early the following morning" after the end of scene 1; yet, the script indicates "*the sound of spring rain*" at the end of scene 1 and "*the sound of summer rain*" at the end of scene 2. Thus, an entire season elapses in scene 2. Besides, the rules of visibility associated with classic realism, including the realist conventions of representing white individuals, are broken from the very beginning. Ian, aging and sickly, is a less-than-perfect representation of Western whiteness. White bodies, film scholar Richard Dyer writes, need to be whole, firm, and healthy in order to "disappear" into the transcendent mind.[76] And while classic realist drama is full of sickly and disabled characters—Henrik Ibsen's Dr. Rank and Oswald Alving come to mind—only rarely has their sickliness or disability been embodied on stage as such.[77] By contrast, Ian's ailing body is untypically exposed to view. Consider the following exchange in scene 1:

IAN Don't like your clothes.
CATE (*Looks down at her clothes.*)
IAN You look like a lesbos.
CATE What's that?
IAN Don't look very attractive, that's all.
CATE Oh. (*She continues to eat.*) Don't like your clothes either.
IAN (*Looks down at his clothes. Then gets up, takes them all off and stands in front of her, naked.*) Put your mouth on me.
CATE (*Stares. Then bursts out laughing.*)
IAN No? Fine. Because I stink?
CATE (*Laughs even more.*)
IAN *attempts to dress, but fumbles with embarrassment. He gathers his clothes and goes into the bathroom where he dresses.*
CATE *eats, and giggles over the sandwiches.*[78]

In a comic reversal of Laura Mulvey's well-known scenario, masculinity rather than femininity becomes the object of the spectator's gaze. As Ian fails to retain the position of observing subject, his white masculinity becomes marked as damaged, and hence particular. Cate, by contrast, is never subject to such utter exposure. Additionally, the connection that Kane draws between realist representational conventions and gender norms qualifies her deconstruction of realism as feminist, despite her stated refusal to be described as a feminist playwright.[79]

Scene 5, in which Ian gets trapped in the floorboards, completely at Cate's mercy, is the culmination of the play's representational logic. Ian—literally reduced to a broken object among the debris—is not only too damaged and incapable of controlling his physical environment to embody normative whiteness; he has died, yet he continues to eat and defecate. Like some of Parks's Black figures, he is both profoundly displaced and unable to shed his flesh and his carnal needs even after his death. The end of the scene, where Ian thanks Cate for taking care of him while she looks away dejected, has been the focus of the feminist conversation about the play.[80] In 1995, this dark ending did not fit easily in the influential understanding of feminist mimesis as representation that does not repeat established gender conventions but is instead "geared to change," a change that would arguably lead to a better future.[81] Nonetheless, playwright Caryl Churchill, whose own work informs that definition, talked of *Blasted* as hopeful and redemptive.[82]

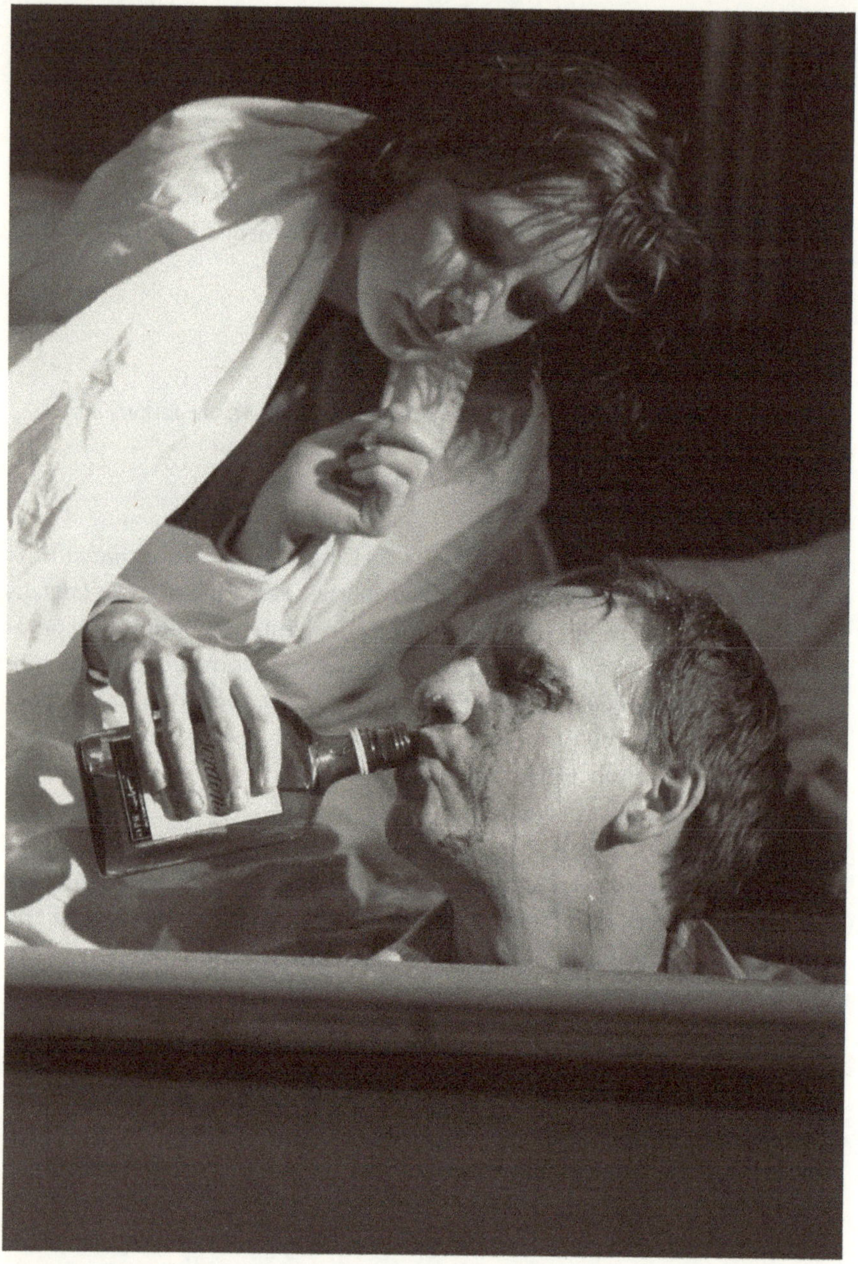

Figure 2. Kelly Reilly (Cate) and Neil Dudgeon (Ian) in the 2001 revival of *Blasted*, by Sarah Kane, Royal Court Jerwood Theatre Downstairs. Photo by Donald Cooper. Reproduced by permission from Donald Cooper.

While one could argue with her assessment, the question about the ending is important because it has to do with the avant-garde, and feminist, trope of utopia: what future (if any) does Kane envision? What subjects inhabit it?

Theorists of utopia remind us that utopia and dystopia are not opposites; rather, they exist on a continuum. Dystopia, writes Dragan Klaić, "implies utopia as a subverted or suppressed desire. [. . .] [E]ven dystopian drama is in fact utopian [. . .] dystopia has become in our times a *via negativa* to express utopian strivings."[83] From this perspective, whether the "no-place" (the literal translation of "utopia") where *Blasted* ends is dark or redemptive may be less important than how it accommodates normative whiteness. In *Blasted*, this is where normative whiteness encounters its limit. Importantly, this no-place is marked feminine because, as we learn from an earlier episode, it is the space where Cate is transported during her seizures:

> IAN Thought you were dead.
> CATE Suppose that's what it's like.
> [. . .]
> IAN Can't stand it.
> CATE What?
> IAN Death. Not being.
> CATE You fall asleep and then you wake up.[84]

This no-place is also feminist because it replaces the modern ideal of autonomous personhood, which assumes (among other things) an able body, with personhood based on mutual support and interdependence.[85] Again, this alternative personhood is embodied by Cate, a rare character in Western drama whose impairment is both explicitly staged and does not translate into passivity or victimization. Instead, resourceful, tenacious, and capable of reciprocating violence, she carries the utopian/dystopian charge of the play. Thus, in scene 4, Ian, who cannot bear his helplessness, asks Cate to help him kill himself. Cate, holding an abandoned baby, refuses: "My [disabled] brother's got blind friends. You can't give up."[86] Interdependence, signified by Cate's taking care of the baby and by her reference to blindness, defines her character from the beginning. She has only agreed to meet Ian in the hotel room because he "sounded unhappy."[87] When Cate fails to keep the baby alive, she is thrown into a crisis of faith, yet she continues taking care of Ian. His "Thank you," which concludes the play, suggests he has accepted interdependence. It is a utopian ending, but unlike liberal and avant-garde utopias inhabited by rational and disciplined bodies, Kane's is inhabited by fleshy, feeling subjects.

Kane's intricate play with the dramatic conventions of time, space, and characterization was not properly conveyed in the first production. The tight budget did not allow the construction of an expensive-looking hotel room, and the set looked like a cheap bedsit—a space readily associated with naturalistic performance.[88] Also, not until after the first production's run did Kane add the detail of summer, spring, and winter rain, trying to foreshadow the oncoming break with the first scene's naturalism.[89] As a result, the critics who saw the first production were completely unprepared for the suspension of realism in scene 3. Likewise, the play's reversal of norms of visibility, through exposing Ian's imperfect body and withdrawing Cate's from view, was not always understood either. In fact, Kane harshly critiqued the Hamburg production of *Blasted* for exposing Cate naked on stage after Ian rapes her.[90] Indeed, failure to figure out how to handle the violent acts on stage was a major problem in the first production, too, motivating critics' judgment that those acts were gratuitous. At the Theatre Upstairs, the small studio space of the Royal Court Theatre, the proximity between performers and spectators made the violent imagery overwhelming, even though the same proximity made the stage technology visible. Even critics who understood that Kane's intention had been to critique violence rather than reproduce it said that she failed to do so. For instance, according to Sarah Hemming, who reviewed the production for the *Financial Times*, *Blasted* "neither glamorizes violence, nor renders it acceptable by placing it in context; in fact, her play is a bold attempt to deal with it neat." That attempt, Hemming wrote, did not work.[91]

Not until Kane and Macdonald began working on *Cleansed*, her third play, did it become clear that portraying violence as the source, rather than the outcome, of identity categories, would never succeed unless that violence was staged in an ostensibly nonrealist manner. And so, in *Cleansed*, a sunflower bursts through the floor as the characters Graham and Grace make love. In another scene, blood flows from Graham's body as his beloved Grace is beaten by an invisible mob: a striking representation of the kind of radical sympathy that *Blasted* failed to accomplish; a fellow-feeling so strong that, as characters recognize their shared humanity as a shared capacity for suffering, the identity distinctions between them become apparent as precarious and contingent.

THE CRITICS' LAST WORD

Long asserted by feminist and postcolonial critics, the insight that looking at ourselves and our others is a social practice shaped by representational conventions also motivated Parks's and Kane's examination of the politics of looking. If this politics stays unexamined, their plays imply, conventions of looking may limit our ability to envision better ways of being together. From the stage, both analyzed how liberal habits of looking, shaped by sentimental and realist conventions, "inscribe a sense of community," in Rancière's terms, in which some inhabit the privileged center and others are pushed to the margins. By experimenting with dramatic and theatrical conventions, they tried to let emerge a different, less hierarchical sense of community. So how could we understand educated critics' initial resistance to their idealistic theatrical experiments?

This resistance could be explained, in part, by their failure to successfully convey their dramatic experiments on stage, and in part by the power of habit that had prompted their first critics' expectation that racial or sexist violence is best critiqued through "corrective," i.e., realist or Brechtian, contextualization. But how do we identify the politics of this insistence in the context of the mid-1990s, a moment of interethnic strife, but also of political hopefulness and economic growth? Francis Fukuyama's inquiry into the politics of identity offers a way to form a hypothesis.

About two decades after Kane theorized identity as an effect of violence, Fukuyama came to a similarly constructivist understanding. In recent texts, he has defined identity as the product of people's perception that their "intrinsic worth" is not being recognized by the larger societies they live in.[92] Put differently, identity is the explanation that people give themselves when they feel that they are not treated with respect. As they see it, the reason they must be so improperly treated is their belonging to a certain class, ethnicity, gender, or another social category. This is why Fukuyama describes identity politics as "the politics of resentment."[93] He is also aware that acknowledging one's intrinsic worth entails specific conventions (or forms) of engagement, and suggests that calls for cultural change from minoritized groups are precisely calls for better recognition of their dignity.[94] But Fukuyama also cautions that "culture and norms are sticky and usually change slowly."[95] And that stickiness could help explain critics' responses to *Venus* and *Blasted*. Given a well-established connection between realism and dignity in African

American theater, as well as a perception of Black performance radicalism as distinct from white experimental art, Parks's rejection of realism and her creative return to Black performance radicalism were bold indeed.

Kane's theatrical experiment too became more acceptable when critics were able to place it in more familiar categories. Eventually, she was declared a founding voice of a new trend, the so-called "in-yer-face theater" that was seen as an heir of sorts to the Angry Young Men's movement of the 1950s and 1960s that also began at the Royal Court Theatre, with its production of John Osborne's play *Look Back in Anger* in 1956.[96] If she were indeed an angry young woman, it made sense that she would share the Angry Young Man's disdain for social mores and for spectators' comfort by creating overwhelming representations of violence. Others tried to normalize *Blasted* by suggesting that Kane seek similarities between her work and Antonin Artaud's "theater of cruelty." At the time, she had not yet read Artaud, but once she did, she responded, to critics' relief, that she felt strong affinity between Artaud's theory and her own artistic sensibility.[97] We may only guess where exactly she saw this affinity, given that, as Martin Puchner has pointed out, it is not clear what Artaud meant when he referred to *theater* in his many essays.[98] Nor does thinking of Kane's experimentalism as an example Artaud's more famous term, *cruelty*, clarify her statement. By *cruelty* Artaud appears to indicate an experience of being with others unmediated by social and representational conventions and certainly unmediated by text, a theater beyond the theater as we know it.[99] In contrast, Kane's ambition "to write a play that could never be turned into a film—it could never ever be shot for television; it could never be turned into a novel. The only thing that could ever be done with it was it could be staged,"[100] indicates a desire to explore the expressive means of the stage to their limit, by first testing the limits of dramatic conventions. In other words, her dramatic innovations drive her theatrical experimentalism.

More important is what such critics signaled by suggesting to Kane that she label her work as Artaudian or by insisting that Parks provide corrective context for her characterization of the Venus. They signaled a demand for balancing experiment and convention when staging social ills, such as racism and sexism. Moreover, they suggested that striking the right balance was the only way to respect spectators' boundaries and therefore their dignity. Recall Sinclair's question to Parks and Foreman: "Did they mean to insult us?" Those spectators wanted to be pushed by experimental playwrights, but they didn't want to be shocked; or if they had to be shocked, it needed to be done in a "properly" experimental fashion, i.e., as Artaud, or the Angry Young Men, or Amiri Baraka would have done it, whatever any of those artists and their works may have signified to any of those displeased critics. In other words, those critics were conscious of their role as active participants in the performer-spectator encounter and wanted to make clear their own sense of which specific art forms inscribed their sense of an ideal community.

In this way, the critics who grappled with *Blasted* and *Venus* anticipated the emergence of another kind of spectator during the next decade: the spectator whom I call *a feeling subject*. In their demand for safe space, that spectator is even less open to experimentalism that could be seen as violating their dignity and much more vigilant toward representation that could violate anyone's dignity. But before I get to this spectator and the discursive context in which they asserted themselves, I discuss another artistic attempt to reexamine sympathy, similar to Parks and Kane in its attention to the socially marked body, yet engaging even more deliberately with the legacy of the avant-gardes: the theater of Forced Entertainment.

2

A Spectator Prepares

FORCED ENTERTAINMENT'S THEATER OF CRITICAL FEELING

There's a word for people like you, and that word is audience.

SHOWTIME (1996), BY FORCED ENTERTAINMENT

Walking in a poor imitation of fashion models, sporting ill-fitting suits, bright Lycra dresses, shiny makeup, and noisy high heels, seven performers stand in line, facing the audience in the semi-lit auditorium with strained, exaggerated smiles.[1] A performer runs backstage, returns dragging another performer by the neck, and forces him to speak in a microphone. The "victim" (Robin Arthur) welcomes the audience in English, French, German, Italian, Greek, and Russian, in a voice expressing pain and discomfort. In the meantime, the "torturer" (John Rowley) is bending the victim's arm and holding his neck tight. "Stop it, I don't know any more," the "victim" pleads. The other actors invite the spectators to laugh at the "victim." After all, everything on stage is done for the spectators' entertainment.

In the second scene, we, the spectators, face the consequences of our complicity. Blindfolded, the actors perform as fortune-telling psychics. The predictions walk an uneasy line between the offensive and the facetious. "There is a very great sense of loss in the auditorium," an actress (Claire Marshall) begins. Another actress (Terry O'Conner) continues: "Somebody lost a father . . . a mother? Perhaps somebody read about a death in a newspaper." The psychological distance between the stage and the auditorium shrinks as the actors' address becomes more specific:

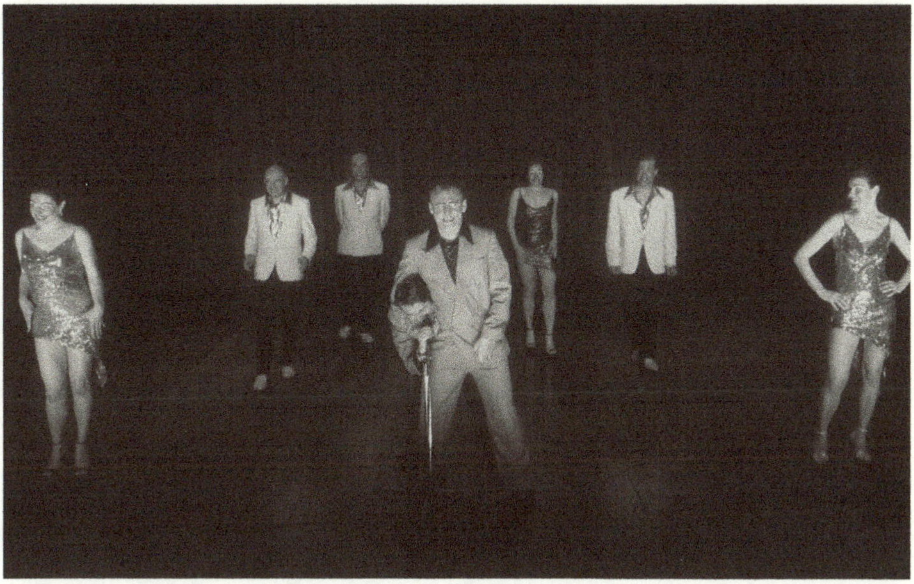

Figure 3. Opening scene of *First Night*, by Forced Entertainment, at The Place, 2001. Photo by Hugo Glendinning. Photo courtesy of Forced Entertainment.

> Somewhere in the back . . . I sense a deep well of bitterness and despair.
>
> Somewhere in the front, I sense joy and happiness.
>
> Somewhere in the middle, there is an overwhelming sense of indifference.

In the recording of the show that I am watching, the spectators applaud the last suggestion the loudest, enjoying the concession that they may be uninvolved, the freedom of detachment that it grants them. But their enjoyment is short-lived: "I'm sensing a very sore penis," John Rowley speaks. "Just to let you know, Sir, it's a lot more serious than you think." The actress in blue (Claire Marshall) continues: "There is someone with us tonight . . . who has a teenage daughter. She is giving you great cause for concern with her attitudes, her friends. Well, don't worry; she will be dead by Christmas." Cathy Naden, the actress in yellow, then takes the black band off her eyes and starts pointing at specific spectators predicting their deaths: kidney failure, suicide, breast cancer, car crash, old age, etc.

In a Forced Entertainment show, watching theater is no simple plea-

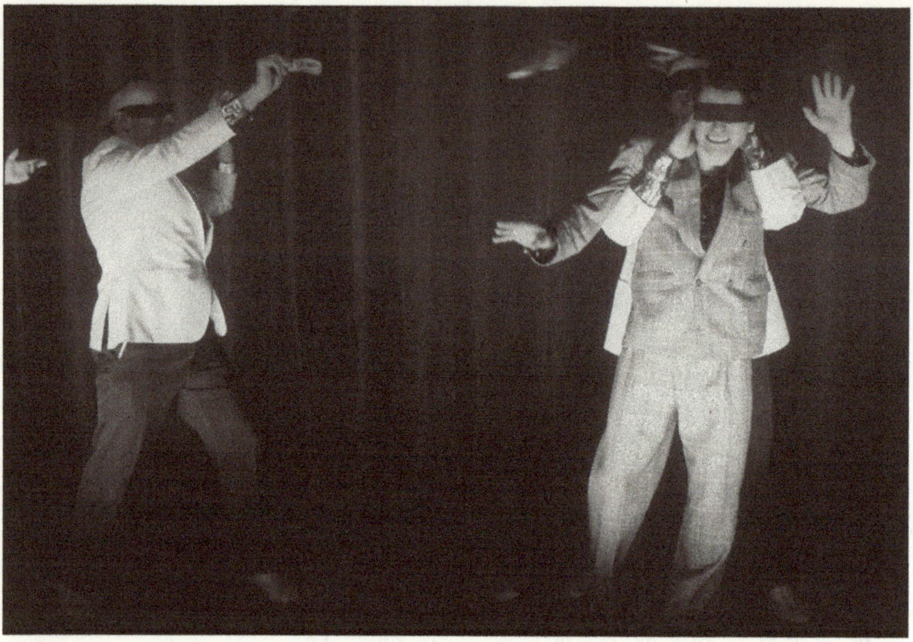

Figure 4. Fortune-telling scene, *First Night*, by Forced Entertainment, The Place, 2001. Photo by Hugo Glendinning. Photo courtesy of Forced Entertainment.

sure. This much we can agree on, as we look back on the nearly four-decade history of this iconic experimental group, which began making theater in Sheffield in 1984. First-time spectators, who may have expected to watch the show in the comfortable privacy of a darkened seat, may find themselves suddenly and unnervingly in the spotlight. Indecorous by mainstream theater standards, the group's methods have understandably divided critics. While some have praised their work for "investigating a new political ethics in the dying days of [the twentieth] century,"[2] others have described it as indulging in a futile postmodern play with signifiers that turns others' pain into spectacle.[3] At issue, for both their admirers and for skeptics, is Forced Entertainment's definition of political theater. As Tim Etchells, the group's artistic director, wrote in 1999,

> The theatre we dreamed of was concerned with ethics and identity, it was deeply and always political but, in embracing the fractured, ambiguous landscape (social, cultural, psychic) of the 80s and 90s in Britain, we knew it

> had to forgo the suspect certainties of what other people called political theatre, that it had to work the territory between the real and the phantasmatic, between the actual landscape and the media one, between the body and imagination. We worked with a growing confidence that a reliance on intuition, chance, dream, accident, and impulse would not banish politics from the work but ensure its veracity—a certainty that old rules did not apply.[4]

Related to this definition is the group's ongoing inquiry into ethical viewing. What does ethical viewing entail in the multicultural, postindustrial Britain at the turn of the twenty-first century? the actors have asked. How does ethical viewing take shape at the theater?[5] This inquiry has also been phrased as an attempt to position the spectator as a witness: someone who is present at the performance event "in some fundamentally ethical way," someone who "feel[s] the weight of things and one's own place in them, even as that place is simply, for the moment, as an onlooker."[6]

In this definition of witnessing, one can see an affinity with Adam Smith's concept of sympathy as conferring personhood on another by recognizing their suffering or joy, a "fundamentally ethical" process in which the observer's own sense of self gets reshaped, however modestly or fleetingly, through the imaginative act of inhabiting the other's circumstances. It is even easier to see similarities between Forced Entertainment's preoccupation with ethical viewing and Suzan-Lori Parks's and Sarah Kane's radical approaches to sympathy that I discussed in the previous chapter. Not unlike Kane, whose play *Blasted* probes a (white) British fantasy of being inherently immune to the interethnic violence that occurs in arguably less civilized places, Forced Entertainment examines the fantasies that mediate the turn-of-the-century Western self's relationship to its cultural others. Likewise, we could propose that by prompting actual spectators to compare their responses to the Venus's dehumanizing exposure with the response of the chorus of spectators, Parks may have intended to make her actual spectators "feel the weight of things [i.e., racial oppression] and their own place in them."

What distinguishes Forced Entertainment's examination of those mediating fantasies from either Kane's or Parks's is the group's paradoxical audience address: one that radically enfranchises spectators while enforcing roles on them with an intensity that can feel coercive. (Anyone who has attended one of their shows has probably seen at least a few fellow spectators leave way before the ending, confused, bored, or disgusted.) The group's ideal spectator, Etchells explains, "play[s] an active role in imaginatively completing the work—reauthoring, speculating, connecting, and creating links among materials that have not been resolved."[7] But spectators are also asked to imagine themselves as people sick with cancer, parents grieving the loss of their children, homeowners whose living rooms are unexpectedly invaded by refugees, and more. This impersonating spectator is central to the company's dialectical model of spectatorship. Even as they are charged with composing a show out of individual vignettes, spectators are asked to do so from within a set of given circumstances, a prescribed position that is by no means neutral. In this way spectators are invited to consciously thread the affect-laden "territory between the real and the phantasmatic" where social politics is negotiated.

This chapter examines this approach as it plays out in Forced Entertainment's piece *First Night* (2001). Fully availing myself of the group's invitation to speculate and reauthor, and to investigate the politics of the distress that the production's form inspires, I read *First Night* as an inquiry into the ethics of living in a diverse, postliberal society. How does it feel to live one's daily life among people different from oneself? the actors seem to be asking. What affects circulate as "we," white Western spectators, grapple with the progressive imperative of loving our racial and ethnic others as we love ourselves?[8] (Admittedly, reading the show as addressed to this specific ideal spectator is a choice that I am making, even as it is informed by my experience of watching Forced Entertainment shows as part of predominantly white audiences.) As it tackles these questions, the group addresses the audience as one more kind of material out of which art can be made, an approach that has precedents in the history of the post–World War II avant-gardes that the group has cited as a source of inspiration for its own work. At the same time, the actors also position their ideal spectator as a Stanislavskian actor called to imaginatively inhabit the circumstances of a *stigmatized character*, one "whose access to discourse must be established as a human right and cannot be assumed."[9] By positioning its ideal audience in this way, I argue, the show tries to make apparent the affective labor that stigmatized subjects perform in Western societies, as well as normative subjects' reliance on that labor to maintain their own, normative, identities.

As in the previous chapter, the ethical question of how to relate to one's cultural others evokes the critical concept of *correct distance*. The correct distance established in *First Night* is deeply embedded in the race-, gender- and class-inflected histories of Western theater and performance. As I explore this embeddedness, I create a genealogy of Forced Entertainment's method: art pieces and intellectual concepts that help us think through the group's experiments. Some of these "precedents" come from the actors' own reflections of their place vis-à-vis their predecessors and contemporaries; others are my own contributions. Thus, I may be taking their encouragement to complete their work farther than they imagined possible.

PERFORMING LIBERALISM'S EXCLUSIONS

The challenges of living in a diverse society must have been very much on the British public's mind as *First Night* opened in October 2001. Four months earlier, race riots had erupted in Oldham and other towns in northern England, following conflicts between white and Asian British groups. The riots were extensively covered by local and national media, who called attention to how racist organizations had exacerbated the deeply entrenched interethnic prejudice among residents of the region. According to the Ritchie Report—an investigation of the social and economic factors that informed the disturbance—by the time the riot began, Oldham had long been a divided city, both because of self-segregation (a desire to live "with one's own kind") and through gang activity. Additionally, far-right activists had been forging an association between the presence of foreign asylum seekers and violence against white British citizens, encouraging the latter to view the Asian immigrants as deceptive asylum seekers. In fact, the first groups of Bangladeshi and Pakistani natives had arrived in Oldham in the 1960s to take jobs in the cotton industry that white workers were finding undesirable. Around the time of the riot, however, a significant number of Oldham's white working-class residents believed that the Asian minority was taking jobs away from them. They also believed that because of their higher birth rates, the ethnic Bangladeshi and Pakistani would soon become the majority in the town. The Ritchie Report found no justification for either of these beliefs.[10] Additionally, only a month before *First Night* opened, the tragedy of 9/11 threw another shadow on the dream of an equitable multicultural society.

This is not to say that *First Night* is about the race riots of May 2001 or about 9/11 in any straightforward sense. Yet the show *is* about those turbulent events, in the figurative sense in which Sarah Kane's *Blasted* is about the ethnic conflict in Bosnia. Like Kane, who tried to write *Blasted* as an act of sympathy to victims of ethnic cleansing in Srebrenica, and in doing so, symbolically decentered the white liberal individual, in *First Night*, Forced Entertainment exposed the limits of Western liberalism at a moment when interethnic violence made palpable the difficulty of seeing those different from oneself as individuals worthy of respect and dignity. A spectator taken aback by the actors' unorthodox address may not immediately notice the intense questioning of Western liberalism in *First Night*. Only in the third scene do the actors spell out a mimetic relationship between mainstream theater audiences and liberal publics. But the group gestures toward an engagement with liberalism from the beginning, through the problematic of pain, represented in the first scene by Robin's being "tortured" by John.

For Sara Ahmed, the ubiquity of pain in public discourse is paradoxical. Although the experience of pain is often presented as private and, to a degree, untranslatable—people do not have the same tolerance for pain—"the pain of others is continually evoked in public discourse, as that which demands a collective, as well as individual response."[11] Moreover, the way we respond to others' pain informs how our social peers perceive us, as compassionate or indifferent, for instance.[12] Because it is capable of situating us in public in a way that matters to our social standing, pain (and emotion generally) is performative, but its precise effect varies depending on the narratives that are being mobilized as we encounter the other's pain.[13] For instance, an organization raising funds for victims of a natural disaster may present their pain as a specifically Christian problem: if "we," to whom the appeal is addressed, are good Christians, we cannot refuse to relieve that pain. Alternatively, in Smith's narrative of sympathy, being able to respond to another's pain makes you a worthy individual, invested in social harmony. And in Forced Entertainment's definition of witnessing, pain comes framed in the avant-garde discourse of immediate presence. "The struggle to produce witnesses rather than spectators," writes Etchells, "is present everywhere in the contemporary performance scene. You can see it in excess/epic style at least, in the public piercings and mutilations by American artist Ron Athey, or in the 'suspensions' on meat-hooks carried out by Stelarc, [an] event in which extreme versions of the body in pain [. . .] demand repeatedly of those watching: 'be here, be here, be here . . .'."[14] For avant-garde artists, the very "unsharability" of pain, as Elaine Scarry characterizes it, its ability to "not simply resist language, but [. . .] actively destroy it," guarantees the truthfulness of the artists' experience. In turn, by acknowledging the significance of the artists' sacrifice, the spectators become promoted to witnesses.

The enduring association between pain and truth, Ahmed suggests, explains why pain works so well across widely different discursive contexts. But the mere fact of showing pain does not guarantee its truthfulness. Instead, pain is perceived as truthful or false depending on how it is shown in public and how observers respond to it. For instance, Smith remarks:

> We are disgusted with that clamorous grief, which, without any delicacy, calls upon our compassion with sighs and tears and importunate lamentations. But we reverence that reserved, that silent and majestic sorrow, which discovers itself only in the swelling of the eyes, in the quivering of the lips and cheeks, and in the distant, but affecting, coldness of the whole behavior. [. . .] We regard it with respectful attention, and watch with anxious concern over our whole behaviour, lest by any impropriety we should disturb that concerted tranquility, which it requires so great an effort to support.[15]

In the liberal script of sympathy, the sufferer's and the observer's dignity depend on their ability to maintain composure during the sympathetic encounter. Not so in the avant-garde encounter described by Etchells, where, he tells us, inflicting excessive pain on oneself is "epic," the guarantee of the artist's commitment to truth.

It is this link between pain and truth, especially as it has been framed in avant-garde discourse, that Forced Entertainment troubles in the "torturer-victim" scene in *First Night*. In that scene, the actor's pain, perhaps true, perhaps truthfully enacted, complicates spectators' responses. How could we even tell the difference? As John twists Robin's arm and Robin strains to welcome us in all the languages he can muster, we could assume that Robin's pain is enacted. There is a cartoon-character quality to Robin's moaning, which is further enhanced by the dark eye shadow he is wearing. And actors, after all, do not usually purposefully injure each other or themselves on stage. But how do we know that we are watching is theater and not performance art, which often stakes its superior hold on the real precisely by allowing for physical injury? It is not unusual for Forced Entertainment to blur the line between theater and performance art, so our uncertainty remains unresolved. And even if we were quite confident that we were watching a theatrical performance, how could we be certain that John is not causing Robin pain unintentionally? Perhaps in rehearsals they worked to find out Robin's pain threshold, but it is possible that at this moment Robin, for whatever reason, is especially sensitive.

The actor's pain thus becomes a visceral metaphor not for truth or "the real," but for their elusiveness, for the space between "[another's] body and [one's] imagination" that for Etchells is the proper space of political theater, and the ground on which ethical viewing is to be defined. Because we cannot ascertain the truth about Robin's pain, we have to make a choice: either decide that Robin is enacting his discomfort and do nothing, or tell John to stop because Robin appears too uncomfortable, which risks exposing ourselves as naive spectators. Thus, at this moment, being a witness does not mean accepting the truth of the performer's pain. It means choosing without guidance how to interpret Robin's pain—as true or as enacted—and accepting the consequences of one's choice. Unlike in sentimentalism, there is no one here to model the appropriate action that this moment may require.

Choosing to view Robin's pain as enacted (as I did when I first saw *First Night* at the Museum of Contemporary Art in Chicago in 2005) compels us to actively produce belief in the theatrical illusion on stage. In other words, rather than suspend our disbelief that what we see on stage is real—the defining move of theater spectatorship—we must keep reminding ourselves that what we see is "only theater." But as the fortune tellers come on stage, the precarity of this strategy becomes evident. What if the spectator who is told they will die from cancer has already been battling cancer? What if the spectator who is told they will commit suicide is already struggling with clinical depression? At that moment I feel for those hypothetical spectators, and for all my fellow-sufferers with whom I bear the actors' assault. I extend to them the sympathy that I could not extend to Robin, and momentarily, I also feel that I had been right to deny him sympathy. He has never been a "victim." He was just pretending to be one. Thus, the self-serving logic of sympathy—the biased way it divides society into "us" and "them," as the perception of who could be in pain shifts from one participant in the encounter to another—becomes apparent to me. And perhaps, as I notice that self-serving logic, I become present in the "fundamentally ethical way" that Etchells talks about.

Notably, in that scene, the group returns, with a critical difference, to the surrealist and Dadaist strategy of manufactured chance. Whether making poems out of words cut out from newspapers and then randomly rearranged (for instance, by tossing them up in the air and accepting the way they fall as the poem's structure) or raising found objects (*objets trouvés*), such as Duchamp's urinal, to the status of sculptures, Dadaists and surrealists tried to create art free from "the means-end rationality" of bourgeois society. According to Peter Bürger, by relying on chance, those artists hoped to avoid bending their art materials to their own preconceived objectives, instead bending their artistic will to the material.[16] (Bürger also found this strategy inherently compromised, pointing out that the artists who employed it subscribed to a means-end rationality too, the end being their resistance to the normative, individualistic concept of the artist as one who controls the artistic process.[17]) In the fortune-telling scene, Forced Entertainment "manufactures chance" out of its spectators' possible responses to the predictions in the fortune-telling scene. The "predictions" of cancer and suicide that they hurl at the auditorium seem to rely precisely on the audience's awareness that for some spectators those words may hit too close to home. But in doing so, the actors, I believe, are not trying to elicit a truthful, arguably unmediated emotion from those hypothetical spectators. Instead, this controversial strategy makes apparent how emotions inform our sense of what is or is not real—as in my shifting assignment of "victimhood" from Robin to "us" spectators—and how our reliance on this affectively informed distinction contributes to social divisions.

The politics of Forced Entertainment's return to the avant-garde becomes even clearer when we consider the group's use of the happening. According to Etchells, *First Night* was inspired by Peter Handke's 1966 play *Offending the Audience*, which addressed spectators as ill-mannered impostors, in an obvious breach with mainstream theater decorum, much as Forced Entertainment does in the fortune-telling scene. Handke has described his play as a reduction of theatrical speech to stimuli. As the play was performed, he said, "many spectators didn't even listen to what was being said. They heard the rhythms, and apparently rhythms somehow reduce the distance between speakers and listeners. These rhythms turn directly into emotion, bringing objects closer."[18] "My point," he explained, "was to use words to encircle the audience, so they'd want to free themselves by heckling; they might feel naked and get involved."[19] Additionally, he wanted to convey to the audience his sense that reason and emotion cannot be separated.[20] In other words, by verbally abusing them, Handke hoped to draw spectators' attention to their unfreedom, manifested in their compliance with bourgeois social norms, including the imperative to watch a performance in respectful silence. Breaking with those norms would make spectators "naked," i.e., "truthfully" present. Hence, by offending the audience, Handke hoped to transform the theatrical encounter into a happening. Indeed, for Susan Sontag, confronting the audience in an abusive manner "seems to provide, in default of anything else, the dramatic spine of the Happening."[21] And for Judith F. Rodenbeck, the purpose of such aggressive treatment is to reveal the spectator as "a cluster of motor reflexes," a subject more susceptible to affect than inclined to reason.[22] At the core of this approach, Rodenbeck proposes, is an understanding of the human subject as a neurological machine, a set of manipulable data that could be meddled with "to perfect the mechanization of affect."[23]

But to achieve its purpose, the happening, too, relies on manufactured chance, the chance that spectators will submit to the artist's abuse. In turn, this all-important reliance on the spectator's willingness to cooperate informs the distinctive performer-spectator contract of this genre. Ideally, in the happening, artist and audience freely choose to become disenfranchised objects. To make apparent the oppressive effects of the bourgeois commitment to reason, the avant-garde artist needs an audience ready to become "a cluster of motor reflexes," at least for the duration of the performance event. Hence, the artist's creative agency is authorized by spectators willing to relinquish their own agency in the name of an artistic experiment. At the same time, the artist puts themselves at the mercy of the audience's unpredictable reactions. Or, as Bürger frames it, by manufacturing chance, the artist tries to "submit" to their "material," which, in the happening, is the audience itself.[24]

For Rodenbeck, in the first decade after World War II envisioning the human subject as a cluster of manipulable affects was an emphatically political act. For one, the Holocaust had been just such an atrocious experiment in reducing persons to organisms responding to stimuli. Additionally, the invention of the computer and the spread of the television network in the 1950s spurred a reframing of the individual as a consumer whose choices and perceptions could be influenced through emotional manipulation.[25] Hence, in the midcentury happening, in "freely submitting" to the artist as their material, the spectator-performer had a degree of agency that is absent from the image of the consumer as a product of market stimuli, or the image of the Holocaust victim. The happening thus was an exploration of the freedom available to a postrational Western subject. In the visual art of the period, writes Rodenbeck, this postwar subject was often represented as a black box, a motif reflecting the increasingly ubiquitous shapes of computers and television sets.[26] Rodenbeck describes Robert Rauschenberg's box-like sculptures of the 1950s, such as his *Music Box (Elemental Sculpture)*

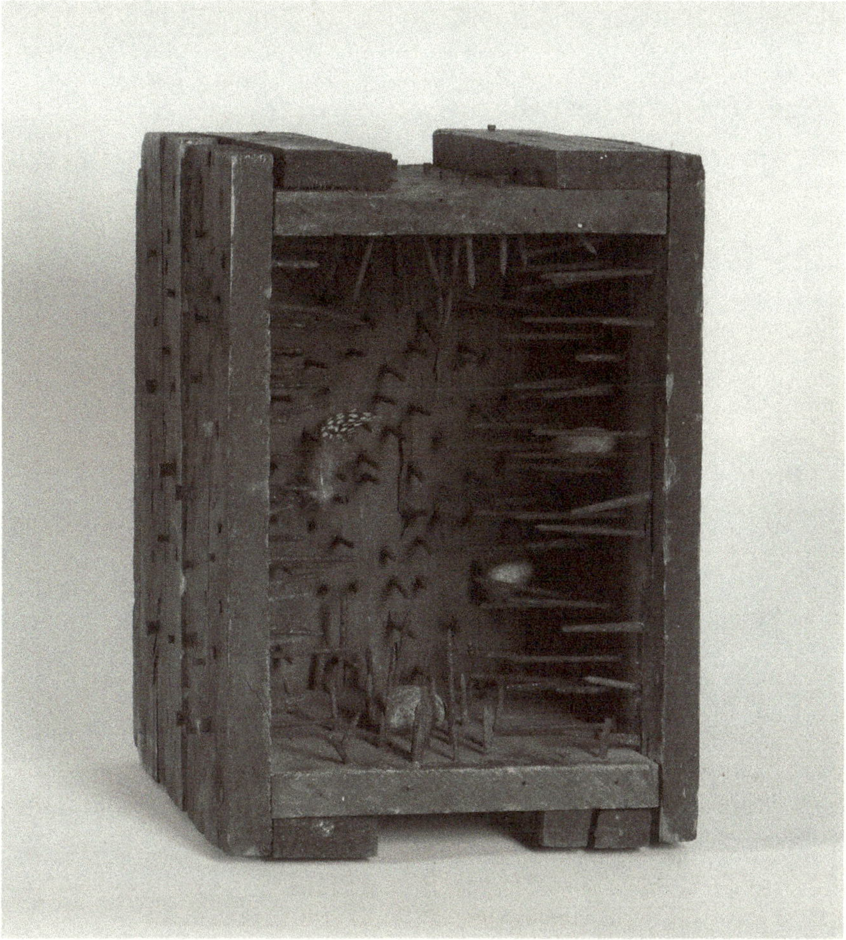

Figure 5. Robert Rauschenberg, *Music Box (Elemental Sculpture)*, ca. 1955. Wood crate with traces of metallic paint, nails, three unattached stones, and feathers, 11 x 7 1/2 x 9 1/4 inches (27.9 x 19.1 x 23.5 cm). Collection of Jasper Johns. ©Robert Rauschenberg Foundation. RRF Registration# 53.027.

(ca. 1955) (whose protruding spikes also suggest the Procrustean bed), as representative examples of this aesthetic. *First Night* signals the same preoccupation with torturous manipulation through the mandate to consume in its final scene, where Robin, unable to escape his victimhood status, gets stuck into a rectangular, box-like shopping bag with only his head visible at the top.

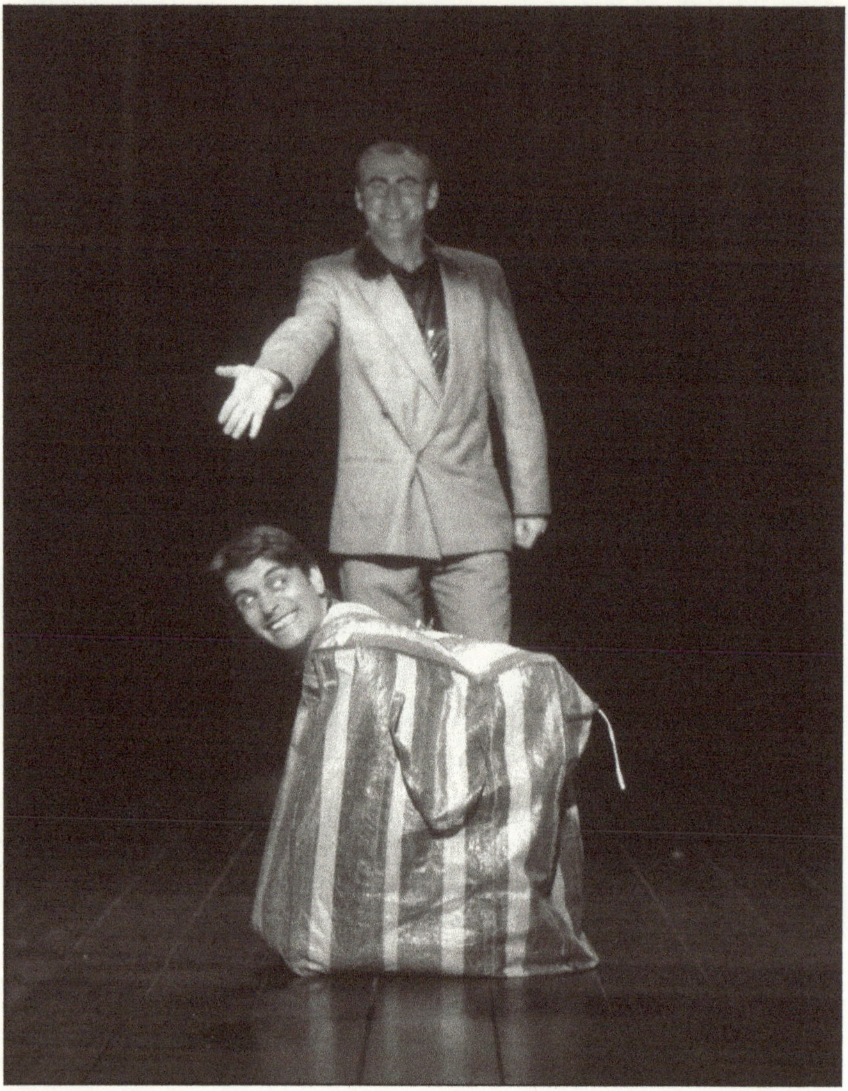

Figure 6. Final scene of *First Night*, by Forced Entertainment, The Place, 2001. Photo by Hugo Glendinning. Courtesy of Forced Entertainment.

That Forced Entertainment should be returning to this postrational subject in the torture-victim scene (a spin of sorts on the Milgram experiment[27]) and beyond is not surprising. The company defines its work as post-televisual, describing it as theater for anyone "who was brought up in a house where the TV was always on."[28] Throughout their work, the actors have also been grappling with the question of how consumerism complicates ethical spectatorship and how the liberal democratic ideal of the individual, as a person with dignity, becomes strained as individuals become objects for viewers' enjoyment. For instance, in *Nights in This City* (1997), the actors took spectators on a bus tour around Sheffield, goading them to stare at locals who had not consented to be made part of the group's show.[29] Indeed, rationalizing Robin's pain as not real because "we are at the theater" is an example of spectatorship as a consumerist act. But while for midcentury artists, the consumerist subject was still a new phenomenon that had yet to be studied, resolved, and experimented with, by 1984, when Forced Entertainment was founded, this subject and their "black-box" aesthetic had become part of late-twentieth-century *common sense*.[30] Technology "is in your blood," Etchells wrote in a 1999 essay about television. "[It] will move and speak through you, like it or not."[31]

This difference—the idea of the subject as a cluster of affects having been normalized—seems to be one factor informing the specific way that Forced Entertainment returns to the midcentury avant-garde. For while their theater is often cruel, it is not a *theater of cruelty*. Their ideal spectator is not a de*person*alized knot of reflexes or an Artaudian object who has joyfully shed all individual agency. Instead, the group's ideal spectator is compelled to im*person*ate. She will accept or at least try on, willy-nilly, the *persona* offered to her by the actor fortune-tellers, though this persona could be quite repulsive. "There are no racists in the auditorium, are there?" "There are no wife beaters here, are there?" Terry O'Conner asks at the end of the show, her sarcastic tone implying that such people are in fact sitting among us (and perhaps within us). What these questions and Etchell's emphasis on the phantasmatic imply is another aspect to the postwar consumerist subject. This subject is made not just of affects and reflexes, but of dreams: media-induced dreams of consumption and media-induced fantasies of one's others. And so, by forcing its spectators to impersonate, Forced Entertainment lays bare the post-televisual subject's *common sense*: the fictions that shape this subject's understanding of their place in the world. In laying those fictions bare, the group suggests that becoming aware of our common sense as constructed may be a path to ethical viewing.

Those media-induced fictions are precisely what complicates the response to Robin's "victimization" in the opening scene. At that point, the racial and gender aspects of the performance contract that the audience has just entered into have not yet been made explicit. Both actors, torturer and victim, are white, which could be why John's invitation to laugh at Robin comes across as a somewhat acceptable response. But how would that change if a Black actor were performing the victim? Given the violent history that shaped the Black body as a body in pain, and at the same time created the stereotype of the violent Black male, casting a Black actor as the victim or, for that matter, as the torturer, might have prompted different readings, and Terry's question—"There are no racists in the auditorium, are there?"—might resonate even more poignantly.

There is another complication, too. Nothing suggests that Robin is forced to be on stage as the victim, so we can assume that, suffering or not, he is there of his own free will. The clear-cut conflict of liberal values central to sentimentalism is absent. If Robin has agreed to be the victim on stage regardless of whether that may cause him pain, and if he is getting paid for his performance, should we even worry about whether he is in pain, or whether his involvement in the scene violates his dignity? It is not simply a consumerist subject but, more accurately, a neoliberal subject, who is raising the latter question. By 2001, in a post-Thatcher Britain that social theorists would soon call neoliberal, personal dignity—the liberal right whose protection, from Rousseau on, has formed the core of modern democracy—was being actively reinterpreted.[32] Within a neoliberal framework, dignity transforms from an inalienable right into a profit resulting from our appropriately directed efforts. The torture-victim scene questions the implications of this shift. What is our responsibility as Robin labors for our pleasure, possibly getting hurt as he does so?

The uncertainty of whether sympathy is the appropriate response to a scene that, at first glance, seems to call for sympathy may prompt a response that, *pace* Tracy C. Davis, could be called *theatricality*: the deliberate suspension of sympathy toward an individual in pain that enables insight into the systemic causes of their suffering.[33] As a response to suffering, theatricality also derives from classic-liberal theory, questioning sympathy's unwanted effects on the sufferer's dignity. "Nothing is so mortifying as to be obliged to expose our distress to the view of the public, and to feel, that though our situation is open to the eyes of all mankind, no mortal conceives for us the half of what we suffer," Adam Smith wrote.[34] The sufferer in the quote feels acutely the gap between his feelings and the spectator's, despite the latter's effort to put himself in the sufferer's circumstances. As the spectator becomes aware of this gap and of himself as acting according to prescribed conventions, theatricality occurs. The possibility of such distancing from the conventional sympathetic encounter, Davis also contends, becomes the foundation of Brecht's performance contract where the suspension of sympathy becomes a tool for Marxist analysis.[35] In fact, my hesitancy about the scene's meaning and my ensuing consideration of a neoliberal redefinition of dignity suggest that I may have been watching with theatricality.

But theatricality, as Davis defines it, does not properly describe the contract that Forced Entertainment offers to its audience in *First Night*. Perhaps because the actors view the post-televisual spectator as one inured to televised suffering, watching without sympathy is not the response they encourage. Like Parks and Kane, instead, they seem to be looking for aesthetic forms that would encourage fellow-feeling for those whose victimization or "aptitude" for violence has become normalized through established aesthetic forms. Hence, the post-televisual subjects must learn to impersonate. This becomes evident in scene 3 of *First Night* where the mimetic relationship between liberalism and the mainstream theater encounter is made explicit.

In scene 3, the actors come onstage again and stand before us in a row, holding the letters W-E-L-C-O-M-E-! They thank the audience for coming and assure us that they, too, feel welcome onstage tonight. But soon the discomfiting dynamic of the previous two scenes settles in. "I'd like to say at this point," Terry O'Conner begins, "I'd like to say that some of our personal lives are in tatters." "But you don't want to hear about that, do you?" adds Richard Lowdon in a conciliatory tone. Their exchange calls attention to the liberal divide between the individual's private space and her social performance as a member of the public, while also highlighting the realist convention that the actors' offstage personas be set aside while they enact their characters on stage. Both kinds of performance, the social and the theatrical, have been critiqued by materialist critics for concealing the labor invested in preparing public performance. Ibsen's *A Doll's House* (1879) uncovered the public-oriented, private female labor of the bourgeois home, while helping establish the concealment of the actors' offstage labor as a principle of stage realism. In contrast, Brecht and midcentury experimental artists aspired to make the performer's labor public, while also drawing attention to how technology (for instance, the conveyor belt) molded the laborer into a particular kind of subject.[36] Like those predecessors, Forced Entertainment suggests that mainstream theater molds the spectator into a voyeur: someone who feels entitled to ignore the actor's offstage labor. This attitude, we quickly learn, deserves a punishment.

"I'd just like to say that what happens backstage is just as much fun as what happens out here on stage," K. Michael Weaver continues, "but quite frankly it's none of your business." The private space of offstage labor now becomes a titillating mystery, but having presumably failed to inquire about it, we will not be made privy to its secrets. "It's so boring anyway," John mumbles apologetically, trying to restore conventional theatrical decorum. But Claire continues, unforgivingly, "The curtains parted and there we were: spread out in a line for your enjoyment." As will become clear shortly, the privilege of remaining ignorant of the actors' offstage woes establishes the average spectator (white, middle-class, and educated) as a liberal individual. Put more simply, according to scene 3, being a liberal individual means being able to ignore the labor that others do on your behalf. The conceit of *First Night* is that everyone in the auditorium fits this description.

After an awkward pause, which Claire bears with an unflinching look and a frozen clownish smile on her heavily made-up face, the actors assure us that there won't be anything unpleasant or disturbing in tonight's performance. (Apparently, we are supposed to have already gotten over any unpleasant feelings that the fortune-telling scene may have provoked, or perhaps this is a signal that we should blot it out of our memories.) "Nothing will give the men an embarrassing erection that they will have to cover over with their coats," Terry elaborates. After a spell of laughter from the audience, she adds, equitably: "Nothing will get the ladies so wet that they'll have to cross their legs in order to conceal the smell." And certainly, Richard promises, "nobody's gonna be shut into a box that's much too small for them, have the lid shut down with hammers and nails." "No actors are going to be blacking up," John continues, "in order to portray kings in very, very old long stories." "Yes, quite so," Robin confirms amicably. "Perhaps now is the time to say," he adds enthusiastically, "that you, you people down there, you are the real stars of tonight's performance, and, really, without you, we would be nothing." "Really," Claire confirms more soberly, but with the same discrepant smile on her face, "without you, we are quite literally nothing." "I am reminded of an old saying," Cathy joins in, "which goes something like this: all the world is a stage, and we are some of the people on it." "So it don't matter, does it, ladies and gentlemen, that we are up here on the stage, and you are not. Because the whole world is one," Jerry giddily chimes in, giving the famous Shakespearean quote an egalitarian gloss. But before we have had the chance to absorb this euphoric burst of egalitarianism, Robin gently and pragmatically qualifies Jerry's statement: "Yes. But tonight, we are going to be staying on this smaller stage." "Yes," Jerry agrees, "and you [the audience] are going to be staying on that bit, which isn't this bit." "And if you got personal problems out there," Terry adds, "they are none of our business."

The contract that the actors have just drawn between them and us, their spectators, has all the trappings of a liberal social contract. We, actors and spectators, are arguably equal participants in the night's performance, which is conceived as a democratic process. The actors are thus our representatives (elected through the purchase of tickets) charged with clarifying from the stage issues that concern us, such as the ethical questions raised by the competition between the liberal and neoliberal ideologies. But, as the pragmatic Robin points out, echoing political theorists, the absolute equality among people governing themselves is an ideal that in practice gets limited in various ways.[37] Thus, even as we are all together on the stage of the world, tonight, Robin points out, only the actors get to be "on this smaller stage." And if we followed closely the comedic fast pace of the actors' exchange, we would also catch their reference to the gender, class, and racial limits of the liberal ideal. Under this contract, we are told, the actors will do nothing to provoke (visible or olfactory) signs of gender difference from becoming conspicuous in the audience. To be equal, in other words, we need to bracket off our gendered bodies and forget about racial difference: "No actors are going to be blacking up," the actors have promised. Liberal equality, as numerous critics have pointed out, would be unthinkable without such strategic forgetfulness.

But not long before Forced Entertainment began working on *First Night*, part of the British public was becoming increasingly unwilling to practice liberal forgetfulness, drawing attention to the status of Black Britons in the social contract. One way this reckoning became manifest was in changing attitudes toward blackface. Around the time *First Night* was devised, the practice of blacking up in public had become newly contentious. As performance historians have pointed out, in the nineteenth and early twentieth centuries, white British audiences, just like white American spectators, were captivated by grotesque representations of blackness. Offered by touring

American performers such as Tom D. Rice, and by English actors such as Charles Mathews, blackface shows catered to an audience fascinated with the diversity and vastness of America. A sense of superiority to Black people was probably a factor in the genre's success in Britain, as it was in the United States, but as historians have proposed, British spectators of minstrel shows also felt at a certain remove from the moral implications of blackface, especially because Britain had abolished slavery before the United States did.[38] Additionally, a rich folk tradition of blacking up, including mummer plays and morris dances, may explain why blackface was still widely practiced in Britain in the last decades of the twentieth century.[39]

At the turn of the twenty-first century, however, a growing awareness of racial and ethnic diversity as integral to a contemporary British identity urged performers to transform or discontinue the practice of blackface. If blacking up once signified respect for folk tradition, as well as freedom of expression, it was now being reevaluated in terms of its impact on Black Britons. Their dignity had come to matter in a way that required a change in aesthetics. In 2000, Rotherham became the first council in Britain to ban blackface in all professional and amateur productions in its buildings. A decade later, the British actor's union formally acknowledged that "the practices known as 'blacking-up' and 'yellow-face' are offensive to many performers and cannot be justified except in very limited circumstances." In the meantime, mummers and morris dancers began experimenting with other colors, for instance, painting their faces blue.[40] Or as Rancière may have put it, a palpable shift in sensibility had occurred: for part of the British public, it was now "self-evident" that the equality of Black Britons, as individuals with dignity, demanded that these traditional performances be modified.[41]

As I watch the recording of the show, yet again, a "promise" made to the spectators in scene 3 also makes me think of the connection between dignity and space in the classic liberal contract. "Nobody's gonna be shut into a box that's much too small for them, have the lid shut down with hammers and nails," Richard says. He is most likely alluding to the Procrustean bed, a metaphor for the cruelty of judging everyone by the same, arbitrarily chosen standard. Indeed, by scene 3, many spectators might feel as though the actors are judging them, by some tacit standards of their own, for sins that the actors are just beginning to name. Yet, as Richard mentions that torturous box, right after Terry has talked of spectators who cannot contain their erections or bad smells, I begin thinking of theater boxes. What does it mean to be told at the theater that you smell or that your body fails to meet the norm in some other way? As it poses these questions, the show evokes the long history of segregated seating in British and American theaters, where, across different periods, social hierarchies were not only solidified into theater architecture but were enforced through shaming.

In her economic history of the nineteenth-century British stage, Tracy C. Davis writes about the efforts undertaken by theater managers and regulatory agencies to make theater venues safer for citizens' health. Typhoid and cholera epidemics were the objective impetus behind such efforts, but the specific steps taken across various theater houses had more to do with social perceptions than with threats to health. The odors emanated by lower-class spectators were deemed especially troublesome, and theaters who attracted such customers in large numbers drew the regulators' special attention. In those theaters, too, the architectural segregation of customers—boxes against gallery, stalls against pit, and occasionally separate entrances, based on ticket pricing—was particularly entrenched. In contrast, theaters whose managers were able to attract primarily middle-class and wealthier customers (or hoped to do so) gradually abandoned the boxes in favor of the more egalitarian-looking dress circle.[42]

In the United States, as is well known, segregated performance venues and movie theaters confined Black spectators to the third balcony—the farthest away from stage or screen, narrow and close enough to the ceiling to make the spectators feel cramped and claustrophobic. Sometimes they had to access this balcony through a separate entrance.[43] Even where a designated "colored" space did not exist, as in the movie theaters of early-twentieth-century Chicago, ushers would sometimes steer Black spectators away from white ones because, according to the ushers, white spectators found Black spectators' smell offensive.[44] White women's presence at the theater was also controlled, though more subtly. With the introduction of matinee performance in the late nineteenth century, middle-class white women could go to the theater unattended without risking their respectability. And yet, Dorothy Chansky has analyzed numerous cartoons and texts in popular periodicals that ridiculed female matinee spectators, describing them as unable to focus on the show because they were eating noisily and talking.[45]

Compare the overregulated spaces to which those spectators were relegated and the freedom with which the classic liberal subject inhabits and moves between coffee shops, salons, and playhouses. Recall also Smith's insistence on the unbridgeable distinctiveness—the insuperable psychological space—between the sympathizing observer and the object of his sympathy. The seating and scheduling practices described by Davis, Chansky, and others made literal the connection between disenfranchisement and the inability to control one's space. How did being reminded so bluntly of your disenfranchisement influence those spectators' ability to sympathize with normative and stigmatized characters on the stage and screen? By telling their spectators that their smelly, aroused bodies ostensibly fail to meet the norms of propriety at the theater, the actors not only place us metaphorically in the seats of stigmatized spectators of the past, they highlight the performative power of shaming. By being shamed, Sara Ahmed suggests, the class, racial, or gendered other's behavior is marked as shameful before a public of normative subjects; by being publicly treated as disgusting, the other becomes disgusting, an object to be kept on the fringe of the conforming community.[46]

The power of the privileged group to define its boundaries in this way is perhaps most poignantly illustrated by stigmatized subjects' acceptance of those boundaries as proper and decorous. For instance, through the Black press, early-twentieth-century Black Chicagoans instructed recently arrived Southern migrants about public etiquette, advising them to keep their voices low and take care to not incidentally brush into someone, particularly if the migrants were in their (presumably dirty) work clothes.[47] Unwittingly, those migrants were being compelled to perform lack of cleanliness by staying away from arguably cleaner subjects. Likewise, in a 1916 note first published in *The Crisis*, the Black intellectual W. E. B. Du Bois scolded his fellow Black spectators for laughing inappropriately while watching a performance. "Any actor is pleased when the responsiveness of his audience shows him he has got his lines 'across,' but the most frenzied Othello can hardly conceal his bewilderment when his attempt to strangle Desdemona provokes shouts of merriment," he wrote. "Is this state of affairs due to ignorance or thoughtlessness? To a combination of both, I fancy. We cannot afford either."[48] His urge to edify those erring theatergoers is particularly striking because he is recounting an incident at a venue for "colored people." Even there, among fellow Blacks, he felt the burden of white judgment and insisted that all Black spectators watch theater with this judgment in mind.

Du Bois knew that Black spectators could not afford to laugh at *Othello*, because, mediated by the fiction of Blacks' inferiority, their merriment would inevitably appear as ignorance. But he also understood that embracing a fiction you cannot shed (or, as Parks may have said, a fiction that won't quit) may enable critical insight. Out of this understanding, he developed the counterintuitive, embodied way of being in the world that he named *double-consciousness*. Not long after he had formulated that concept, his contemporary Virginia Woolf articulated a structurally similar critical perspective, informed by her own experience of not fitting in a man-made world. She named that perspective *a splitting-off of consciousness*. Those concepts describe Blackness and femininity as the performative effects of being told you don't fulfill the liberal ideal. Hence, returning to them can help illuminate Forced Entertainment's attempt to engender an ethical stance out of being made to feel bad in public. I begin with Woolf because Etchells indirectly gestures to her feminist critique of space when in his essays he ponders the question of ethical viewing. "You can see the plea for witnesses," he writes, "in the use of personal and unlikely public spaces by Bobby Baker—kitchens, medical centres, schools. In [her] work one gets [. . .] an invitation to be here and now, to feel exactly what it is to be in this place and this time."[49] In turn, Baker credits Woolf's prose, and particularly *A Room of One's Own* (1929), in which Woolf develops the concept of splitting-off of consciousness, as a formative influence on her own work.[50] And while Forced Entertainment does not refer to Du Bois in any way, his description of being "here and now" in a place where you are told you do not belong and the critical-race critique of liberalism he develops from that space complement Woolf's feminist critique.

WATCHING THEATER WITH QUEER FEELING

The feminist perspective that Woolf called a splitting-off of consciousness developed on the literal and figurative margins of the early-twentieth-century, male-dominated academia. In her foundational essay *A Room of One's Own* (1929), Woolf describes a female novelist who tries to walk through the campus of a private male college while composing a lecture about women and fiction. Her attempt at a contemplative stroll is repeatedly thwarted by male characters who inform her that she is out of place there. The grass is reserved for students and scholars only, and the library is inaccessible to women. As she zigzags through the college, continually redirected, literally put in her place by men with authority, she observes herself not being able to get absorbed in composing her lecture, as her femaleness gets continually and punitively impressed on her. Transcending her body—the imaginative act enabling the presumed objectivity of the liberal thinker—is not an option for her. Under these circumstances, a critical feeling takes shape:

> Again if one is a woman one is often surprised by a sudden splitting off of consciousness, say in walking down Whitehall, when from being the natural inheritor of that civilization, she becomes, on the contrary, outside of it, *alien and critical*. Clearly the mind is always altering its focus, and bringing the world into different perspectives. But some of these states of mind seem, even if adopted spontaneously, to be less comfortable than others. In order to keep oneself continuing in them one is unconsciously holding something back, and gradually the repression becomes an effort.[51]

A feeling of not fitting in, imposed from without, produces an undesired, uncomfortable, yet fertile distancing: such splitting off of consciousness, troubling and draining, gives women's writing the power of suggestion, Woolf concludes.[52] As she is barred from assuming the arguably disembodied, objective position of the male liberal intellectual, a radically embodied feminist perspective begins to emerge, providing the thesis of the novelist lecturer's essay. Women's fiction, like all female knowledge, is informed by the social critique a woman develops as she is continually reminded of being "alien" in spaces of learning created for men.

Ahmed might call this specific feminist perspective *a queer feeling*: one that emerges from experiences of not fitting into normatively structured spaces (not to be confused with *feeling queer*, i.e., experiencing the world as a sexually nonnormative subject).[53] Queer moments, Ahmed explains, may occur when, as one fails to properly inhabit a normative space, one embraces and enjoys the negativity of shame, "of that which has been designated shameful by normative culture."[54] This is what happens as Woolf's female novelist tries to get lost in her thoughts by walking leisurely through the male college: she is made aware of a normative script that she fails to follow. As she embraces the discomfort of being pushed around, she happens on a new critical perspective, one that opens up an alternative intellectual space, while making evident the contingency of liberal thought on having a male body.

Like Woolf's splitting-off of consciousness, Du Bois's concept of double-consciousness originates in an academic space designed to welcome some and marginalize others. As readers of his work will recall, Du Bois first used that term in his essay "Of Our Spiritual Strivings," initially published in the *Atlantic Monthly* in 1897. In the essay, Du Bois recounts an episode that he views as the primal scene of his blackness. At school, during an exchange of visiting cards, a tall white girl refuses to take his card. For Du Bois, this felt as though a veil had been drawn between him and white people. From then on, he would continually strive to tear that veil down. Considered in classic-liberal terms, the episode shows the white girl refusing to imagine herself in Du Bois's circumstances. By rejecting his card, she tacitly, but effectively, presents his blackness as an insurmountable difference in their life circumstances. By thus denying equality to Du Bois, she molds him into a subject with double-consciousness: "a stranger in [his] own house," one constantly looking at himself through the eyes of white others, deprived of the fantasy of being a unified subject.[55] Du Bois then recalls responding "felicitously" to the girl's formative gesture, making it his life's objective (and eventually the objective of all Black Americans) to match and surpass white Americans at all things coded white: science, the humanities, art, and sports.

Yet already in this essay, double-consciousness is described not just as a plight that has to be overcome on white terms; it is also a gift of insight. "After the Egyptian and Indian, the Greek and Roman, the Teuton and Mongolian, the Negro is a sort of seventh son, born with a veil, and gifted with second-sight in this American world," Du Bois writes.[56] This notion gets further developed in "The Souls of White Folk" (1920):

> Of them [white folk] I am singularly clairvoyant. I see in and through them. I view them from unusual points of vantage. Not as a foreigner do I come, for I am native, not foreign, bone of their thought and flesh of their language. Mine is not the knowledge of the traveler or the colonial composite of dear memories, words, and wonder. Nor yet is my knowledge that which servants have of masters, or capitalist of artisan. Rather I see these souls undressed and from the back and side. I see the working of their entrails. I know their thoughts and they know that I know. This knowledge makes them now embarrassed, now furious![57]

Across these two texts, written over twenty-three years, double-consciousness emerges as a richly ambivalent concept. Du Bois vacillates between his awareness of having blackness performatively enforced on him and yearning for an ideal, essentialist blackness in the tradition of Western romanticism.[58] Having been made "a stranger in his own house," he conceives of a place where the Black race "naturally" belongs, an imaginary community (*pace* Benedict Anderson) of great ancient tribes.[59]

But in both essays, the romantic nationalist Du Bois shares space with an equally compelling Du Bois who is a queer thinker. As he proclaims Black pride in "The Souls of White Folk," he seems aware that, to be successful, such rhetorical gestures may require some form of acknowledgment from the white status quo. It is perhaps his knowledge that such acknowledgment will not be easily granted that explains the ambivalence in his phrasing. Again, in "Of Our Spiritual Strivings," the Negro is described as "*a sort of* a seventh son [. . .] gifted with a second sight in this American world" (my italics). The hesitant "sort of" and the historical and geographic particularity of "this American world" take us away from the mythic time of Egyptians, Teutons, and Mongolians to the unexalted reality of living as a Black person in the early twentieth century. The Negro's gift of second sight thus derives from his inability to transcend the material circumstances of racism and become (seen as) properly mythical: a seventh son unprefaced by disclaimers.

The Black thinker who emerges out of this situation is thus, of necessity, an anticategorical thinker. He is neither a foreigner nor a traveler; his knowledge doesn't fit servant/master, capitalist/artisan, or other binary models.[60] As a knowing subject, he is neither separate (i.e., distanced) from his object of study—whiteness—nor assimilated into it. He is *the bone* of white thought and *the flesh* of white language: a position that (as racist violence reminds him daily) is conspicuously different from the transcendental Cartesian *cogito*, the product of the abstract mind's imagined victory over the misleading senses. In the language of late-twentieth-century theory, such knowledge may be retrospectively described as *queer*: knowledge that is at once "antiseparatist [and] antiassimilationist," as Eve Sedgwick may have put it.[61]

Neither the similarity of context in which the queer feelings of split-consciousness and double-consciousness emerged, nor the similarity in naming, are accidental. Such feelings seem to arise around the edges of liberal discourse, and "consciousness" was a buzzword as pre-Freudian and eventually the Freudian models of the mind were becoming popular in Western intellectual circles.[62] It is probably not a coincidence that as Forced Entertainment began thinking about how liberalism's promise of equality was accomplished in their own times (or failed to be), they tried to evoke similarly queer feelings in their spectators by suggesting that their undisciplined bodies do not fit in the auditorium.

But why adopt a Stanislavskian approach to evoking such queer feelings? Watch *as if* you may be fighting cancer; watch *as if* you had a difficult teenage daughter; watch *as if* you were sexually aroused in public; watch *as if* you were a racist, the actors keep instructing us. Stanislavsky's naturalism is typically thought of as part of the bourgeois institution of theater that the avant-gardes tried to deconstruct. Indeed, Rodenbeck points out, this is just how Stanislavsky entered post–World War II avant-garde discourse: as the aesthetic model that had to illustrate, through comparison, what avant-garde art was *not*. The avant-garde was *not* an aesthetic proclaiming an "authentic" subjecthood, based on emotions, with which spectators could sympathize. Instead, Rodenbeck argues, the avant-garde, and especially the happening, let the human subject experience themself as "fundamentally mediated and contingent."[63] For artists like Kaprow, this amounted to a truthful aesthetic experience.

The same preoccupation with showing subjecthood as mediated and contingent seems to motivate Forced Entertainment's return to Stanislavsky's process of creating a role, whereby his actors explored how placing themselves in the given circumstances of a character might evoke specific feelings. In this process, the contingency of feelings on the adoption of a specific perspective becomes apparent. Whereas avant-garde artists may have seen in the System an attempt to produce affective authenticity on stage, Forced Entertainment saw a strategy to expose the contingency of feelings on the subjects' specific perspective. In other words, the actors return to Stanislavsky not to affirm the "authenticity" of spectators' feelings for their others, but to show us how such contingent and manipulable feelings mediate both our perceptions of ourselves and our perceptions of others as different.

In thus redirecting Stanislavsky's method from the stage to the auditorium, *First Night* inadvertently calls attention to the racial politics of the System. (We are told, for instance, that trying to place ourselves in the circumstances of stigmatized subject by blacking up may be not a good idea.) Indeed, although race was not in any way central to Stanislavsky's thinking about naturalism, he grappled with it on at least one important occasion: his attempt to create a realistic Othello. Looking at his struggle to realistically inhabit the circumstances of Shakespeare's Black Moor shows how his understanding of race and realism evolved together. In turn, the insights Stanislavsky gained from working on *Othello* help clarify the *correct distance* between self and other in Forced Entertainment's approach to spectators.

Like Smith, who emphasized the distinctness between the sympathizing individual and his object, Stanislavsky considered merging between actor and character to be impossible. "You can understand a part, *sympathize* with the person portrayed, and put yourself in his place, so that you will act as he would," the theater director Tortsov, a fictional surrogate for Stanislavsky, says in Elizabeth Reynold Hapgood's English translation. "That will arouse feelings in the actor that are analogous to those required for the part. But those feelings will belong, not to the person created by the author of the play, but to the actor himself."[64] While in the Russian original Stanislavsky does not use the verb "sympathize," it aptly describes the actor's creative act. Literally, Stanislavsky says, "You may *understand*, *feel* your part, you may put yourself in the character's place and start acting as the character would. This creative action will recall, in the artist himself, feelings analogous to those of the part. But these feelings belong not to the character created by the poet but to the artist himself."[65] To understand is to feel, Stanislavsky suggests, articulating his own elegant definition of sympathy.[66]

Feeling a role, Stanislavsky further explains, is inseparable from creating the appropriate physical aspects of a character's behavior. This reflects his recourse to pre-Freudian psychology, as he tried to think through the relationship between action and emotion. Théodule-Armand Ribot, from whose theory of the mind Stanislavsky borrowed his concept of *emotional memory*, proposed that such memories were stored in the *subconscious*, a behaviorist predecessor of the Freudian *unconscious*. Stanislavsky's indebtedness to behaviorism explains his attention to the physical behavior suitable to each character: a felicitously chosen physical action, he believed, would lure the actor's elusive emotional memory into revealing itself, resulting in a lifelike performance.

This logic resonates with nineteenth-century theories of sympathy that held that some practices and behaviors were more conducive to sympathy than others. As Gay Gibson Cima writes in her account of nineteenth-century antiracist activism in the United States, "[e]vangelical and mainstream Christians held that women were particularly gifted at sympathetic identification and that through their embodied, imaginative suffering a diverse nation could be forged into a unified one. [. . .] This national project was so important that men were encouraged to become more like women in terms of sympathy; men's fashion wardrobes even began to include corsets, so that their very bodies would more closely resemble women's."[67] A suitable costume, in other words, could incline the body, and hence the mind, to specific feelings. Working on *Othello* enabled Stanislavsky to test this hypothesis firsthand.

Elise Marks has proposed that watching *Othello* allowed late-nineteenth- and early-twentieth-century European spectators to vicariously "'*un*domesticate' themselves, 'liberat[ing] briefly' another self [. . .] normally restrained by Western propriety."[68] Stanislavsky's first attempt at understanding the Moor was similarly primitivist. To prepare his own production of Othello, in which he played the part of the Moor, he traveled to Paris, where he befriended an Arab immigrant. Stanislavsky told the man about his intention to direct Shakespeare's play, and the man invited him to spend time with him and other members of his community so that Stanislavsky could observe their body language, clothes, and manners. "After that," writes Stanislavsky, "I saw Othello as a cross between [the actor Tomaso] Salvini and my new friend, the handsome Arab."[69]

In this description, we see Stanislavsky treat the person who would become his prototype for Othello with all the good intentions and self-serving obliviousness of a classic liberal. To point out the obvious, he mentions Salvini by name, but not the Arab, despite his claims to friendship. He also blatantly exoticizes the Arab, describing his "movement of the hands and body like a graceful deer."[70] Having finally attempted the role on stage and (in his own estimate) failed, he concludes that he failed precisely because he exoticized Othello, rather that treating him as an individual whose outsider status had put him into an extremely difficult situation.

Therefore, when he next approached Othello, he scrupulously attended to the character's thoughts and feelings. Creating the appropriate physical life of the character remained important, but secondary to the importance of understanding how the European history of racism and anti-Islamic bias may have informed the conflict between Othello and the white Venetians. How does the Venetian Senate feel about having to entrust their lives to a Black man "whom they despise," as the Turkish fleet is invading Cyprus? Stanislavsky asked. Did Desdemona fall in love with Othello the individual, or Othello the exotic warrior? How did it feel for Othello, who must have known that Venetians saw him as inferior, to be invited into Brabantio's home?[71] Having tackled these questions, he then asked himself, "What circumstances of my own inner life—which of my personal human ideas, desires, efforts, qualities, inborn gifts and shortcomings—can oblige me, as a man and actor, to have an attitude toward people and events such as those of the character I am portraying?"[72] Thinking about how the characters' social circumstances—including their racial politics—inform their private relations and public encounters thus became key to his thinking about realism. In the course of this reconsideration, Stanislavsky's character analysis begins to approximate Du Bois's and Woolf's examinations of the racist and sexist societies they lived in. Othello emerges as deeply uncomfortable with his position, yearning to be accepted, and full of unwanted insight into the ways of the proudful Venetians.

In *First Night*, we see a similar negotiation of the distance between the liberal self and the stigmatized other, reframed as a viewing position. We spectators will not be put in costumes, be enclosed in boxes, or have our faces blacked up as we ponder our relationship to our racial and ethnic others. We are cautioned against reducing those others to their looks and mannerisms, as Stanislavsky did with the Arab man in Paris. Rather, in a performance contract that reckons with theater's inequitable history, we are urged to see ourselves as theater misfits, as people who do not fit well in the auditorium. In turn, accepting our part as misfits may move us to become aware of the territory "between the body and imagination," the social fictions that inform our sense of who belongs or doesn't, even as we are "just" sitting in our seats.

The performative work of these fictions is made evident in the second-to-last scene, in which the actors get the closest to talking about the Oldham riots, without explicitly doing so. At the beginning of the scene, Robin is tortured again. Jeremy holds Robin's arms behind his back, John stuffs playing cards into Robin's shirt and mouth and moves as though he were raping him. Standing on each side of Robin and his molesters, Richard and Michael goad us into laughing. We do. It is clear that Robin is not really getting raped: all the actors are fully dressed and wear black bands over their eyes, as in the fortune-telling scene. An incongruous music theme, suggestive of a wondrous fairy-tale world, accompanies their actions. Funnier still, Robin manages to get out of Jeremy's grip, pinning Jeremy's arms down, and making Jeremy the target of John's aggression.

Though taken by surprise, the unnerved Jeremy soon gets out of the victim's role by stepping into that of a fortune teller. "I am getting something; I am picking something up," he shouts out in an urgent voice and points toward the audience. His spiteful predictions are our payback for having laughed at him. An unspecified man is told that by the time he gets old, he will be so fat and ugly that no one is going to look after him. A woman in the audience will try to buy her favorite newspaper tomorrow, but it will have sold out, and she will have to settle for a worse one. Soon enough, predictions of greater woes follow. A man who lives in a nice neighborhood will see it deteriorate as gangs of immigrants move in, burnt-out cars appear in the streets, and the buildings are defaced with graffiti. And when he comes home from work one day, he will find out that a family of refugees from a foreign war has set up camp in his living room and started a fire with his books so they can cook a stew. Another man will fare even worse, trying to get home one day only to find that the police have blocked the street to his house because terrorists have gotten inside and are holding his family hostage.

The hilarious but vivid fantasy of a violated living room in a nice (i.e., middle-class) neighborhood strikes at the heart of the bourgeois sensibility theatricalized in so many classic realist plays. Where once it was a resentful wife or a vengeful one-time friend who threatened the quiet domesticity of the bourgeois home, it is now "the refugee." To make things worse, it is not a single refugee, but a whole family of refugees, who, ignorant of advanced technologies such as the kitchen stove, unwittingly yet relentlessly destroy one of the most enduring signs of bourgeois cultivation: the books in the living room. No wonder that in Jeremy's angry outburst the refugee quickly becomes "a terrorist." In the aftermath of the Oldham riots and 9/11, this slippage would have resonated particularly strongly.

According to Ahmed, such fantasies, suggestive of the fantasizing subject's fear of losing their status, are integral to the politics of fear that racist organizations thrive on.[73] Fear, she writes, aligns bodily and social space and in doing so effects "a collective": us versus them.[74] In the scene above, Jeremy's predictions in response to his humiliation lay these dynamics bare. Having lost his status as a torturer and found himself in the role of the victim, he tries to reestablish himself by threatening the spectators with an immigrant invasion. Implicitly, he tries to convince spectators that he and we are on the same side, that there are others who deserve the spectators' degrading laughter. While we laugh at him, "our fellow Englishman," "they," the foreign refugees, unlawfully intrude on "our culture," "our homes," "ourselves."[75] Thus the figure of the migrant/terrorist helps Jeremy clarify to us our "true" identity. And as Jeremy does so, he draws attention to how the actors have been using fear—the fear of being singled out as a racist spectator or as one who smells—to forge a cohesive whole out of *First Night*'s individual spectators. For however each of us may react to the actors' provocations—with laughter, boredom, disgust, anger, or in another way—"we" are all vulnerable to being embarrassingly singled out. Of course, the "we" of the audience can be only somewhat cohesive. How might a Bangladeshi man or woman, or a white man or woman from Oldham, pro- or anti-immigrant, have responded to Jeremy's performance? As Ahmed reminds us, fears of intrusion and cultural degeneration attach to some bodies more than others, because the circulation of fear is mediated by already established stereotypes.[76]

As the scene shows us to ourselves as a collective connected through fear, it also questions "our" ability, as Western liberals, at the turn of the century, to fulfill the multicultural imperative of loving the other. As Jeremy suggests, in our minds we may still be living in Ibsen's living rooms, the exclusive spaces of classic liberalism, even as a different kind of character (an immigrant, a Black Briton) calls for a different imaginary and a different social contract. Loving our others as we love ourselves will probably entail new spaces, new public habits, new fantasies circulating among us. All that, Forced Entertainment suggests, also entails queer feeling: becoming strange to ourselves like Du Bois and Woolf in their moments of enforced self-estrangement. This is what ethical viewing is about.

ADVANCING TO SOME KIND OF DEMOCRACY IN TINY LITTLE GRANDMOTHER-LIKE STEPS

In a 1998 interview, Robin Arthur described Forced Entertainment's creative process as advancing "in tiny little grandmother-like footsteps."[77] The reason they moved forward so slowly, Claire Marshall clarified, was because the group saw itself as "some kind of democracy."[78] I cannot think of a better metaphor to describe the way the company negotiates the *correct distance* between selves and others than that of an elderly woman carefully picking her way through the fantasy- and affect-rich terrain of life in diverse societies. This woman is a postmodern figure. She returns to the past neither to reject its lessons as no longer useful, as an avant-gardist would, nor to radically rewrite it as a justification for her utopian social project, if she even has one. Instead, the past—always somewhat reshaped as she delves into it, provoked by her present-day concerns—becomes a repository of social and aesthetic practices that she can draw on as she tackles the specific challenges of her present moment.

This dynamic relationship between past and present characterizes Forced Entertainment's return to the avant-garde, Stanislavsky's System, Woolf's and Du Bois's critiques of liberalism, and the segregated spaces of nineteenth- and early-twentieth-century playhouses and cinema halls—not as authoritative precedents used to legitimize the group's own theatrical experiments, but as models to be tried on as the company continually looks for the correct distance between selves and others at the beginning of this century. In their theater, the correct distance to the other, as well as to the past, does not entail getting to an unmediated truth. Rather, finding that distance entails one's willingness to own uncomfortable narratives. And in making the spectator aware of how watching theater is embedded in such narratives, spectatorship is exposed as a discursive and affective practice with subtle yet important social implications. In other words, by inviting spectators to impersonate, *First Night* makes apparent the agency involved in spectatorship, a kind of agency based, in part, on failure. As in Du Bois's and Woolf's critiques of liberalism, in *First Night*, too, insight is contingent on failing the liberal norm, i.e., on spectators' willingness to inhabit the failures of liberalism's promise of equality as they manifested in the history of theater practices.

It is possible that this kind of spectatorship relies on a spectator who is not too concerned with having their worthiness affirmed, perhaps because they have never had it drastically challenged. Indeed, for almost four decades now Forced Entertainment has been able to rely on a self-selected audience, in Britain and abroad, willing to have their *common sense* contested. In the case studies that follow, we see that postmodern view of the past—and the critical spectatorship based on it—rejected as relativist and indulgent, a luxury that those dedicated to social equity cannot afford. A feeling subject, mobilized by the imperative of ending injustice once and for all, proposes a new grand narrative of history as trauma and a new aesthetic of protest based on militant victimhood.

3

The Behzti *Riot as a Contemporary Avant-Garde*

The Sikh riot against the Birmingham Repertory Theatre's production of *Behzti (Dishonour)*, by Gurpreet Kaur Bhatti, which broke out on December 18, 2004, has become a frequently recounted episode in the history of contemporary British theater. According to a chronology provided by the Commission for Racial Equality, which was involved in the case from the very beginning, the controversy began in August 2004 when members of the Birmingham Sikh community learned that the Birmingham Repertory Theatre would be staging a play about hypocrisy and double standards among British Sikhs. Worried that aspects of the play may cause tension within their community, Sikh leaders approached the West Midlands Police, asking them to mediate between the community and the theater. In response to their request, the police organized a series of meetings between Sikh representatives and the theater and even got the theater to agree to let the representatives attend a rehearsal, much against the wish of the artists, who did not yet feel ready to perform before an audience.

The Sikh representatives praised the playwright's critique of Sikhs' moral failures. Such critique, they said, was integral to Sikhism. Yet they were deeply disturbed by the playwright's decision to set a rape scene and a murder scene in the Sikh temple, the gurdwara, even though neither scene contained any graphic detail. Staging these acts in the gurdwara, they claimed, was an assault on Sikhism's essential dignity, and therefore a racist act.[1] Perhaps, they suggested, these scenes could be set in a Sikh community center. Bhatti, however, felt that such a change would violate the artistic integrity of her play and refused to make it. Instead, seeking to be fair, the theater decided to distribute a leaflet before each show, conveying to the audience the opposing Sikhs' position. Unsatisfied by this solution, the Sikhs informed the police that they would be holding peaceful demonstrations. As the play opened on December 15, 2004, small numbers of Sikhs began protesting quietly outside the theater, while other Sikhs, in Britain and beyond, defended the production. Three days later the number of protesters grew to about 400 and some attempted to enter the theater, injuring three police officers, breaking windows, and damaging equipment. All spectators, including parents and children who had come for the theater's Christmas show, had to be evacuated. Bhatti and her family received death threats, and on December 20 the theater canceled the play because it could not guarantee spectators' safety.[2]

Many have discussed at length the political implications of the controversy. Indeed, "the *Behzti* affair" (named after "the Rushdie affair"[3]) has become an emblematic example of the tension between freedom of expression and cultural sensitivity in Western multicultural societies. Intriguingly, to my knowledge no commentator has seriously considered how the *Behzti* controversy was shaped by the theater artists' and the protesters' aesthetic choices and perspectives. In fact, from the outset, the clash between the artists' right to expressive freedom and the Sikh community's demand that their religion be respected was also tied to each party's sense of the connection between liberal rights and aesthetic contracts. As I noted, for Bhatti, staging rape and murder in the gurdwara was a matter of artistic integrity. As the conflict escalated, director Janet Steele made the same point, claiming that artistic integrity also entailed artistic autonomy. "We were the victims of a political scenario," Steele commented; a scenario that relegated the discussion of the play to "the news pages" rather than to "the arts pages, where it belongs."[4] In other words, she claimed that even if art engages in social commentary, as *Behzti* does, its presumed essential autonomy from politics should protect it from legal accountability. This is just the kind of modernist argument that Peter Bürger scoffs at in his *Theory of the Avant-Garde*. In contrast, and much like Bürger, the protesting Sikhs asserted a view of art as a social praxis, always embedded in the broader political discourse of its time. Or, in Rancière's terms, between the artists and the Sikhs, there was no consensus—no *common sense*—about the boundary between art and social reality, and hence about art's accountability for its social effects, whether accidental or intended.

That a controversy about religious imagery manifested as a clash between a modernist and an avant-garde paradigm may come as a surprise to those who share Bürger's Marxist attitude to religion as "the opiate of the masses." But Mike Sell, who has critiqued this aspect of Bürger's theory, contends that many avant-garde movements have drawn on religion as a source of "critical perspectives, resistant cultural practices," and utopian social visions.[5] Likewise, by drawing on Sikhism, the protesting Sikhs provided a critical perspective on mainstream British theater as a liberal institution that practices multiculturalism only within the limited framework of a liberal social contract. That contract, as analysts of the Muhammed cartoon controversy have pointed out, entails a specific theory of representation that liberalism considers rational, while rejecting alternative theories as irrational.[6]

At the core of the *Behzti* controversy was the status of the gurdwara on stage. Was the staged gurdwara an artistic representation, as the artists claimed, or did it remain an actual gurdwara, as the protesters argued? As the question suggests, the artists and the protesters approached the play from within two different systems of signification: a system that posits an essential distinction between objects and their representations, and an alternative system that asserts continuity between them. Only within the latter does it become possible to read the staging of rape and murder in the gurdwara as an offense to Sikhism's essential dignity. But as Birmingham Catholics joined the protesting Sikhs, demanding legal limitations on expressive freedom when such freedom could be interpreted as blasphemy, the controversy assumed the more familiar shape of a tension between secularism and religion. Yet, crucially, the protesters and their allies framed their objection to *Behzti* as a demand for respecting cultural diversity. Drawing on Mike Sell's analysis of the avant-garde's "theatrical authenticity," I call this strategy an instance of theatricalized credibility.

This chapter argues that the *Behzti* controversy cannot be fully understood without proper attention to the two disparate systems of signification that informed the conflicting interpretations of the gurdwara. Because critics failed to account for how those systems shaped the controversy, they had a hard time establishing the *correct distance* to both the play and the protest, and as a result could not grasp their larger implications. As I try to demonstrate, understanding how those systems informed different spectators' interpretations of the play illuminates an aspect of the controversy that previous analyses have overlooked: the playwright's radical feminist return to Sikh scripture that, I believe, accounts for the intensity of the Sikh reaction against the production. By noticing yet not publicly acknowledging that feminist critique, the protesters managed to frame their protest as antiracist, without appearing sexist. More importantly, in the name of antiracism, the protesters also tried to assert that alternative system of signification as one that a truly multicultural society should legitimize. I further argue that the participants' attempts to establish their credibility by publicly performing their minoritarian positions *as racially marked* illuminates the larger discursive shift that this book seeks to understand: a shift from equality, understood as a liberal value, to equality as the acknowledgment of minorities' sense of their intrinsic worth.

• • •

Occurring only three years after 9/11, the *Behzti* controversy was framed by concerns about the longevity of Enlightenment values and the fate of multiculturalism that became so prominent in the aftermath of the terrorist attack on the United States. Participants in the debate quickly assumed one of two positions: a liberal anxiety about the future of Western democratic values, including the separation of church and state, or a critical-race critique of the British multicultural model. That these two positions were perceived as antagonistic, rather than complementary, was made evident by the heated responses to home officer Fiona Mactaggart's attempt to dissolve tension by presenting the Sikh protest as an expression of free speech: "When people are moved by theatre to protest [. . .] it is a great thing [. . .] that is a sign of the free speech which is so much a part of the British tradition."[7] It seems that Mactaggart was trying to remind the British public that freedom of expression applies equally to a theatrical production and to critiques about it, even when such critiques take shape as protests. Also notable was her attempt to prevent racist outbursts against the protesters by representing their actions as integral to "the British tradition." Many, however, took issue with her proposition that a protest that had violently closed down a theater could be viewed as an example of free speech. Outraged, they accused Mactaggart of dangerously slipping into cultural relativism: "It looks like we are going to have to fight and win the Enlightenment thinkers' battle for freedom of thought all over again," warned Salman Rushdie, drawing a parallel between the cancellation of *Behzti* and the fundamentalist Islamic reaction against his novel. "One must never forget that the battle was not against the state, but the Church."[8]

Aesthetics did become part of the debate to the extent that everyone involved recognized the play specifically as art, rather than as representation more generally. Numerous theater artists, especially those involved in the production, echoed Rushdie's view of a fundamental distinction between the artists and the protesters. According to the artists, freedom of expression did not apply equally to a religiously motivated protest and to an artwork. In the words of Dominic Dromgoole, the artistic director of the Oxford Stage Company, "nonconformity is as natural to theater as conformity is to religion," hence "it is theatre's role not to be bullied by religious or ideological sensibilities."[9] According to playwright David Edgar and theater historian Helen Freshwater, the artists' insistence on theater's autonomy reflected the relatively weak protection of the freedoms of expression and speech in Britain, compared, for instance, to the protection these rights enjoy in the United States under the US Constitution. "It's worth remembering," Edgar wrote, "that up until the abolition of stage censorship in 1968, British playwrights couldn't show two men in bed together, mention venereal disease, criticize the royal family, insult friendly foreign powers or represent God."[10] Likewise Freshwater points out that "freedom of speech in Britain was merely 'a legal leftover'—what remained after the application of the laws which cover libel, obscenity, privacy and official secrets—until the 1998 Human Rights Act became domestic law in 2000."[11]

In contrast, the protesters insisted that exceptions apply when "sacred icons" are represented on stage. Besides, they stated, "freedoms are never absolute, least of all in multicultural, multiracial societies where responsibilities to co-exist must limit them."[12] This statement resonated with at least some commentators. In a letter to the *Guardian*, Sarita Malik argued that freedom of speech, as practiced in the West, is "deeply racially coded" and the Sikh community's response to *Behzti* signaled a need to rethink how this freedom is practiced in a multicultural society.[13] Similarly, for Gurharpal Singh, a professor of theology at the University of Birmingham, the protest highlighted the "assymetrical pluralism" in the British state's approach to diversity. Although Britain had proven itself willing to grant minorities exceptions from "general rule-making," it had resisted a transition to "deep multiculturalism," i.e., to "a radically plural and diverse British democracy" that would require rethinking the Western values underlying the status quo.[14] But even as she largely shared Malik and Singh's position, political scientist Monica Mookherjee added an important nuance to the discussion. While Singh emphasized the group rights of minorities, Mookherjee drew attention to the rights of individuals within a minority group. The tension between the status quo, based on Western Enlightenment values, and the demands of cultural minorities, Mookherjee wrote, could not be democratically resolved without guaranteeing the individual's right to dissent. In her view, the *Behzti* controversy highlighted the advantages of *progressive* multiculturalism, a political arrangement whereby minority groups are granted rights *as groups*, while individuals are guaranteed the freedom to challenge their group's values and positions.[15] Missing from this conversation is an assessment of how a transition to deep multiculturalism or progressive multiculturalism might inform (and be informed by) artistic practices. In a society truly appreciative of Sikhism's distinct values, would a play such as *Behzti* be unacceptable, as the protesters argued? Or would a progressive approach to multiculturalism guarantee Bhatti's right to represent her religion as she saw fit? And above all, how exactly had the production disrespected Sikhism's sacred icons?

That theologians and political scientists such as Singh and Mookherjee did not raise these questions is understandable. But in-depth analysis of how the play's aesthetic choices informed the controversy has been scarce even in theater and literary commentaries about the play, which tend to describe *Behzti* as an artistic failure. "*Behzti* is unlikely to feature on any list of great British plays," wrote the feminist literary scholar Priyamvada Gopal. "*Behzti*, it should be made clear, suffers from uneven style, inconsistent switching of registers, and at the end, a cramming together of events that would startle even a hard-core aficionado of Bombay's action films and family melodramas, long used to suspending disbelief."[16] Though less harshly than Gopal, theater scholar Brian Crow suggests that *Behzti*'s aesthetic serves the play's critique of Sikhism poorly. "In *Behzti*," he writes, "there is nothing in the characterization, dialogue or action to indicate anything positive within contemporary British Sikhism [. . .]. There is no sense of any presence within the *gurdwara*, or within Sikh culture generally, that counterbalances the comic or more sinister depravity of its priest, elder, and female initiates."[17] At the same time, Crow quotes the observation of Roshan Doug, then poet in residence at the Birmingham Rep, that *Behzti* was especially successful in attracting "young Asian, and especially female Asian, audiences precisely because of their willingness to deal openly and trenchantly with important issues that dominant members of the community wish to suppress."[18] But despite this favorable reception, Crow concludes that Bhatti "was arguably misguided in using the tragicomic and satirical dramatic form [. . .] if she was really serious about engaging in constructive 'debate' [. . .] a wide cross-section of the Sikh community."[19]

While I disagree with Crow—the play, as I will show, does depict a positive example of Sikhism, and its comedic form is integral to its critique of corruption among Sikh leadership—I find his comment revealing about how he understands the social responsibility of theater. Crow, too, appears to think of theater as a social praxis, one whose objective is to build consensus through "constructive debate." He also suggests that some aesthetic modes—particularly satire and comedy—may be less conducive to such debate than others. This understanding of art—as a palliative intervention in social ills—informed not only the critical reception of *Behzti*, but also the immediate critical response to Sarah Kane's *Blasted* and Suzan-Lori Parks's *Venus*. Such criticism implies that because these playwrights did not provide the kind of representation of Sikhism, blackness, or Britishness that their audiences would have found acceptable, those playwrights were responsible for the controversies their plays caused. As I explain in more detail in chapter 4, the implication that artists are a priori responsible for any effects of their work that spectators may find offensive is a major aspect of the sensibility of the social actor I call the feeling subject.

But it is precisely by not trying to appease the protesting Sikhs that Bhatti and her collaborators provoked a productive, if not constructive, debate on multiculturalism in Britain, just as Parks and Kane, by not following representational rules that would have guaranteed their spectators' comfort, incited a debate about the politics of representing racism and sexism on stage, and about the politics of theater criticism. In all three cases, affect-rich performances effectively highlighted a link between social tensions and aesthetic preconceptions, by stirring a range of feelings among diverse groups of recipients, while refusing to build consensus. And this, according to Elin Diamond, can be the mark of a truly feminist intervention.[20]

COMEDY AND BHATTI'S RADICAL FEMINIST RETURN

In her foreword, which she wrote before the production's opening night, Bhatti justifies her decision to write a potentially offensive play as stemming from her Sikh commitment to truth. "Truth is everything in Sikhism," she begins. "The truth of action, the truth of an individual, God's truth."[21] This commitment takes shape in the story of the ambitious but disillusioned widow Balbir and her well-meaning, naive daughter Min, as they decide to go to the gurdwara for the first time in many years, on the birthday of Guru Nanak. While Balbir intends to reconnect with her community, hoping to make an advantageous match for her daughter, Min hopes to feel spiritually uplifted through the rituals of Sikhism. Min's hopes are thwarted as Mr. Sandhu, the leader of the gurdwara and the culprit responsible for Balbir's social isolation, rapes Min in his office and then proposes to marry her. In raping Min, he is assisted by another Sikh woman, the middle-aged Teetee, whom he once also raped but who agrees to assist him to procure a lucrative business opportunity for her underperforming son. Violence, it becomes clear, is an established way of doing business in the gurdwara. The plot resolves as Balbir, helped by a repentant Teetee, kills Mr. Sandhu with Sandhu's kirpan (a ritual sword), arguably restoring both her daughter's and the Sikh community's honor.

Bhatti's decision to expose a horrific discrepancy between Sikhism's prescriptions and practices primarily through the perspectives of women and their experiences (of violent sexual initiation into adulthood, difficult marriages, unsatisfying motherhood, and socially isolating widowhood) aligns her play with a robust line of feminist inquiry into Sikh gender politics. Scholars identify the source of this discrepancy in the deep intermingling between Sikh scripture and the influential unwritten Punjabi codes of behavior that often prevail in the daily practices of Sikhism. From its inception in the late fifteenth century to the death of the tenth guru in the early eighteenth, Sikhism, as recorded in the *Guru Granth Sahib*, the Sikh scripture, articulated a powerful message of social equality. Women, regardless of their class, caste, or marital status, participated in worship on the same terms as men. Women and men could wear the same five symbols of Sikhism—uncut hair, a comb to keep the hair neat, a steel bracelet, breeches, and a kirpan—and were equally encouraged to fight oppression. Likewise, early Sikhism rejected caste distinctions, and scholars have argued that since caste was in part based on complexion, Sikhism also promotes racial equality.[22] But according to feminist scholars, by the turn of the twenty-first century, Punjabi customs had overtaken the progressive message of Sikh scripture:

> [I]n many gurdwaras a married Sikh female is not allowed to partake in the *amrit* (initiation) ceremony unless she is accompanied by her husband. Further, while women are encouraged to cook, clean, and wash dishes for the Sikh communal meal (*langar*), they are not permitted to enter the *sanctum sanctorum* of the temple [. . .] where the Guru Granth is placed.[23]

Also, despite Guru Nanak's explicit rejection of the notion that menstrual blood is a sign of pollution, "today during their menstrual period, women are not allowed to do prakash [the morning ritual of opening the Guru Granth] or sukhasan [the evening ceremony of closing the Guru Granth]."[24] (This particular discrepancy is addressed in *Behzti* when, seeing the blood on her clothes after she has been raped, Balbir slaps Min's face, thinking that Min has come to the temple on her period.) As a result, one feminist approach to Sikhism, especially common among third-generation women from the Sikh diaspora, has taken shape as a radical return to Sikh scripture, deliberately read as autonomous from Punjabi-influenced Sikh practices.[25]

This approach is not unique to Sikh women's search for empowerment. In *Politics of Piety* (2005), Saba Mahmood analyzes how Egyptian Muslim women have similarly found social empowerment through close reading of the Quran, a practice that has sometimes motivated them to act differently from established Muslim custom.[26] At the same time, such radical returns to texts belie the simplicity and straightforwardness implied in the phrase "close reading"; they only make sense if we understand the specific factors that motivated them in the first place. Famous Western examples—notably the Protestant returns to the Bible, which produced multiple interpretations and denominational variation, or the American and Russian literary formalisms, which despite their proclamations of political neutrality found themselves entangled with various political agendas—also reveal close reading as deeply mediated by culture and ideology. In *Behzti*, Bhatti, like her contemporaneous Sikh feminist scholars, undertakes a return to Sikh scripture. But because she does so through the conventions of Western comedy, she immediately draws attention to the mediated nature of such a return, particularly to the politics of undertaking this return as a British-born Sikh woman in multicultural Britain.

Behzti depicts a Sikh community that has betrayed the Sikh scriptural mandate for egalitarianism and organized itself according to strict patriarchal principles. Men lead worship and the community's economic and social life; women work in the kitchen and support men's decisions, vying with each other for the leader's attention and the social and material rewards he can grant. While Sikh scripture explicitly prohibits the isolation of widows, after Balbir's husband's "dishonorable" suicide, the community has abandoned her and Min to isolation and poverty. Mr. Sandhu's acts of adultery and sexual violence and his brother's history of drug abuse are explicitly prohibited by the Sikh ethical code. Greed, which motivates Teetee's decision to assist Mr. Sandhu in raping Min, is viewed by Sikh scripture as the gravest of vices and the source of all human conflict.[27] In contrast, Min, who has not been formally instructed in Sikhism, effortlessly practices the selflessness that Sikhism values as the highest virtue. She devotedly nurses Balbir, who, having suffered a stroke, needs help walking, bathing, and going to the toilet. And although Balbir's discontent sometimes drives Min to aggression (on one occasion she tapes Balbir's mouth with Sellotape to stop her from berating her), Min never dreams of having a different life. As she prepares to go to the gurdwara, she tells Elvis, the young Black man who sometime helps her take care of Balbir, that she will pray "that things can stay [the same]. For me and for her."[28] Like Min, Elvis gladly assists elderly and disabled people, for which he gets modest payment from the state: "I shave and wash and wipe them till they look like million dollar grannies and granddads," he tells a woman in the gurdwara.[29] In the last scene, Elvis consoles the distressed Min and persuades her to join him in a dance that subtly recalls the weddings at the end of Shakespearean comedies: celebrations of communities coming together after having overcome a deep moral crisis. But in *Behzti* this familiar comedic trope celebrates a biracial and distinctly multicultural vision of "true" Sikhism.

This happy resolution is preceded by a standard comedic narrative of mistaken identities. At the gurdwara, a disoriented Elvis momentarily feels attracted to Polly, a forty-eight-year-old Sikh woman "who is losing her once sensational looks."[30] In a brief but passionate encounter, they exchange a kiss. Elvis then talks to the Gianni, Mr. Sandhu's brother, seeking advice on how to tell Min he loves her. Polly, who overhears part of the conversation, thinks that Elvis is talking about his feelings for herself, rather than for Min, but eventually learns the truth. Disappointed, Polly tries to hit Elvis. As they struggle, Teetee walks in and demands an explanation, and Polly declares, equivocally, that Elvis has insulted her. Threatening Elvis, Teetee proclaims:

> Remember one thing boy. There is a man's soul in this woman's body. Our men are cruel to our women but we get used to it and follow the rules, letting each slap and tickle and bruise and headbutt go by. And at the end of this rubbish life, we write the rules. We find the beauty in our cruelty.[31]

Ironically unaware of the implications of her statement, Teetee has just acknowledged that her relative powerlessness in her community is the result of her own choice to cede power to undeserving men. In other words, she has misunderstood her true identity as a Sikh woman. Her statement foreshadows the play's resolution where she and Balbir regroup to put an end to Mr. Sandhu's corruption and violence, reassuming the position of Sikh warriors that the scripture opens to women and men alike. In this way, the comedy of mistaken identities works as a feminist tool, calling Sikh women to account for their complicity with an abusive status quo.

The comedic characterization also serves Bhatti's feminist critique. In the beginning, the four female characters are all comic types. Foul-mouthed Balbir is an ill-tempered, cynical hag; Min is "a faithful but simple lump of lard [. . .] a sturdy, but ungainly ingénue, prone to outbursts of extreme excitability."[32] When we first encounter Polly and Teetee, they are going through the shoes that worshippers have taken off at the entrance to the gurdwara, stealing some and commenting ungenerously on their owners. As the plot unfurls, the female characters acquire depth through the tried and tested realist recourse to unsatisfactory, and often traumatic, experiences in the characters' lives. Faced with the choice of protecting Min from the inevitable violence that she knows threatens her, Teetee transforms into a tragic figure; the dissatisfied Balbir rises in status not through her daughter's marriage, but though fulfilling her religion's commandment to protect the weak and avenge dishonor; and Min completes her arc of an ingénue by refusing to succumb to cynicism in the aftermath of a crisis that has ended her naivete about the ways of the world. This shift—from comic types to individuals confronting tragic dilemmas, and in the end, triumphantly assuming the dignity guaranteed to women in Sikh scripture—may be what Gopal describes as "unevenness of style" in *Behzti*. Yet the stylistic shift can be interpreted differently: the female characters have only temporarily been reduced to comic types by the constraints of their misogynist environment.

It is the concluding scene, however, that best illustrates Bhatti's strategic use of comedy. In this scene, titled "Gurdwara—Resurrection," the female characters celebrate their hard-fought return to true Sikhism not just with Min and Elvis's biracial dance, but also by revealing a community of initiated Sikh women. Balbir shows her bloodstained hands to her daughter, and following a brief conversation that is inaudible to the audience, but that presumably informs Min of Mr. Sandhu's death, they exchange greetings in Punjabi:

BALBIR: Vahegurudji kha khalsa . . . [God be with you; literally, initiated Sikhs belong to God.]

MIN: Vehagurudji khi fateh. [All victories are God's.][33]

In comedic terms, this, too, is a happy outcome, even as a man has just been murdered: a previously disrupted community is brought back together, having rid itself of major flaws and resolved grave misunderstandings.

As a commentary on societal faults, Western comedy has not been hostile to nonnormative ideas. Rather, as Eric Weitz observes, "comedy and the comic have shown the ability to open spaces for the unique and effective challenge of received ideas and encrusted sociocultural conceits."[34] Indeed, *Behzti* recalls the work of numerous late-twentieth-century Western female playwrights, artists, and comedians (including, among others, the lesbian duo Split Britches, the transnationally performing activists the Gorilla Girls, and television celebrities Tina Fey and Samantha Bee) who have used comedy and satire as tools for feminist critique.[35] But Weitz also notes that regardless of its political range, comedy "cannot quite shake its reputation for guarding the status quo by ridiculing difference and confirming allegiance to the social order."[36] In *Behzti* Bhatti skillfully uses both the conservative baggage of comedy and its potential for radical critique. The establishment of a newly equitable female community at the end of the play suggests a radical feminist utopia. But by finding its justification in a return to scripture, rather than in a revision or in a new text altogether, this feminist community, counterintuitively, also positions itself as conservative: committed to the conservation of "true" Sikhism. Viewed in terms of her foreword, Bhatti's comedic feminist approach serves her Sikh commitment to the truth, because feminism enables her to reveal Sikhism's true egalitarianism.

THE PERFORMATIVITY OF INJURY

But as formalist critics insist, the medium is the message. And while Bhatti's use of comedy did defamiliarize Sikhism, exposing contradictions between its sacred text and its practices, comedy also made her play vulnerable to accusations of cultural insensitivity. Regardless of how conservatively it may resolve its major conflict, comedy typically indulges in irreverence, and *Behzti*'s claim to represent "true" Sikhism is certainly irreverent to established custom. Besides, comedy, with its typical emphasis on lower-body functions, physical awkwardness, and incontinence, presumes undisciplined bodies that fail to conform to social and religious norms. The prologue of *Behzti*, where Balbir sits naked on a chair and Min, in inelegant house clothes, helps her take a bath,[37] their language mimicking King Ubu's canonical crudeness ("No bloody soap, shitter!"[38]), could be generously interpreted as fitting with Sikhism's worldliness and explicit rejection of asceticism.[39] But the deliberate lack of refinement in the characters' words and gestures decisively veers away from a Sikh understanding of beauty that, Nikky-Guninder Kaur Sing tells us, is based, among other things, on a canon of poetry drawn from a range of eastern religions and compiled by the Fifth Guru. The language of this poetry is "one of reverent wonder"; it is "a melodious instrument for stimulating the senses and the mind into intuiting the Infinite One. The ears hear the Divine Word. The tongue tastes its deliciousness. Every pore of the body bathes in its passionate color."[40]

Behzti, as the crude comedic language implies, clearly does not try to fit into this aesthetic, and protesters found this offensive. For instance, several protesting Sikh women, none of whom had seen the play, told the *Birmingham Post* that they were very disturbed by the information that in one scene a turban is placed on a shoe rack. They found this choice utterly disrespectful of Sikh culture.[41] For conservative Sikhs, however, the (mis)placement of the turban paled before the production's representation of the gurdwara. As Sewa Singh Mandha, the chairman of the Council of Sikh Gurdwaras in Birmingham, stated:

> In a Sikh temple sexual abuse does not take place; kissing and dancing don't take place; rape doesn't take place; homosexual activity doesn't take place; murders do not take place. I am bringing to the attention of the management of the theatre the sensitive nature of the play because by going into the public domain it will cause deep hurt to the Sikh community.[42]

But does such "deeply hurtful" insensitivity equal actual harm to conservative Sikhs, as the protesters claimed? In other words, does it equal harm that can (or should) be legally recognized as harm? More specifically, could a play about a minoritarian culture, such as *Behzti*, create such enduring negative perceptions of Sikhism that as a result the community may become disadvantaged in a measurable way? For Western theater scholars, accepting this proposition would mean accepting that a dramatic performance in a mainstream venue can produce a speech act. This would entail grappling with J. L. Austin's definition of performative speech acts and its legacy in 1990s speech-act theories.

Austin defined as *performative speech acts* utterances that effect changes in social reality. He also asserted that speech acts that are conventionally considered performative become "hollow or void" when spoken by an actor in the course of a theatrical performance. A performative speech act on stage, he famously claimed, has no binding effect because it is "parasitic upon its normal use."[43] Thus, a marriage performed as part of a play does not have the binding effects of a marriage performed in a court or church ceremony. Despite the legal specificity of the marriage ceremony, Austin implies that what applies to marriage on stage also applies to any theatrical act: while theater could influence our perception of a specific social issue, theatrical acts cannot effect change in the social world beyond the stage in the immediate way that a legal ruling does that.

Any theater scholar will recognize Austin's pronouncement as an instance of the long-standing Western antitheatrical prejudice. But for feminist theater scholars, speech-act theory presents special difficulties. Judith Butler's concept of gender as performative, rather than essential, has had immense influence on our scholarship, even as Butler seems to have inherited Austin's bias against the theater. Like Austin, she distinguishes between performativity (the continuous reiteration of social norms, such as gender, that may reveal their contingency) and theatricality (the dissimulation of this contingency so that social norms appear stable and universal).[44] Feminist theater scholars have duly noted that even as Butler reads Austin deconstructively (interrogating the discursively constructed authority from which performative speech acts draw their power), she leaves untroubled his designation of theatrical speech as the constitutive *other* of performative speech acts. Accepting this would imply that feminist theater could only indirectly contribute to social change rather than body it forth,[45] and feminist theater aspires to do both. For feminist theater artists and critics, a theatrical illusion, even one using "the master tools" of mainstream aesthetic modes such as realism, can effectively illuminate gender hierarchies and sexism.

In the 1990s, the effects of Austin's antitheatricality on theater scholarship were further impacted by the growing authority of performance studies research that has drawn heavily on speech-act theories. In academia, performance studies has sought to distinguish itself from theater studies by emphasizing research on nontheatrical performance, though overlap has been common in practice. In designating theater as unable to produce performative speech acts, these theories provided new justification for an already well-established suspicion of theater in conventional venues that performance studies—especially in the influential articulation by the experimental theater director and scholar Richard Schechner—inherited from post–World War II avant-garde artists. As a result, at the time *Behzti* was first produced, many performance scholars shared the view that dramatic theater in mainstream venues cannot produce radical social effects.

This view is compellingly expressed in Baz Kershaw's study *The Radical in Performance*, first published in 1999. Ten years after the fall of the Berlin Wall, Kershaw, along with other materialist scholars, was asking how the dissolution of the Soviet sphere, which had provided the communism-versus-capitalism axis on which much post-1960s materialist theory drew, had influenced our understanding of political theater as defined in the 1960s and 1970s. For Kershaw, the collapse of this axis was the final stage in a process of depoliticizing conventional theater that began under Thatcherism in the 1980s. Thatcher's cuts in spending for the arts, as part of her politics of austerity, had transformed British theater into "a playground for the newly privileged" and "a marginal commodity in the capitalist market place."[46] This is why Kershaw directed his search for the radical beyond mainstream venues, focusing instead on street and prison performances. In these performances, he looked for moments where performers and spectators found themselves suspended between two ways of understanding the post-1989 West: one "modernist," the other "post-modernist."[47] Such suspension between paradigms, he argued, may enable a radical perspective.

Indeed, much about *Behzti* seems to support Kershaw's view that British mainstream theater after Thatcher has been hostile to radicalism, especially Janet Steele's surprise that the show provoked a protest and her disagreement that a forceful political statement may have been the artists' objective. But when, counter to what Kershaw may have predicted, the show provoked dissension, the dissension seemed to fit his description of post-1989 radicalism as the experience of being suspended between "modernism" and "post-modernism." While liberal critics insisted on the universal value of freedom of expression, the protesting Sikhs emphasized a minority culture's viewpoint, or what in postmodern terms we could call *a petit narrative* of minoritarian sensitivity. Yet Kershaw's post-1968 suspicion of theater in mainstream venues, though grounded in a strong critique of Thatcher's politics and widely shared in late-twentieth-century British theater criticism,[48] eventually limits his analysis. Although he declares himself reluctant to create "a wholesale binary opposition" between theater and performance, his decision to focus on "'the [pro–status quo] limits of theatre' and the potentially radical 'excesses of performance'"[49] eventually does just this, positioning cases like *Behzti* as exceptions that only confirm the general truthfulness of the binary. By not admitting that theater, too, can be "excessive" in terms of established norms, he provides no hypothesis about how such a controversy could have occurred.

Such a hypothesis is suggested by David Edgar, who in a 2006 article about *Behzti* and related controversies wrote that

> In recent years, fears about the influence of sexual and violent images, a growing concern for the victims of crime and emerging movements against the insulting of religions have widened the range of acceptable restrictions on freedom of expression in the arts. These new, non-legal pressures rely on the blurring of the boundaries between representation and enactment or promotion, so that to dramatize is often seen as to condone. The right of consumers not to be offended is now prioritized over the artist's ability to foster imagination and empathy.[50]

To paraphrase his insight in terms of speech-act theory, Edgar observes that the field of performativity has expanded, endowing previously unlikely instances of representation, such as a play in a mainstream theater, with the reality-shaping force of a speech act. This expansion, he suggests, relies on two conditions that seem to be motivated (but are not necessarily) by distinct political concerns. One is a heightened awareness of how representation may trigger a posttraumatic response, often associated with a leftist concern for the rights of victims (including victims of social injustices such as racism and sexism) and the disabled. The other is the paying customer's demand, nowadays associated with neoliberalism, to not be offended or made uncomfortable by art. In other words, whereas in 1999 Kershaw sees consumerism as a limit to radicalism, Edgar's account, written seven years later, suggests that by expanding the field of performativity, consumerism and concern for victims have engendered a new kind of radicalism.

That in 2004 theater artists and critics and other intellectuals were so surprised by the protesting Sikhs' response reflects in part the conflation of radicalism and leftist politics in post-1960s critical theory. Indeed, Austin's theory of speech acts emphasizes the power of conservative institutions, such as heterosexual marriage. Yet in the 1990s, constructivist thinkers such as Butler, who are typically considered leftist, successfully reworked Austin's theory in the service of a progressive engagement with representation. By then, however, the post–World War II institutions enabling leftist politics in the West, such as labor unions, had been steadily eroding, replacing efforts at class allegiances across ethnic and racial lines (however difficult such allegiances may have been) with identity politics. According to the self-defined communist Slavoj Žižek, and to the self-defined cultural conservative Fukuyama, this move benefited the new neoliberal status quo.[51] If workers' dignity was once affirmed by guarantees of proper pay and good working conditions, their dignity—now interpreted as the acknowledgment of their intrinsic worthiness not as workers, but as white, Black, Sikh, etc.—was to be affirmed by not offending their particular sense of whiteness, blackness, or Sikhism.

Whether or not one agrees with this view of identity politics, changes in how British Sikhs organized between World War II and the early 1980s on the one hand, and since the 1980s on the other, illustrate a variant of the transition that Žižek and Fukuyama have described. According to Gurharpal Singh and Darshan Singh Tatla, until the early 1980s British Sikh politics was dominated by class issues. After that, and especially since Operation Blue Star (1984)—the Indian government's campaign against the Sikh nationalist Khalistani movement, in the aftermath of which Indira Gandi was murdered by her Sikh bodyguards—class politics was increasingly replaced by concerns with ethnicity, race, and religion. This coincided with the general economic uplift of the community that made Sikhs a positive example of British multicultural politics. However, Singh and Tatla point out that even when British Sikhs identified primarily along class lines, their class politics had reflected the social dynamics in Punjab and India more generally, rather than social dynamics in Britain. By end of the 1990s, when third- and fourth-generation Sikhs began successfully entering mainstream British politics, ethnic issues became increasingly important for culturally conservative Sikhs who wished to preserve the distinctiveness of Sikh culture.[52]

It was in the 1990s, too, that British Sikhs became known for expertly using the discourse of multiculturalism in ways intended to maximize social and political gains for their community.[53] Or, as critics of neoliberalism might have said, Sikhs became adept at employing social-justice arguments in a distinctly neoliberal way: to earn a competitive advantage over other communities, rather than equality in a classic liberal or Marxist sense. For instance, as they demanded that *Behzti* be closed, the protesting Sikhs emphasized their position as taxpayers. According to the authors of the "Statement by Sikh Groups on *Behzti*," the setting of the violent scenes in the gurdwara illustrated how "the white arts establishment [. . .] subtly impose[d] its racism in the name of 'artistic license' *with the funds of the public*."[54] Their phrasing echoes a statement about art funding that Lord Palumbo, chairman of the Arts Council of Great Britain from 1988 to 1994, attributed to Margaret Thatcher: "She knew the arts were important. 'Don't talk to me about government money,' she would say. 'There is none. It's taxpayer's money.' She wanted every pound put into the arts to return two pounds to the Treasury."[55] In Thatcher's statement, the taxpayer, previously understood as a contributor to public welfare, is reframed as an investor awaiting return on their money. Likewise, the taxpaying public referred to in the Sikh protesters' statement is a public of investors. Sikhs are taxpayers and thus investors, the logic goes; therefore, they have every right to demand that a theater that receives public funds should make art to their taste.

Lest this neoliberal logic should appear too cynical, neoliberal taxpayers are also an affective public: they invest affects, as well as money, anticipating specific emotional returns in addition to financial gain.[56] For the Sikh protesters, the anticipated return was art respectful of their minoritarian religious sensibility. "Most religious [*sic*] sensitive audiences [. . .] have been offended by the play's depiction of the Sikh religion," the protesters stated.[57] As the Birmingham Rep's *Behzti* failed to deliver these anticipated returns, the play became a speech act.

But no matter how strongly a non-Sikh critic may disagree with such neoliberal logic, that critic's commitment to diversity and/or respect for pluralism would suggest that they try to understand, as best as they can, the worldview that caused so many Sikhs to feel offended by Bhatti's play: the worldview according to which a staged gurdwara is the same as, or at least not different enough from, a gurdwara in a Birmingham neighborhood.

SECULAR SEMIOTICS, RELIGIOUS AFFECT, AND THE SIKH PROTEST

For many supporters of the Birmingham Rep's production, the protesters' assertion that the staged gurdwara is an actual gurdwara proved difficult to grasp. For instance, Anthony Frost found the Sikh leaders' position unjustifiably literal.

> A play like *Behzti* is not a documentary and audiences are normally quite able to distinguish symbolic representations from actuality. [. . .] [The play

> does not] purport to be actually taking place *in* a gurdwara, but rather (on an open and simple set, and by the use of certain indicative props and musical sound effects) it is bringing a gurdwara to mind for the purposes of the narrative.[58]

For Frost, the distinctions between fictional and actual spaces and between documentary and fiction are clearly common sense, and denying their common-sense nature could have no other purpose than to shift attention away from the play's critique of sexism among British Sikhs.[59] But as feminist and postcolonial theories, among others, have taught us, accepting an idea or a state of things as common sense signals the need to reexamine entrenched assumptions and habits of thought.

What Frost designated as a common-sense distinction between an actual and a represented gurdwara and what Edgar designated as a (formerly) common-sense distinction "between [the] representation [of racism or sexism] and [its] enactment or promotion" are examples of a more fundamental Western distinction between an object (or idea) and its representations. In their book *Is Critique Secular?*, Talal Asad, Wendy Brown, Judith Butler, and Saba Mahmood discuss how that fundamental distinction, perceived as common sense in Western democracies, informed Western critics' misunderstanding of why Muslims were so offended by the *Jyllands-Posten*'s publication of caricatures of Muhammed in 2005. Western secular critics, the four authors wrote, viewed the Muslim protests against the caricatures "as a sign of Islam's incapacity to 'handle criticism.' This alleged incapacity, in turn, was treated as a sign of orthodoxy, secularism's putative opposite."[60] More specifically, Western secular critics saw the offended Muslims as

> hav[ing] committed a category mistake, collapsing a necessary distinction between the subject (Muhammed as sacred) with the pictorial object (public representations of Muhammed). If the protesting Muslims had been schooled in this distinction, they might have been able to appreciate that what is really sacred (the idea of prophecy) remains untouched by the satirical representations of Muhammed (considered as mere signs, not as part of the Prophet himself).[61]

Secular criticism considers its analytical procedures rational, i.e., free from religious doctrines and their affects. According to the four authors, however, secular rationalism relies on "a semiotic ideology in which signs stand apart from the meanings they signify," and this ideology is rooted in Western Protestantism.[62] Hence, secularism is not truly neutral to religion; rather, it is inadvertently partial to Protestantism. This semiotic episteme, Saba Mahmood continues, "fails to attend to the affective and embodied practices through which a subject comes to relate to a particular sign—a relation founded not only on representation, but also on cohabitation."[63] This embodied and affective relationship to signs describes a Muslim's relationship to the figure of Mohammed. Mahmood writes:

> Those who profess love for the Prophet do not simply follow his advice [. . .] but also try to emulate how he dressed; what he ate; how he spoke to his friends and adversaries; how he slept, walked, and so on. These *mimetic* ways of realizing the Prophet's behavior are lived not as commandments but as virtues where one wants to ingest, as it were, the Prophet's persona into oneself.[64]

Because devout Muslims host the Prophet in their own embodied minds, they experienced the caricatures ridiculing Mohammed as a deep personal wound. "This wound requires moral action, but its language is neither juridical, nor that of *street protest*, because it does not belong to an economy of blame, accountability, and reparations," writes Mahmood.[65] "The action that it requires is internal to the structure of affect, relations, and virtues that predisposes one to experience an act as a violation in the first place."[66] Mahmood does not recommend a specific corrective approach; she worries about important nuances that may be lost if such an injury is subject to interpretation within a Western legal framework, which is a product of an entirely different epistemology.[67] Instead, she suggests that Muslims try to make their injury intelligible to non-Muslims, especially secular Westerners, through other, nonlegal, means. This could bring about a transformation of sensibility in all parties involved.[68]

Two aspects of Mahmood's discussion appear particularly relevant to the *Behzti* controversy: her description of devout Muslims' relationship to the Prophet as "mimetic," i.e., embodied, affective, and hence not subject to the semiotic logic; and her suggestion that a street protest may not be the best way for such Muslims to make their injury public, because a street protest in the West is understood as demanding a legal remedy, which she thinks would be ineffective in this case. That the protesting Sikhs, too, described their relationship to the gurdwara as mimetic, but deliberately opted for a street protest, exposes the difference between Mahmood's and their politics concerning religious rights. Mahmood calls for respect between Western secularists and Muslims based on their understanding of each other's philosophies, respect that is deeply enough felt on both sides that it does not need to be legally enforced. In contrast, the leaders of the Sikh protest demanded legal changes that would affect not just the representation of Sikh religious symbols, but would gain privileges for all religions in Britain. Such legal changes, they implied, are necessary precisely because secular law, as is, does not provide sufficient protection for minority rights based on a mimetic relationship to symbols.

Here is how the argument went. "It was not the substance or message of [Bhatti's] play that invoked the wrath of so many Sikhs, but the deliberate, sensational and offensive use of sacred icons," wrote Jasdev Singh Rai, a medical doctor and human rights activist who emerged as one of the strongest voices in the controversy.

> For the Sikhs, the Guru Granth Sahib, the text in complete form, is sacred. The Granth Sahib is the embodiment of the Sikh gurus and is treated as our living spiritual guide. The gurdwara is where the Guru is in residence. [. . .] All the Sikh gurus used practical rational examples to attack superstition and blind ritual. Yet Sikhs will throw out a person who walks into a gurdwara hall with shoes and uncovered head. The sacred is different to [*sic*] the rational.[69]

Rai describes a mimetic relationship among the Guru Granth Sahib (the Sikh scripture), the gurdwara, and the devout worshipper, similar to the relationship between Muslims and Mohammed as explained by Mahmood. The scripture is not a representation but an embodiment of the guru; the gurdwara is the living guru's home (which is why, for instance, every night Sikh religious officials literally put the scripture to bed[70]). The worshipper, therefore, needs to enter the gurdwara with all due respect to this most honored host. In other words, the scripture, the gurdwara, and the worshipper are not distinct entities, as they may be viewed according to the semiotic logic of liberal secularism. Instead, they are intimately and affectively connected, and Sikhs are expected to enact this connection through the appropriate embodied repertoire, including entering the gurdwara barefoot. The theologian Nikky-Guninder Kaur Singh confirms Rai's statement. In Sikhism, she writes, "a heightened sensuous experience is a requirement for metaphysical knowledge."[71] In turn, this affective connection to religious symbols explains why conservative Sikhs felt that responding to the play with articles in the press or interviews on radio and television would not be enough. They felt that the Birmingham Rep's hurtful treatment of the living guru's home required that they put their bodies in front of the theater.

• • •

Not much footage of the protest is freely available, but the little that is reveals important aspects of its aesthetics (albeit mediated by the TV camera). The footage included in the Channel 4 documentary *Holy Offensive*, about the clash between freedom of speech and cultural sensitivity in diverse liberal societies, shows a clip from the early stages of the protest. Sikhs are walking around, chatting with their friends. A musician is beating a big drum. A young man is dancing to its rhythm and smiling for the cameras. The protesting Sikhs are performing their disagreement joyfully and lightheartedly, illustrating a concept of critique as an embodied and affective practice, just as Bhatti did in her comedy. A second clip, from the night of the riot, registers the changes in embodiment and affect. Sikh protesters and police are densely packed in front of the theater. The human figures seem metonymically reduced to turbans and police helmets, as some protesters, now notably angry, try to break through the row of police officers and get access to the theater.

To theorists of affect, the simultaneous presence of joy and rage in the protest would make sense. Affects help individuals form groups, writes Jeremy Gilbert, and "joyous affects" in particular "increase the potential power of bodies, enabling them 'to form new and potentially powerful encounters.'"[72] Rage, too, has been long associated with struggles for empowerment, especially with human rights demands in the West. However, in the context of human rights struggles, rage has been perceived not so much as an *affect* as an *emotion*: an affect that has been processed by reason. Thus, feminist rage or workers' rage implies that these enraged groups are already aware of themselves as affective publics, and of the specific material conditions justifying their rage. But to a Western liberal sensibility, rage, when an affect and not an emotion, particularly when rage leads to violence and destruction, signifies not the reasoned demands of individuals gathered in a public, but the irrational excess of a mob.

The Sikh leaders were apparently highly attuned to how the outburst of violence could be interpreted, so they made a deliberate effort to manage public opinion. Thus, although throughout the protest the cameras

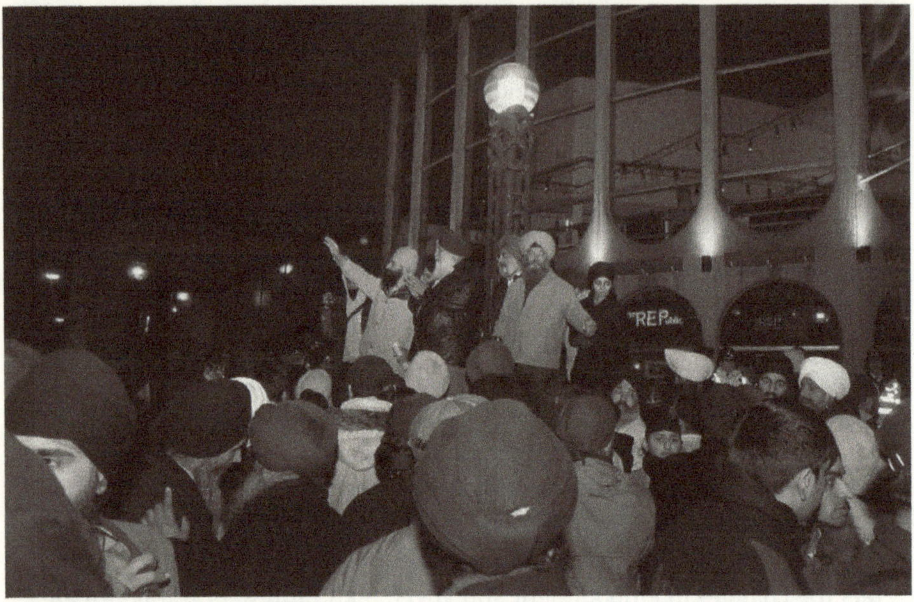

Figure 7. The Sikh protest against *Behzti (Dishonour)*, by Gurpreet Kaur Bhatti, in front of the Birmingham Repertory Theatre, December 2004. Photo from the *Birmingham Mail*.

caught few images of Sikh women among the male protesters, on the day following the riot a woman, councilor Kim Kirpaljit Kaur Bron, wearing a traditional headscarf, addressed reporters. In the footage she is encircled closely by five men, four of whom wear turbans: an image of gender egalitarianism as understood and authorized by the Birmingham Sikh religious establishment. With emphatic calmness, Bron reads her statement from a piece of paper: "We congratulate the theater for taking the decision it took [i.e., cancelling the show], after we exercised our democratic right of protest. Withdrawing the play *Behzti*, for whatever reason, is appreciated." At this moment the camera shifts away from councilor Bron and her fellow Sikhs to the vandalized building of the theater, and reporter Alex Thompson comments: "The Sikh community in this city has yet to explain how smashing up a theatre is, quote, our democratic right of protest."[73] Clearly, the Sikhs' strategy did not work. To liberal commentators, including Thompson, the protesters became "a violent mob": a characterization that would be repeated in numerous news reports about the protest.

Street protests are, of course, fundamental to Western democracies, but how such protests are interpreted also exposes entrenched Western biases. For instance, criminologist Michael Rowe argues that public disorder in twentieth-century Britain, particularly since the 1980s, has been racialized, having been framed as a deviation from the fundamentally law-abiding British national character.[74] Reflecting on the violence involved in the Muslim reaction to the Danish caricatures, Talal Asad, too, points out that

> The European history of boycotts [. . .] and strikes [. . .] with all their accompanying violence, has been a story of the struggle for modern rights. And yet in the present case [the Muslim response to the Danish caricatures] European commentators described the two differently: the one as an expression of freedom, the other as an attempt at restricting it, and thus as yet another sign of the conflict between two civilizations having opposed political orientations. In liberal democratic thinking the principle of free speech cannot be curtailed by the offense its exercise may cause—so long as it is not defamatory or a threat to social order.[75]

That the Sikh protest thus became entangled in Europe's and Britain's racialized histories of disorder and in debates about freedom of expression confirms and adds nuance to home officer Fiona Mactaggart's view of the protest as belonging very much to a British tradition of fighting for human rights. But despite this entanglement, the Sikhs were also drawing on their own well-established repertoire of protest that, prior to the *Behzti* controversy, had successfully shaped British public policy to their liking.

Cultural separatism has been inherent to Sikhism since its beginnings. The founding Guru Nanak mandated that his followers "stand out from the crowd," and one way they have done this is through their distinctive attire.[76] For most male Sikhs, the turban is synonymous with Sikh identity, and the inability to wear it is perceived as "a sign of collective dishonor."[77] During the second half of the twentieth century, British Sikhs ran several campaigns seeking protection for their rights as a minority. All of them centered on elements of costume: the right to wear turbans, kirpans, and beards at the workplace, at school, and in other public spaces, regardless of dress code. Mass protests were integral to these campaigns, taking place simultaneously in Britain and in other countries with large Sikh communities. As early as 1970, Sikh policemen have been wearing their turbans, instead of the uniform hat, while serving on the police force, and the juxtaposition of turbans and police hats in footage from the *Behzti* protest must have recalled the 1960s and 1970s Sikh campaigns to at least some television viewers.[78] As a result of these campaigns, in 1983 British Sikhs obtained protections under the Race Relations Act, which would not be extended to other religions until twenty years later.[79] However, the campaigns, focused on seeking specific exceptions to the prevailing law, also gave British Sikhs the reputation of being "the paradigm case of a special-interest group which can always negotiate an opt-out from general rule-making."[80] In view of the present discussion, it is also important to emphasize the strong aesthetic aspects of Sikh minority rights campaigns. Their demands for "exceptions" have taken shape as demands to *appear* in public in a specific way, a detail suggestive of the mimetic relationship between religious principle and practice that Mahmood identified among devout Muslims.

The influence of this repertoire is evident in the *Behzti* protest: from the growing number of Sikhs who gathered throughout its duration (and the leaders' statements that hundreds of thousands more would join, should the theater continue resisting their demands[81]), through the transnational resonance of the controversy in Sikh communities around the world, to councilor Bron addressing the press. A performance scholar may analyze such features of protest as choices of casting (a female speaker), costume (traditional clothes), and blocking (how protesters occupy space). They may refer to their totality as a "scenario." In the case of the *Bezhti* protest, however, the term "scenario" acquires an even more specific meaning. In 1978, a school in Birmingham refused admission to Gurinder Singh Mandla, arguing that his insistence on wearing a turban violated the school's dress code. Gurinder's father, Sewa Singh Mandla, filed a complaint with the Commission for Racial Equality, claiming that his son had suffered racial discrimination. The resulting legal case, *Mandla v Dowell Lee*, was key to Sikhs gaining protection under the Race Relations Act.[82] Sewa Singh Mandla, of *Mandla v Dowell Lee*, was also one of the leaders of the *Behzti* protest. His leadership role demonstrates the continuity between the protest and earlier Sikh activism; it also confirms director Janet Steele's suspicion that the Sikh attack on the production was part of a calculated political strategy.

Yet, as Gurharpal Singh, who first followed the connection between earlier Sikh activism and *Bezhti*, has observed, the *Behzti* protest was qualitatively different. This time conservative Sikhs did not seek an "exception," but sought to radically renegotiate the limits of expressive freedom.[83] Indeed, in the immediate aftermath of the riot, Mandla told BBC reporters, "Freedom of expression carries with it a responsibility, and if you don't discharge this responsibility in an appropriate manner, then it's an abuse of that *privilege*. Fiction or no fiction."[84] In liberal democracies, freedom of speech is a right, not a privilege, despite the specific ways in which this right may be limited by national law. From a Western liberal perspective, Bhatti's freedom to stage her play, regardless of how offensive it may prove to some or all spectators, instantiates both freedom of speech and gender equality as rights. In contrast, councilor Bron's role in the protest represents Mandla's understanding of freedom of speech as a privilege, granted only if specific conditions are fulfilled. From the perspective of Western theater history and performance theory, Mandla's proposed redefinition of freedom of speech and freedom of expression as privileges, rather than rights, appears as an avant-garde act: not just because of its inherent challenge of liberalism, but (as I have been arguing) because of the specific aesthetic through which this challenge was made public.

THE SIKH PROTEST AS AN AVANT-GARDE ACT

But first, we need to qualify Mahmood's distinction between the semiotic and the mimetic systems of signification. For as soon as we begin thinking of the Sikh protest in terms of performance, avant-garde or not, it becomes clear that aligning theater with the semiotic system, as Anthony Frost (among others) did, and the Sikh protest with a mimetic model, is untenable, especially if we see these models as opposites. An embodied and affective relationship to signs is, of course, central to performance. This relationship is frequently studied under the label of semiotics, but Saussurian semiotics, to which the semiotics of performance is indebted, differs from the secular semiotics described in *Is Critique Secular?* According to this secular semiotics, Mahmood writes, the Muslims' offence at the Danish caricatures displayed "a fundamental confusion about the materiality of a particular semiotic form that is only arbitrarily, not necessarily linked to the abstract character of their religious belief."[85] Saussurian semiotics, too, accepts that the relationship between representation and referent is arbitrary, rather than necessary or natural; however, it also asserts that form is meaning. For a Saussurian semiotician, "the materiality of a particular semiotic form" matters even as its relationship to the referent is arbitrary. Thus, it matters a whole lot that the Danish caricatures represented Mohammed as ridiculous (this, Mahmood specifies, was the issue, rather than the *Jyllands-*

Posten having broken the Muslim interdiction against depicting Mohammed[86]) and not, for instance, as dignified.

For theater people, the limits of the semiotic system as *the* system of rational representation become apparent when we consider theatrical approaches that make special efforts to align themselves with rationalism, such as Brecht's epic theater. Brecht's dedication to rational Marxist analysis led him to emphasize the importance of the materiality of signs and of the feelings that accompany individuals' relationships to representation. As his essays demonstrate, he thought of rational analysis as an affective and embodied practice. In his theater, rational thinking—the ability to see the world clearly—is pleasurable, and this pleasure is at once physical and mental (and, as feminist scholars have argued, masculine): inseparable from the enjoyment of drinks, food, and cigars during a performance. The important nuance is that the Brechtian pleasure of seeing the world clearly is an affect processed through reason, i.e., an emotion. Such emotion, or, as Wendy Brown puts it, "informed passion," is the feature of a liberal public, a definition that includes the ideal Brechtian audience despite all of Brecht's antibourgeois sentiment.[87] We find yet another model of rational representation in some avant-garde performance, such as Meyerhold's biomechanical theater, where the rational actor mimetically models their actions after the mechanical movements of a complex but well-coordinated factory machine. In that model the actor is rational not because they reason, in the reflexive manner of Adam Smith or John Locke, but because they are efficient. (Meyerhold's biomechanics was inspired in part by Frederick Winslow Taylor's theory of "scientific" management that aimed to improve the productivity of factory workers.) As in Brechtian theater, in biomechanics, pleasure binds the actors in a collective. But this is not the pleasure of Brechtian analysis, at once cerebral and somatic. Instead, this is the pleasure of coordinated movement, skillfully executed in synchrony with others. Kimberly Jannarone, who has analyzed the politics of mass gymnastics, argues that its pleasures are illiberal, because mass gymnastics enables the individual to temporarily lose themselves in an ideal collective body, giving material representation to abstract concepts such as "the nation." This could be especially appealing in times of acute social fragmentation.[88] Meyerhold's project, though not a mass performance, held a similar appeal. He staged the ideal Soviet body politic at a time when only extreme coercion held Russian society together. As such examples illustrate, in performance, rational thinking, variously interpreted as intellectual reflection, efficiency, or both, involves mimesis, as well as semiotics, as complementary rather than opposite systems of signification.

Among the liberal commentators who wrote about *Behzti*, at least one, Tom Sellar, considers theater's nuanced relationship to semiotics and rationalism:

> As we emphasize rational critical debate and reflexively defend free speech, those who care about art must also make sure that the stage itself never succumbs to literal-mindedness under public pressure. The semiotic clarity essential to defending a production like *Behzti* in print or debates doesn't necessarily make great theatre—a form whose power and inner logic so often come from metaphor and magic.[89]

Inadvertently or not, Sellar's statement supports the Sikh hypothesis that there are cases of exception to the semiotic logic: the sacred may be one such exception, but so too is "great theatre." In each case, the exception is tied to affect. Devotion, the believer's relationship to the sacred, is an affect, and so, in Sellar's view, is the appreciative spectator's experience of a strong performance: reason makes way for magic. Sellar's statement also indirectly reminds us that, as a right, freedom of expression is not predicated on the rationality, or lack thereof, of the idea that is being expressed.

Yet the central place of affect in both theater and the sacred does not necessarily validate the protesting Sikhs' claim that *Behzti* failed to uphold the distinction between an actual and a represented gurdwara. In fact, the production team took measures to uphold this distinction, consistent with Sikh theology. As Randhir Singh Bains wrote in a letter to the *Guardian*, "the play was indeed set in a Sikh temple, but it was not played in a real temple. To claim that it violates the sanctity of a Sikh temple is, therefore, nonsense. A building without the presence of the Guru Granth Sahib is just that—a building."[90] Indeed, aware that according to Sikhism the physical presence of a copy of the scripture on stage would transform it into an actual temple, Steele and Bhatti decided that no such copy would be used as a prop.[91] And here is an important twist: no Sikh elder ever said outright that there had been a copy of the Guru Granth Sahib on stage, although Jasdev Singh Rai strongly implied it. In the excerpt from his comment for the *Guardian* quoted above, he first explains that the presence of scripture in any physical space renders this space a Sikh temple ("The Granth Sahib is the embodiment of the Sikh gurus [. . . .] The gurdwara is where the Guru is in residence"), and then says that "by setting the play—unnecessarily in Gurdwara, Bhatti disrespected the sanctity of the Guru."[92] It would have been easy for Sikhs who did not see the play, including many of the protesters, to assume from this phrasing that a copy of the Sikh scripture was on stage. In a longer essay, written several years later, Rai is equally elusive about the presence of the scripture in *Behzti*: "The director brought the Gurdwara and the Guru Granth Sahib's text into [*sic*] the stage where rape and corruption were being staged."[93] That the "text" was brought onto the stage is true: in the course of the play the characters quote excerpts from the Guru Granth Sahib. From a theological perspective, however, quoting scripture does not transform the place where the quoting occurs into a temple.

Rai's elusiveness, regardless of its ethical implications, is theoretically significant. In the absence of a theological justification for his claim that a sacrilege has been committed, he creates his own justification masked as theology. In his texts, quoting scripture becomes the new minimal condition for transforming any space into a gurdwara, and setting rape and murder in such a space now counts as sacrilege. In other words, in the absence of established norms that would have rendered the Birmingham Rep's representation of the gurdwara a performative speech act, Rai creates new ones. Foremost among them is theater's embodied and affective relationship to signs that makes possible the momentary blurring between representation and reality in spectators' minds. Rai thus *harnesses theatricality as the enabling discursive condition of the performativity of religious symbols* in his revised theory of the relationship between the sacred and the mundane. This move places us on avant-garde terrain.

In his study of the manifesto as a distinctive aesthetic invention and major medium of the avant-garde, Martin Puchner observes that, unlike Austin's speech acts that derive their power from the authority of the law (or Butler's performativity of gender that draws its power from patriarchal custom), the avant-garde manifestos of the late nineteenth and early twentieth centuries, because they were anti–status quo, had no authority to draw on. Therefore, these manifestos assumed as the source of their authority the utopian future that they projected: "The speech acts of the manifesto thus are launched in the anterior future, claiming that their authority will have been provided by the changes they themselves want to bring about," writes Puchner. "But this future perfect construction is nothing but a hope, a claim, a pose, a desire that often comes to naught."[94] Puchner calls this assumed authority the theatricality of the manifesto. He argues that the manifesto's performativity, i.e., its power to produce reality effects, relies on its theatricality: on assuming an authority it does not yet have. In other words, lacking legitimate power, the manifesto willfully creates its own conditions of performativity.

In Rai's revised theory of religious performativity, theatricality serves as an enabling condition and not as a source of authority. But like the avant-garde manifestos, Rai's texts, too, devise their own, equally theatrical sources of authority: while the former tap a utopian future, Rai turns toward an idealized past. In his second major text about *Behzti*, the 2008 essay "The Monologue of Liberalism and Its Imagination of the Sacred in Minority Cultures," Rai tries to prove the superiority of his position by donning the mask of a theater scholar. As in his earlier essay, he bristles at suggestions that conservative Sikhs may be irrational and unsophisticated spectators who can't grasp the difference between reality and representation. "Neither is rationalism alien to eastern cultures," he writes in his 2005 essay "Behind Behzti." "Science and mathematics thrived both in the great age of Hindu civilization and Islamic ascendancy. Eastern cultures have long traditions of theater, reform movements and of absorbing criticism. But when a creative work offends the sacred, it loses its message."[95] In "The Monologue of Liberalism," he reasserts the refinement of Sikh spectators. "The traditional Indian audience," he writes (and, by implication, conservative Sikhs) "is sophisticated, having inherited a pattern of theatre which rejects universality and sustains the general principles of plural life."[96] According to Rai, this "pattern of theatre" derives from an "ancient Indian arts theory, [according to which] the entirety of existence is itself theater. The constructed theater of man is only another drama within it."[97] This claim—that there is no ontological difference between theater as art and theater as life—appears to support his statement that a real and represented gurdwara are equally sacred. That ancient Indian arts theory, Rai continues, also articulates rules that "determine how, when and what can be out on stage in one form or other. The rules require that the plays avoid grim realism, tragic ends, sexually explicit actions, political revolt and offence"[98]—all features that *Behzti* undoubtedly displays. In Rai's view, these rules allow for critique while guaranteeing that pluralism is respected. By breaking them, *Behzti* fell into the trap of Western humanist universalism, which, Rai warns, threatens the coexistence of diverse groups and their beliefs.[99]

But even if Rai's understanding of this ancient Indian art theory is correct, why should one judge by its standards a play written for a British theater and its diverse audience? For Rai the answer to this question stems from his belief that culture is genetically transmittable across time and geography. Sikhs are Indians and unless they have been infected with Western universalism, an Indian art sensibility inevitably informs their art making and reception: "[t]housands of years of cultural orientation are not lost merely by migrating to another country," Rai contends.[100] He finds the strongest evidence for the power of cultural genetics in the riot. "Sikhs protested. It is interesting that on the twelfth day, British born non-practicing young Sikhs emerged from the pubs in Birmingham, saw the pain of their community and took matters into hand. They attacked the theater. Although brought up in Britain, they do not share the British middle-class reverence for theater as a 'sacred' place."[101] This unapologetic depiction of the riot as an expression of cultural rejuvenation is important, and I will return to it shortly. But I first want to address the "elephant in the room" in Rai's art theory.

Just like their distinctive attire, Punjab—the real and mythic place of Sikhism's origins—is central to the Sikh identity. "In the traditions and culture of today's British Sikhs," write Singh and Tatla, "the 'remembered' [Punjabi] village still occupies a pre-eminent position, and this recognition must underlie any serious understanding of British Sikh society."[102] Given that Sikhs have been so adamant about their cultural uniqueness, why did Rai choose the larger category of "Indian theatre" to explain the protest against *Behzti* rather than the more specific category "Punjabi theatre"? Like "Indian theatre," "Punjabi theatre" includes artists from various ethnic and religious groups; nonetheless it seems to be the more relevant category in view of Rai's theory of genetically transmitted cultural values. But attributing Sikh protesters' theatrical sophistication to Punjabi theater would have been challenging. As literary scholar Gunjeet Aurora explains, "Punjabi theatre is a relatively young entity in the Punjabi cultural landscape. The tradition of theatre is not strongly rooted in Punjab as it is in some other parts of India."[103] Further inconveniencing Rai's agenda, Punjabi theater, according to Aurora, "exhibit[s] a marked influence of English drama which was taught in colleges and available to the reading public in Punjab during British rule."[104] Because its cultural hybridity is a product of British colonial rule, post-independence Punjabi artists have alternately embraced and rejected the conventions of pre-independence Punjabi drama, writes Aurora.[105]

Rai seems to share little of these artists' ambivalence, and despite his frequently professed love for pluralism and tolerance, he erases Punjabi drama from his theory and replaces it with a narrative of Indian theater that better serves his objectives. To students of the Western avant-garde, the radical rejection of a historical narrative that fails to serve the avant-garde artist's purpose (typically referred to as a break with ["bourgeois"] history) and its replacement with an alternative, often prehistoric past is a familiar strategy. Artaud's turn to precolonial Mexico, where he looked for a model of performance more alive than modern life itself, is one well-known example. Rai, likewise, does not need a history that would explain the conflict between the Birmingham Rep and the protesters (such as the history of Punjabi gender customs replacing the gurus' egalitarian message, told by Sikh feminists). Instead, Rai needs a narrative that presents the protesters, including those who never saw the play, as spectators whose sophistication is evidenced by their refusal to be taken in by that Western theater's insincere professions of commitment to cultural diversity. He finds that narrative in "an ancient Indian arts theory."[106] For Rai, the violence that erupted in the protest does not in any way undermine this sophistication; rather, in the act of violence it finds its fullest expression. Moreover, by exercising their "natural" sophistication as spectators, the young British-born Sikhs "returned" to their prediasporic roots, rejuvenating the British Sikh community.

This combination of tropes—militancy, violence, racial exceptionalism, and racial rejuvenation achieved through performance—is familiar to Western avant-gardes, though in reality the violence they perpetrated was mostly epistemological and perceptual. But the Sikh warrior—a culturally hybrid phenomenon that emerged during British colonial rule over India when the crown successfully courted the military support of Sikhs against Hindus during the Indian Mutiny (1857–8)[107]—is not just an image of racial exceptionalism, as Rai presents it, but also a racially marked image. In the West, Sikhs have not infrequently become targets of racist violence, both because of their complexion and, particularly since 9/11, because of their turbans, which have attracted the ire of anti-Muslim extremists.[108] This begs the question of the legitimacy of considering the Sikh protest within an avant-garde framework. Not only are the history and theory of the avant-garde both deeply informed by Western examples, but, as others have demonstrated, this history and theory are inherently tied to racial and racist thinking. For instance, Mike Sell has pointed out that Henri de Saint-Simon, commonly credited as the avant-garde's original theorist, praised Napoleon for upholding slavery in Martinique, Tobago, and St. Lucia, and despite his belief in the perfectibility of all races, also maintained that there are separate and unequal species of humankind.[109] Sell further writes that the European avant-gardes commonly emerged as responses to a perception of the racial decline of Europeans caused by feminist and egalitarian ideas. In fact, he proposes, one reason why avant-garde artists such as the futurists opted for a militant, often aggressive, and hence arguably masculine style of public performance was that they believed such a style could counter racial decline.[110] Concerns about racial decline, however, did not stop avant-garde artists from turning to minoritarian cultures for strategies to overcome the deadening monotony and uniformity that, they felt, permeated modern life. This turn was evidenced by their fascination with the "primitivism" of non-Western people, such as the French bohemians' selective appropriation of the European Roma's nomadic culture, which was often perceived as a deliberate affront to Western modern values, especially rationalism and productivity.[111]

The Iranian psychoanalyst Gohar Homayounpour uses the term "fascinated rejection" to describe a similarly intense Western interest in present-day Iranians as essentially nonmodern, irrational (because religious), and exotic.[112] Nonwhite and non-Western artists and thinkers drawn to the utopian thinking and aesthetics of the avant-garde have had to struggle with their designated place of being the Western avant-garde's fascinating other.[113] Such struggle, Homayounpour argues, could be complicated by the non-Western subjects' own investment in the self/other dynamic of Orientalism. For while being othered is often denigrating, there are also "pleasures in being looked upon as erotic, exotic, and strange." Hence, to assume their place in discourse and politics as the Western subject's equal, the non-Western subject needs to give those pleasures up. "We [non-Westerners]," asserts Homayounpour, "have to come face to face with our inevitable ordinariness."[114]

Indeed, according to Adam Smith, relating to others as one's equals relies, in part, on the participants' shared ordinariness, which Smith describes as a shared aesthetic sensibility (and Rancière as a common sense). "Our first ideas of personal beauty and deformity are drawn from the shape and appearance of others," writes Smith. "We begin [. . .] to examine our own passions and conduct, and to consider how these must appear to [others], by considering how they would appear to us if in their situation."[115] The reciprocity he describes—"considering how [others] would appear to us if [we were] in their situation"—is informed by a shared sense of beauty and ugliness. As he talks of this shared sense, Smith makes several important remarks. "The most customary [i.e., ordinary] form [. . .] is in each species of things [. . .] the most beautiful."[116] But the "customs" that inform our perceptions of beauty are culturally contingent. "A fair complexion is a shocking deformity on the coast of Guinea," he remarks. "In China if a lady's foot is so large as to be fit to walk upon, she is regarded as a monster of ugliness."[117] Yet, such customs do change, particularly under the influence of "eminent artists" and "agreeable men of high rank."[118] In sum, according to Smith, rank and culturally contingent custom inform our shared perception of "ordinariness," which, in turn, enables reciprocity, equality, and social cohesion.

Thus, Bhatti's choice to tell a story about Sikhism through the conventions of Western comedy may have enabled a sense of ordinariness for at least some in her audience, even as that sense seems to have also obscured her radical return to Sikhism. While her characters are culturally distinct, comedy makes their faults appear familiar: faults that white British spectators can sympathize with. Homayounpour's attention to the importance of a sense of ordinariness to reimagining minoritized people as the Western subject's equals also puts in a different light critics' opinion (discussed in chapter 1) that Suzan-Lori Parks should have written a play about Saartje Baartman in a more established aesthetic mode. Because in her lifetime Baartman was the target of Western audiences' "fascinated rejection," a play that aimed to be an act of restorative justice would have conferred on her a sense of ordinariness, those critics implied.

But, as has become clear by now, the protesting Sikhs, or at least their leaders, did not want to be perceived as ordinary; they did not want to participate in the performance encounter on liberal terms, but to challenge those terms. Hence, they used their cultural exceptionalism strategically. Rather than argue against their exoticization and racialization, the protesters used the performative power of race to their advantage, arguing that their disagreement with the Birmingham Rep over religious symbols was in fact a racial issue. As Rai wrote,

> Freedoms are never absolute, least of all in multicultural societies where responsibilities to coexist must limit them. Most British people recognize this, which is why the career of the football commentator Ron Atkinson was ended when he made a racist remark. Britain's Asian communities are generally less fazed by colour prejudice, but are sensitive to offence of the sacred: culture and the sacred defines Asians.[119]

The football pundit Ron Atkinson had resigned earlier in 2004 after making a racist comment on TV about the French Black player Marcel Desailly. As reported in the *Guardian*, "referring to the underwhelming performance of the French defender, Atkinson said: 'He's what is known in some schools as a fucking lazy thick 'n——r.' Atkinson's conversation was picked up by microphones that should have been switched off."[120] The setting of rape and murder in a gurdwara, Rai argues, is equally racist. Therefore, acts of religious desecration, as understood by the adherents of specific religions, should be treated as hate speech, and hence as a limit to the freedoms of speech and expression, in the same way that racist remarks, such as Atkinson's, are not protected under laws guaranteeing freedom of speech.

This may appear to be a spurious conflation of religious conviction and racial identity. As Judith Butler remarks in *Is Critique Secular?*, neutrality to religion is integral to the Western secular state. This means that in such states "(a) religion ought to be protected as a *private* issue and that (b) no religious beliefs should drive *public* law or policy."[121] But while secular societies consider religion a private matter, they view race as a phenomenon with both private and public dimensions. The distinction derives from a Western conviction that unlike race, religion is a matter of personal choice. As a result, Wendy Brown explains, most Western countries have stricter laws against racial offense than against religious offense.[122] The Sikh religious identity, however, like that of many observant Muslims, acquires a public dimension due to the dress code integral to Sikhism. It has been also pointed out that in the West, religious difference has been racialized, as in the infamous example of Jewish Europeans.[123] In granting Sikhs protection under the Race Relations Act, Britain recognized this complex interplay of race and religion. Nonetheless, race in this case was also used as a mask or camouflage—a militant tactic. For while Sikhs have experienced racism, the theater's representation of the gurdwara, which in no way contradicts Sikh religious doctrine, cannot be persuasively interpreted as racist.

This strategic presentation of a religious issue as a racial issue becomes even more evident in Birmingham's Catholic bishop's support for the protest, whereby he stated that an offense against the religious symbols of *any* religion should be considered an offence against *every* religious group in Britain and legally sanctioned. Evidently, the bishop seized on the idea of equivalence between the sacred and racial difference proposed by the Sikh leaders. Catholics are a recognized religious minority in Britain, but not an ethno-religious minority like the Sikhs. Therefore, the bishop's attempt to rhetorically extend Sikhs' protected status under the Race Relations Act to all religions, including Catholicism, was an avant-garde act, radically disregarding the distinct histories of Sikhism and Catholicism in an effort toward a major legal and cultural shift, a contestation of the limits of expressive freedom in secular Britain. Thus, the Sikh protest, together with the Catholic support for it, at once employed the radical tactics of the Western avant-gardes, including epistemic violence and institutional critique, and exposed those avant-gardes' racial histories. And just as earlier white avant-gardes modeled their practices on those of so-called primitive or nonmodern groups (whether or not the artists understood them), the Birmingham Catholics attempted to mark themselves as ethnically different by association, through forging an alliance with the Sikhs.

Finally, even the relationship between the feminist politics of *Behzti* and the Sikh protest fits into an established Western critical conversation about the relationship between feminist and avant-garde performance. In his book *Cutting Performances* (2012), which undertakes a feminist historiography of the US avant-garde during the 1960s and 1970s, James M. Harding examines how female artists' deliberate breaks with so-called polite behavior often exposed a major blind spot in male radical performance: male artists' unawareness of the entanglement between capitalism and the patriarchal social system. By making indecorous art, Harding argues, female radical performers demonstrated that "*an anticapitalist aesthetic becomes a trope of the avant-garde only to the extent that it is simultaneously antipatriarchal, only to the extent that the two are indistinguishable.*"[124] His attention to the way a sense of decorum (or lack thereof) informs the gender politics of radical performance resonates with Smith's observation about the importance of custom to social cohesion. Put differently, the feminist provocations that Harding writes about highlighted radical male thinkers' reliance on an unacknowledged custom of social cohesion among themselves: the exclusion of feminist acts as indecorous.[125]

A similar dynamic operated in the *Behzti* controversy. The protesters made explicit Bhatti's antipatriarchal break with Sikh decorum in the seemingly conventional *Behzti*. Her feminist perspective exposed the gendered limits of Sikh egalitarianism as practiced in turn-of-the-century Britain. In turn, the rioters' "indecorous" assault on the theater exposed racial and antireligious biases among the liberal defenders of expressive freedom. Thus, like Harding's analysis of 1960s feminist performance, the *Behzti* controversy exemplifies radical performance as situational, i.e., dependent on the discursive context in which the performance event takes place, rather than on a set of aesthetic and political features.[126] In other words, the politics of performance is dependent not solely, or even primarily, on the artists' intentions, but also on spectators' acts of reception.

THE TAKEAWAYS

As avant-garde acts tend to do, the *Behzti* controversy created a crisis in representational politics and critical thought.[127] Established paradigms were challenged by a community of spectators employing a representational system that was radically different from the system used by professional critics. As the protest made clear, when a clash between such widely different systems occurs, the criteria by which critics may judge an aesthetic as "mainstream" do not apply. Instead, as we evaluate the politics of an artwork, we need to consider not just the range of responses it has attracted, but also the tacit theories of representation that underly each response.

Theorists of reception have long argued that a text or production acquires meaning within distinct interpretive communities of readers and spectators.[128] But the presence of more than one representational system among interpretive communities radicalizes theories of reception. Critics who have struggled to figure out the "desire of the other," i.e., the spectator, within a framework where theorists and spectators are both conceptualized as Western liberal individuals, now have to account for the desire of an other who refuses to communicate within the semiotic liberal framework. The mimetic system the protesters drew on shrank the distance between aesthetic choices and the embodied spectator, giving weight to the protesters' claim that *Behzti* had hurt them; it had hurt them differently than a Western legal notion of harm could express, but it had hurt them deeply. And while the protesters using the mimetic system were mostly Sikh, such systems are not exclusively used by people who practice non-Western religions or belong to specific ethnic groups. As the Birmingham Catholics (and, eventually, Anglicans) allied with the Sikh protesters, they all articulated their position from within a similar understanding of representation: not just as a disagreement with the theater's methods, but as a wound inflicted by racism.

Recall Shannon Jackson's observation that race has the power to collapse the analytical distance between signifier and signified on which the semiotic system relies. Because racism is experienced as trauma—a topic I discuss in the next chapter—staging a play about racism, if not properly handled, can get confused as promoting racism, as David Edgar observed too. The British and American histories of racist violence also imbue racial pain with a sense of authenticity. Hence, by positioning themselves as the Sikhs' allies while keeping the Sikhs as the public face of the protest—i.e., as that protest's vanguard—the Birmingham Catholics presented their disagreement with the legal protections of expressive freedom as a racial, and hence a "true," injury that had affected them as much as it had affected the protesting Sikhs.

But the relationship that the Catholics established with the Sikh was not sympathy. The Catholics never claimed that they were able to imaginatively inhabit the circumstances of the hurt Sikhs. Such an act, as I have argued, entails a shared aesthetic sense, and the aesthetics of Catholicism and Sikhism are distinct. Moreover, a claim that the Catholics could imaginatively inhabit the circumstances of the Sikhs could have been interpreted as a racist act of cultural appropriation. Instead, the Catholics claimed that despite their differences, they could feel the Sikhs' pain as their own. In other words, the Catholics didn't claim they felt *for* the Sikhs (as a liberal sympathetic observer may have claimed); they said that they felt *like* the Sikhs, based on their own experiences as religious people in a secular state. Such forging of alliance through pain—a pain felt across distinct cultures and religious practices—is, arguably, a neoliberal development.

Scholars of neoliberalism have observed that, as global market pressures have been fragmenting the liberal democratic public into interest groups, the ways in which political alliances are built have changed. Even when separate interest groups do not share an overarching political vision, they can still join forces around shared or complementary objectives. The temporary cohesion between such groups, as they pursue their shared objectives, entails the circulation of affectively charged signifiers.[129] Thus, Catherine Chaput argues that, given the power of affect to overcome political differences at least for a time, rhetoricians need to shift from "a [semiotic] communicative model wherein rhetoric moves audiences through encoded messages that these individuals decode and act on" to one "following rhetoric as it energizes different audiences throughout diverse situations."[130] The semiotic model assumes that the participants in an encounter—in this case artists and protesters—share cultural and institutional knowledge. But Chaput is interested in a different model: one in which two, or more, interpretive communities may very well understand each other's semiotic codes, but may diverge or converge in their responses on the basis of affect, rather than on the basis of rational understanding or misunderstanding alone. She calls this model *trans-situational*, one in which affects may charge signifiers in ways that overwrite their normative meanings, enabling seemingly unlikely political alliances. This model, she writes, complements rather than replaces the semiotic model.[131]

Applying this model to the *Behzti* controversy helps explain why the Sikh elders, who saw the production and knew the semiotic codes according to which the staged gurdwara was undoubtedly a representation, chose to claim that a blasphemy had been committed: they had a much bigger objective in mind. Their hopefulness that this objective would be achieved and their displeasure at having a woman contest Sikh egalitarianism were the affects that mobilized the Sikhs who protested, and those who rioted, even though many of them had not seen the show and hence could not have had individually informed opinions about its alleged transgressions of Sikh doctrine. Likewise, many liberal commentators who did not understand the semiotics of Sikhism, and hence couldn't appreciate Bhatti's feminist intervention, supported the play anyway, indignant that the protesters wanted to limit the artists' freedom of expression. Finally, the Birmingham Catholics, who didn't have the semiotic knowledge that Bhatti and the Sikh elders shared, formed an alliance arguably based on deeply felt racial injury. Moreover, they implied that such affective alliances—feeling *like* rather than feeling *for* a cultural other—were the true way of practicing multiculturalism. Their feeling *like* the Sikh other was presumably enabled by the Catholics' own understanding of racial injury: as religious people, they knew what it felt like to be racially wounded. This tacit argument imaginatively placed the Sikhs and the Catholics within a shared narrative of racial injury: a theatrical gesture meant to compensate for the lack of shared history between them.

A decade after the *Behzti* controversy, this affective model of building alliances across identity groups—a model that relies on a mimetic system of signification, resembling the system that informed the reception of *Behzti*—would flourish, spurred by developments in social media, such as Facebook (now Meta), that enabled the quantification of emotional responses and the rapid circulation of emotion-rich content. Thus, technologically enhanced, the feeling subject that we could see emerge in the controversies over *Venus* and *Blasted* and even more in the context of the *Behzti* protest—a subject who contests expressive freedom in the name of an equality more perfect than liberalism has ever been able to achieve—became a powerful social activist. The rise of this subject, as a spectator and activist, is the focus of the next chapter.

4 *Feeling Bad about Being White*

YOUNG JEAN LEE'S THEATER AND THE PROGRESSIVE AVANT-GARDE

Young Jean Lee's theater has been described as avant-garde,[1] and there are many reasons why the description rings true. In plays such as *Songs of the Dragons Flying to Heaven* (2006), *The Shipment* (2009), and *Straight White Men* (2014), Lee grapples with contemporary race relations, trying to understand the persistence of racial prejudice. What makes her approach particularly daring is her willingness to write about racial groups not her own, a practice that the legacy of minstrelsy has rendered politically suspect. Lee, moreover, uses avant-garde tropes to describe her own artistic pursuits. While her company was still active (from 2003 to 2016), her website bore the motto "Destroy the Audience," and in several interviews she has spoken of the value that, as a playwright, she finds in going to uncomfortable places and taking spectators with her.[2] In reflecting on *The Shipment*—her show about blackness in the arguably postracial America that some said had been ushered in during Barack Obama's first term as president[3]—critics and artists have been more than happy to grant the play avant-garde status. Thus, in his review for the *New Yorker*, Hilton Als compares the third part of *The Shipment*—a realist play about a dinner party gone wrong—to Luis Buñuel's 1972 film *The Discreet Charm of the Bourgeoisie*.[4] Through this comparison, the ghost of the bourgeois spectator, the *raison d'être* of avant-garde performance, enters the discussion, claiming the play as avant-garde by association. This status has been further reinforced by the venues where *The Shipment* and Lee's other dramas have been performed: nonmainstream houses and international festivals for new and experimental work.

Yet despite anticipating controversy, Lee's work has not caused the furious polemics that Parks's and Kane's plays caused in the mid-1990s and

Behzti in 2004. Importantly, those three works became controversial when staged in mainstream venues: the Public Theater in New York, the Royal Court Theatre in London, and the Birmingham Repertory Theatre in Birmingham, UK. In all three cases, a play's specific aesthetic choices clashed with professional reviewers' and/or nonprofessional spectators' understanding of the (racially, gender-, and religiously defined) limits of decorum when violence is shown on stage. Likewise, the only occasion when Lee's work provoked audiences to protest was the opening of *Straight White Men* at the Public Theater in November 2014, where the loud hip-hop preshow music unexpectedly angered some spectators. Lee explained that the music was chosen to make her regular off-off-Broadway audience feel welcome at the Public, and she was taken aback by the Public's subscribers' insistence that the music was alienating and aggressive.[5] For the most part, however, her spectators have been more than happy to follow her to uncomfortable places. In the case of *The Shipment*, this meant watching from the position of a white liberal reflecting on their attitudes toward people from other racial and ethnic groups. Occasionally, some spectators have even complained that Lee's drama "doesn't make them feel worse about being white"[6] or that it is not as "disorienting" as they expected.[7]

Such spectators may or may not be representative of Lee's larger audience, but, paradoxically, they appear to be her ideal spectators. As their dissatisfaction reveals, they expected exactly what she intended: an unsettling show prompting them to reflect on the privileges that their whiteness grants them. What intrigues me is not her failure to give them what they wanted, but their very demand for this specific experience: for spectatorship as a practice of feeling bad *in public* about one's privileged position in the racial hierarchies of twenty-first-century America. It is through Lee's white spectators' demand to be made uncomfortable, I suggest, rather than through her intentions and artistic choices, that her plays anticipate the aesthetics of twenty-first-century progressivism that would soon become prominent in progressive settings such as university campuses. Since white progressivism is the subject of at least two of Lee's plays—*The Shipment* and *Straight White Men*—I view her theater as a laboratory for progressive aesthetics: a place where white liberal spectators in particular could rehearse new, more equitable ways of being together with racially minoritized people.

This chapter examines this aesthetic as it emerged during Barack Obama's two terms of office (2009–2016), finding political expression in the Black Lives Matter and #MeToo movements. I detail this aesthetic as it manifests in responses to *The Shipment* and in the Yale Halloween costume controversy, a confrontation between sociologist Nicholas Christakis and his students over Yale's attempt to advise students on their choices of Halloween costumes in fall 2015. What these two case studies have in common is a preoccupation with racial aesthetics—how minoritized, especially Black, subjects and their white progressive allies appear in public in Obama's America—that took shape as theatrical concerns about casting and costumes. Drawing on these case studies, I suggest that for social progressives of this period, *feeling bad about being white, in public*, became a bonding affect as important as sympathy has been to liberalism. In this aesthetic, as in the model for cross-racial alliances that it informs, the white individual is as radically decentered as in Sarah Kane's *Blasted* and in the Sikh-Catholic alliance facilitated by the *Behzti* controversy, even as the white individual "cruelly" clings to liberal rules of engagement. I am referring here to Lauren Berlant's phrase "cruel optimism," her description of the liberal individual's tenacious commitment to the "good life" of liberal theory, under the conditions of neoliberalism that according to Berlant have made that life an unreachable ideal.[8] In these case studies, too, we see liberal individuals, cruelly invested in liberal social and discursive practices, confront the feeling subject of progressivism who rejects those practices while calling for a reckoning with liberalism's racial politics.

SPECTATORSHIP AS AN ACT OF PENANCE

The Shipment begins pleasantly enough, with a dance piece. Actors Prentice Onayemi and Mikéah Ernest Jennings come on stage, dancing to Semisonic's rock song *F. N. T.* [Fantastic New Thing].[9] Lee's stage directions specify that the dancers' moves should be "goofy and unidentifiable in genre," although "occasionally, we'll see a flash of a possible minstrel reference."[10] In view of Lee's stated intention to unsettle, the dance is most likely meant to invite us in, help us relax into our seats, so that the opening monologue will take us by surprise. Forewarned or not (depending on whether we have recognized the minstrel references), we then watch the *Ubu*-esque second scene. As the dance ends, Douglas Scott Streater walks forward, dancing to the rap song *I Don't Give a Fuck*. "Seattle! Ladies and gentlemen! Please put cho mothafuckin' hands together for the one, the only, Douglas Scott Streater," the announcer calls.[11] And just in case we missed the significance of the expletive, Streater exclaims: "Laurelhurst! See, that's my shit ya'll."[12] The celebrated "Merdre!" resounds yet again, but Lee must be aware that by now, more than one hundred and twenty years after *Ubu Roi*'s fabled premiere, it must have lost its power to shock. So she gives us another word to ponder: "I'm a Laurelhurst n——a—born and bred," Streater states. "N——a" rather than "shit" seems charged with the task of producing shock, intimating that in Obama's allegedly postracial America, speaking of racial inequality, rather than of lower-body functions, threatens the norms of polite society.

The parallel can be pressed further. *Ubu Roi* (1896) held a distorted mirror to the French bourgeois, portraying him as a Macbeth without a dagger scene, a greed-propelled machine divested of a depth-conferring subconscious and immune to ennobling pangs of conscience. Streater's character similarly divests the white liberal of their self-proclaimed colorblindness: "And all a you people who consider yourselves to be 'colorblind'? Y'all are the WORST mothafuckin' offenders," he declares.[13] But in the end, he (mercifully, one might say) gives the white spectator an alternative dagger scene. What may be truly ennobling, he suggests, is white progressives feeling uncertain about how Black people may perceive them: "And for all you white folks out there who walk on eggshells around Black people, paranoid about saying the wrong thing that's gonna make us uncomfortable . . . shit, I like you. We Black folks been doing that shit for y'all since the day we got here."[14] Streater's monologue thus arcs from an avant-garde provocation to a progressive proposition. He proposes a social contract whereby a white progressive tries to see themself through the eyes of a contemporary Black American. But unlike in classic liberalism, in this revised contract, the binding affect is not assimilative sympathy. Instead, the white individual and their racially marked others are bound together by the white individual's unsettling uncertainty about how their Black interlocutor may perceive them.

The implications of Streater's proposition become clearer when considered in light of Elizabeth Maddock Dillon's definition of Adam Smith's sympathetic individual as a revision of the Cartesian *cogito*. I think, therefore I am, says the Cartesian transcendental subject. "I think *the other thinks* I am, therefore, I am," responds the sympathizing individual, acknowledging his constitutive dependence both on the object of his sympathy and on the impartial judge who ensures the appropriateness of both participants' behaviors.[15] In the new social contract proposed in Streater's monologue, the Cartesian formula takes yet another twist: "I think the Black person thinks

I am *more racist than I think*, therefore I am *white*." Streater's character thus articulates the affect appropriate to the white progressive, complete with a cue about how it is to be embodied: "walking on eggshells around Black people." Put differently, Streater defines Obama-era white progressivism as a practice of reckoning with liberalism's racial politics. His monologue is also a cutting commentary on 2009 postracial claims; in a truly postracial society, he implies, white people wouldn't need to continually assert our colorblindness, as if hoping that the assertion may become true through repetition. Retrospectively, the monologue also reads like a script for the future: by the end of the following decade a white person's impulse to "walk on eggshells around Black people" would have become a progressive mandate.

In the second part of *The Shipment*, Lee continues examining postracial claims, this time by drawing a parallel between nineteenth-century minstrelsy and twenty-first-century media stereotypes of blackness. The minstrel stock character Dandy Jim reappears as the elegant drug-dealer Desmond (Onayemi in a tuxedo and a bowtie). The good-for-nothing "plantation darkie" is back as the fashionably dressed Crackhead John (Jennings, in a three-piece suit, including a floral vest and a red tie). The tough-loving, violent Black Mama (Amelia Workman in a long turquoise dress) is every bit as glamorous as Michelle Obama on the March 2009 cover of *Vogue*. Ryan Anthony Hatch has described Lee's return to minstrelsy as Brecht-like.[16] Indeed, the actors seem to be telling spectators about a minstrel show rather than enacting the denigrating types in good faith. But their critically distanced acting is perhaps better described as *strategic ambiguity*, a term I borrow from media scholar Ralina Joseph.

Joseph devised the term to explain how privileged Black people have tried to draw attention to racist acts in Obama-era America, when calling racism out became unseemly.[17] For Joseph, the semiotics of postracial glamor caters above all to white people's expectations about how Black people, and especially prominent Black women, should behave in public after racial equality has supposedly been achieved.[18] The pressure on socially and economically successful Black people to substantiate this belief, Joseph points out, makes postrace a treacherous performance. The privileged Black woman's perceived failure to confirm the end of racism through her public presence returns that post-Obama figure to her "original" state of unrespectability, stripping her of her glamor, a dynamic Lee makes conspicuous by dressing up the unrespectable Black gangsters of her minstrel show in glamourous attire. Moreover, Lee's return to minstrelsy through the aesthetic of racial glamor suggests that the two are connected. Just as minstrelsy affirmed nineteenth-century white spectators' fantasies of their racial superiority, the aesthetic of racial glamor affirms contemporary white viewers' fantasies of racial equality.

In the script, Lee cautions that the connection between minstrelsy and the aesthetic of racial glamour should be handled with care. The actors should gesture toward minstrelsy in a way that "denies the audience easy responses (illicit pleasure or self-righteous indignation) to racial clichés and creates a kind of uncomfortable, paranoid watchfulness in everyone."[19] This makes her approach strategically ambiguous: conscious of the racial politics of the moment that demands subtlety from the Black critic and punishes Brechtian explicitness. It is perhaps because of the strategic ambiguity in Lee's minstrel show that I was able to enjoy the cast's command of the ugly stereotypes. The actors' well-measured exaggerations comfortingly signaled to me (at least in my self-serving imagination), that we, the actors and I, both knew that there was never any truth to such stereotypes. But this ambiguity may also be what made Lee's dissatisfied "ideal" spectators not feel as uncomfortable about being white as they had anticipated. This, indeed, as Joseph explains, is the risk of strategic ambiguity. Spectators may fail to register it, or alternatively, they may fail to appreciate the performer's tact, accusing them of alleging racist bigotry where there was none.[20] But despite its risks, Lee's use of strategic ambiguity may have also prevented the angry response that Parks's explicit staging of the Venus's victimization evoked in 1996. As actress Adina Porter licked the chocolates that onlookers threw into the Venus's cage, and as she was poked and groped by a chorus of white spectators, she did not seem in control of the racist stereotypes she was enacting; instead, to Black audience members, those stereotypes seemed to control Porter's performance.

Lee's reflexive, metatheatrical approach to blackness continues in the last part of the play, a realist drama. As in the previous parts, here again the show gestures back to earlier works, and when I first saw it, I immediately thought of Edward Albee's *Who's Afraid of Virginia Woolf?* (1962). Like Albee's play, Lee's revolves around a dinner party that ends with the host, Thomas (played by Streater), "getting the guests."[21] These include the socially awkward Omar (Jennings), who is abnormally fixated on healthful eating and so cannot taste the food and drinks that Thomas has prepared; Desmond (Onayemi), who speaks excessively loudly, stares blankly in front of himself, and appears to have taken cocaine before coming to the party; and the

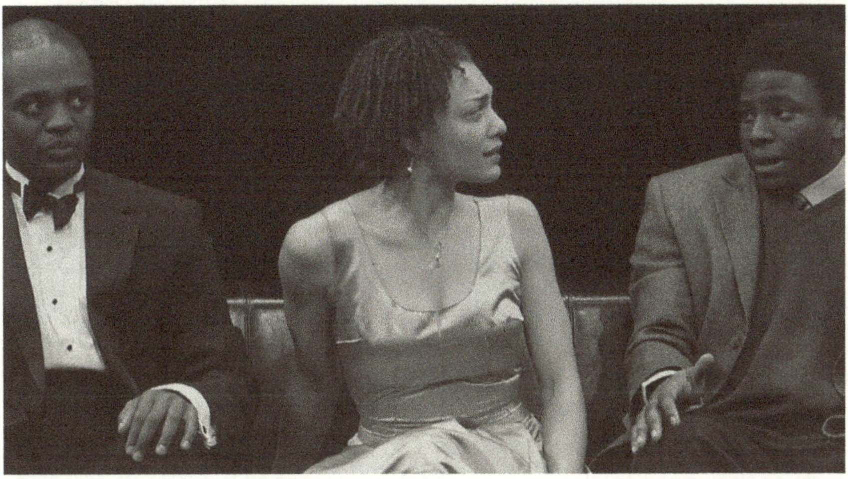

Figure 8. Scene from *The Shipment*, by Young Jean Lee, *The Kitchen*, 2009. Photo by Paula Court.

suave Tomasina (Workman), who, Thomas callously reveals, suffers from incontinence. None of the characters appears capable of forming lasting relationships, and even a party seems to tax their psychological endurance. One can imagine them looking at Albee's dysfunctional couples with wistful yearning.

But while Albee examines his characters' strivings for success and fulfilment during the tumultuous 1960s, in the context of a genteel academic liberalism that espoused but failed to practice gender and racial equality, Lee's characters are mired in the neoliberal moment of the early twenty-first century. The inexpensive, functional set, which seems to have come out of an international chain such as IKEA, the characters' casually elegant clothes, and even their forced conversation convey the impression of corporate elegance, of parties that double as informal job interviews, of upward mobility that entails geographic impermanence at the expense of meaningful friendships. Even the pathologies through which Lee individualizes her characters, including eating disorders and cocaine addiction, seem up to date, compared to Albee's characters' old-fashioned hysterical pregnancies and alcoholism.

At last, Thomas, frustrated with his guests' behaviors and disappointed that no one has remembered it is his birthday, lies that he has poisoned their drinks, and then breaks down and admits that he has been feeling lonely and hopeless. Afraid that he may be suicidal, his angry guests call an ambulance, and while waiting for it, begin playing a game about Black superstition. But as they try to complete the sentence "The Negro believes . . . ," Omar interrupts: "I'm sorry. I'm sorry, but I have to say that I'm really uncomfortable with all of this. I just don't think we'd be doing this if there were a Black person in the room."[22] Through this statement, Omar at once reveals himself as not Black and as a progressive: one who tries to internalize a Black impartial judge and act as that judge may deem appropriate, even when a Black person is not present.

Whatever hypothesis about the meaning of the characters' interactions a viewer may have built so far, this hypothesis now needs to be thoroughly reexamined. For instance, even before Omar reveals that the characters are all white, it is clear that they resort to playing "The Negro believes . . ." because they need to close the rifts that have opened between them; they need to regroup until an ambulance arrives and Thomas can be treated. Once we know that the characters are white, the game becomes legible as a racial strategy for building consent. No matter how self-involved the characters have shown themselves to be, no matter how dysfunctional their relationships, they prove capable of forging a temporary bond in a critical moment by ridiculing Black people. Hence, for all their apparent sophistication, they prove to be no different than nineteenth-century white spectators of minstrel shows, who bonded over their collective ridicule of Black people. While the aesthetic of minstrelsy may have changed, the ending suggests, white Americans' need for it as a tool for building social cohesion may be just as strong in Obama's America as it was in the past. Indeed, David Harvey argues that during the late twentieth century, racism, along with sexism and homophobia, became a major strategy for building consent over neoliberal policies among white Americans from different social strata.[23] Likewise, the play suggests that the narcissistic self-involvement and social fragmentation that have come to be associated with neoliberalism can be overcome, at least temporarily, through taking part in racist entertainment.

But to fully appreciate this *coup de théâtre*, we need to know how the show was conceived. Lee asked her cast what roles they would like her to write for them, and they requested that she writes naturalistic characters "with some serious dramatic arcs"; the kind of characters, they told her, that as Black actors, they rarely got to play.[24] Having done so, Lee even proposed to cross out the first two parts of *The Shipment* altogether, but the actors insisted on keeping them so they could "address all these stereotypes that they're still dealing with."[25] The *coup de théâtre* thus probes the actors' desire for realist roles in the symbolically charged moment of 2009. What did it mean to be a postracial Black in this moment, as the characters appear to be? Did it mean that Black artists could finally work in a realist mode without fearing that realism, often critiqued for its assimilative power, would overwrite their histories and experiences as Black people? Is postracial blackness, realistically performed for a white audience, the ultimate disavowal of racism's history and present?

Lee's use of disability also draws attention to the racial politics of classic realism. In classic realist plays, physical and mental pathologies are strategies for individualizing a character who is otherwise to be perceived as average. Individual pathology thus becomes synonymous with character complexity, transforming middle-class whiteness into a realist aesthetic object. In contrast, Black people have been usually pathologized as sociological types, such as criminals and victims of crime. Only postracial Blacks, *The Shipment* implies, seem eligible to be pathologized as individuals, because the screen media have already constructed them as realist aesthetic objects.

If the play suggests any alternative to the realist and postracial representational entrapments, it could be in the fable at the end of the second part, where Rapper Omar (Onodowan), dissatisfied with his posh yet empty lifestyle, calls to the Lord to show him the way. In response, Grandma from Heaven (Workman) tells the following story:

> There were two cranes. And the first crane had one red berry for an eye, which the second crane pecked out and ate. And that berry expanded to the size of a world inside the greedy crane until its crane-flesh burst open and went flying in every direction. And that world-shaped berry developed boils the size of people, which were red and hungry and which fed upon each other until the juice was dripping down everyone's faces. And the people walked around with parts of their bodies missing—chunks of ear, a bite out of their backs. And the crane that had been eviscerated began to gather up all its molecules to re-form feathers and flesh and eyes and beak, until it found itself whole and healthy on a planet of red berry earth and flesh. And the crane gorged itself until it was round and red as the planet itself. And everyone sat around, crippled and maimed and feeding, until the sun went down.[26]

The figure of Grandma from Heaven is as culturally burdened as any of the other types in the second part of *The Shipment*. A bearer of traditional African wisdom who recurs in African American drama—from Willis Richardson's Aunt Nancy in *The Chip Woman's Fortune* (1923) to August Wilson's Aunt Esther in *Two Trains Running* (1990)—she embodies at once a Black American fantasy of an uninterrupted link to a mythic African preslavery past and the anxiety that this past, full of wisdom but not reason (according to an enduring stereotype), may hinder African Americans' political and economic uplift.[27] As historians have pointed out, this ambivalence about the preslavery past is expressed in the two names of the Black cultural flourishing in the early twentieth century: "the Harlem Renaissance" and "the New Negro Movement." The former connotes cultural rebirth, renewal through reflection on a past that encompasses both African mythological time and the history of slavery. In contrast, the latter signals a hope for a definitive break with that history of oppression, a hope for a new way of being, embodied by a New Negro looking toward the future.[28]

Given her ability to host such discordant perspectives, it is not surprising that this mythic Black woman should resurface in early-twenty-first-century postracial discourse. For the term *post*-race—like the earlier terms "Harlem Renaissance" and "New Negro Movement"—connotes at once the felt necessity to confront the past and the will to overcome it. Maybe because Lee and Workman's Grandma from Heaven is all too conscious of being periodically convoked to give face to such critical ambivalence, she attends to her task with both wisdom and whimsy. The fable that she tells could be read for its moral, perhaps as a fatalistic tale of inescapable greed, in line with the neoliberal theme of the third part. But the fable's dizzying imagery, at once fanciful and grotesque, need not be logically understood. (This character, as I said, is not tasked with offering rational solutions.) Instead, one could marvel at its fast-paced transformations: a crane's eye made of berries becoming boils, becoming people, becoming a crane again, as in Giuseppe Arcimboldo's sixteenth-century portraits of human heads made of vegetables, flowers, fish, and books.

But while such whimsical ambiguity could be abided, at least in some theatrical contexts, in cautiously optimistic 2009, it would become intolerable in the second decade of this century, when a series of murders of unarmed Black people—beginning with the shooting of seventeen-year-old Trayvon Martin in February 2012—forcefully undermined postracial illusions. Three years after Martin's death and just months after the third wave of the unrest in Ferguson, Missouri, which began when the unarmed Black teenager Michael Brown was killed by the police in August 2014, a controversy at Yale over the politics of Halloween costumes spectacularly marked the shift toward a new progressive aesthetic notable for its insistence on representational purity.

THE FEELING SUBJECT AND THEIR UTOPIAN HOME

In October 2015, shortly before Halloween, the Intercultural Affairs Council at Yale sent an email asking students to be considerate when choosing their costumes, pointing out that some choices could offend members of Yale's diverse community. In response, Erika Christakis, a professor of child developmental psychology and associate head of the residential Silliman College, wrote to the students in her charge, questioning whether an administrative body should be regulating students' choices. "Have we lost faith in young people's capacity—in your capacity—to exercise self-censure, through social norming, and also in your capacity to ignore or reject things that trouble you?" she asked. An outraged response soon followed. "In your email, you ask students to 'look away' if costumes are offensive, as if the degradation of our cultures and people, and the violence that grows out of it is something that we can ignore," said an open letter signed by more than 700 students and faculty.[29]

During the public confrontation that followed on Yale's campus on November 5, 2015, an eighty-one-second encounter was captured on a phone and went viral on the internet. In the recording, we see Nicholas Christakis, a physician, professor of sociology, head of Silliman College, and Erika Christakis's husband, trying to talk to students about the relationship between free speech and hate speech, while students insist that he and his wife need to apologize for her hurtful email. One female student in particular talks passionately, while fighting tears back, insisting that free speech ends where she starts hurting. As Christakis apologizes for having unintentionally hurt the protesters' feelings but refuses to apologize for the content of the email, the student says: "It is your job to create a space of comfort and home for the students who live at Silliman. You have not done that. By sending this email, you have gone against you position as Master. Do you understand that?" "I don't agree with that," he answers, even as he is nodding back at her to indicate that he understands her point. "Then why, the fuck, did you accept the position?" she asks in an increasingly high-pitched voice. "Because I have a different vision," he begins answering. But she interrupts, "Who, the fuck, hired you? [. . .] You should step down. This is not about creating an intellectual thing. It is not. Do you understand that? It's about creating a home here. You are not doing that." "You are supposed to be an advocate," a male voice adds. The female student then says that students will be transferring to other institutions because of the Christakises and concludes, "You should not sleep at night. You are disgusting."[30] At that point, she faces the camera just long enough that web hounds were able to identify her: a mixed-race, middle-class suburban woman.[31]

Widely circulated across different media, this encounter captures the major elements of the aesthetic and political shift that I have been trying to theorize. Video clips of varying lengths show Nicholas Christakis, a lone middle-aged white man, trying to model a classic-liberal debate to a passionate and diverse group of students who surround him on all sides. From his outfit (slacks and a casual button-down blue-and-white checkered shirt without a tie) through his body language (nodding to show attentive listening, stretching out his hands in ways suggesting he is trying to position himself as standing with, rather than against, his students despite their differences) to his voice (trying to sound warm and respectful), Christakis represents the liberal white individual in the liberal university: the exemplary ideological apparatus of that kind of subjecthood. His students are outspoken and emotional; they raise their voices, laugh and jeer, sob, and hug each other for support. At times the intensity of their feelings appears threatening, but it never transforms into physical aggression. At one point, a tall Black male student asks Christakis to admit that he is wrong (about defending his wife's position), and his face gets very close to Christakis's face. But when Christakis asks him who he is, he identifies himself and tells him he will probably be taking a sociology class with him. On that, they shake hands and pat each other's backs. One female student of color, too, specifies that she doesn't consider Christakis a terrible person, even as she thinks he has not done his duty toward the students. Such moments of rapprochement, however fleeting, suggest a range of opinions among the students, even if a relatively narrow one. The media, however, would amplify the more intolerant voices, such as that of a young Black woman who calmly tells Christakis that she doesn't want to shake his hand, doesn't respect him, is sick of the "smirk" on his face and of watching her fellow students try to argue with him, because all she sees from him is "arrogance and ego."[32] It is thus in part through editing choices that the controversy acquired the shape of a polarized confrontation, casting the students as a radical group against a representative of the white liberal status quo.

But it was not all the media's doing. By making those choices, the media highlighted, rather than created, the discursive logic of the controversy, which was already on display in Erika Christakis's email and in the letter protesting it. For Christakis, wearing a potentially controversial costume for Halloween—a turban, a feather headdress, blackface, etc., when the person wearing it is not a Muslim or Sikh, a Native American or Black—should not immediately be pronounced an act of bigotry, even though, she acknowledges, the histories of racism and colonialism complicate our judgement on such matters. "I wonder," she muses, "what is the statute of limitations on dreaming of dressing as Tiana the Frog Princess [a Black character from an animated Disney musical] if you aren't a Black girl from New Orleans? Is it okay if you are eight, but not 18? I don't know the answer to these questions; they seem unanswerable. Or at least, they put us on slippery terrain that I, for one, prefer not to cross."[33] Where the Intercultural Affairs Council sees possible insensitivity, Christakis sees productive ambivalence that calls for intellectual engagement. For the students, however, these histories of oppression have a priori drawn unnegotiable distinctions between appropriate and hurtful choices, making even the suggestion of ambivalence a racist speech act. As the Black community mourned the recent murders of unarmed Black people, insensitive representation gained new power to wound. These divergent notions of history—one as a story to be continually examined and revised, the other as an unshiftable burden (or, *pace* Susan-Lori Parks, "time that won't quit")—are at the core of their conflict, and I will be returning to them shortly. For now, I'd like to highlight the differing ways in which the participants in the conflict enacted their positions.

These enactments faithfully followed the conventions of classic liberal and avant-garde performance, including their gender and racial baggage, which becomes conspicuous when we consider the "casting" of the most prominent characters. Notably, Erika Christakis, the true protagonist of the face-to-face encounter, is absent from it and is represented by her husband. As Dillon and others have noted, although classic liberalism deemed the public presence of female bodies indecorous, women could venture out of their assigned private sphere under the guise of print, contributing to public discussion and the liberal imagination.[34] Erika Christakis followed that tradition, publishing her account of the controversy a year later, in the *Washington Post*.[35] Her sticking to print may not have been entirely of her choosing. According to her account, some students had requested advance warning should she walk into the Silliman College dining hall, insisting that the very sight of her caused them pain. In an intriguing and ironic turn, the white woman speaking her mind had become unbearable again, though in a new, postliberal regime.

Yet print endowed Christakis's position with respectability, sparing her the harassment that the mixed-race female student endured once the video recordings became public. The virulence of this harassment made palpable the inequitable position of women of color in public discourse. While Christakis was banished from view for her perceived trespass, the student came under the harsh light of social media as details of her private life were made public without her permission. It is a contrast haunted by performance history: a white woman's public presence is limited to print, while a woman of color is coerced into spectacular exposure. In the course of that exposure, the rawness of the student's presence—her distressed crying and cursing—were interpreted by some as undeniable proof of her entitlement and hence as justification for the racist attacks against her. By choosing to freely express her outrage or by failing to control it, she had embodied the white fantasy of the "angry Black woman," the abject edge of both classic liberal and postracial respectability.[36] The *Washington Post*, too, played into this stereotype through their choice of illustration for Erika Christakis's text. In the photo, a (different) female student of color stands in the middle of the protesting crowd. Her mouth is shaped in an angry shout, and her left hand is raised in a fist with her middle finger sticking out. Ironically, the racist reaction against the mixed-raced student, prompted by the video's circulation, proved the protester's point: insensitive representation has real-life effects, not all of which can be easily ignored or resolved through polite intellectual engagement.

But writing off the protesting students as unrespectable, as they inevitably appear to be according to the conventions of liberal decorum, does little to explain the larger phenomenon exemplified by the Yale controversy. Besides, at that moment, the Black Lives Matter movement was deliberately rejecting the respectability pursued by earlier movements for Black uplift, which the Obamas had also come to represent. As the number of Black victims of violence grew, Black activists felt compelled to abandon both the racially coded public composure, which has been a feature of liberal social engagement since Adam Smith, and the strategic ambiguity practiced by privileged Black people. Persistent racism required a vocal response and freedom to "express rage at [. . .] an unjust system."[37] In view of this, it is fruitful to consider the protesting students' behavior in an avant-garde framework. Indeed, their insistence on the real-world effects of representation (i.e., the ability of insensitive costume choices to injure minoritarian subjects) and their abrogation of institutional decorum during their public engagement with Nicholas Christakis have an affinity to avant-garde tactics of the past. Additionally, considered in avant-garde terms, the students' wish to have Erika Christakis banned from their dining hall directs us, the conflict's audience, to the utopian vision that guided their actions: a vision of a home away from home that the Christakises failed to create.

"This [Silliman College] is my home, and you came in here," a female student tells Nicholas Christakis in the longer video recording. "You adopted me," she continues. "You understand that? You take care of me. You haven't been doing that." Apparently, Christakis, who had been head of Silliman for two months by the time of the controversy, had not been able to remember the names of the 500 students in his charge. This made that student feel "divested of her humanity," especially because she was his main aide. Instead of creating a home, another student charged, "you have created a space for violence." For the students, feeling at home equals an experience of emotional well-being, which includes, among other things, a head who knows you by your name. In fact, nowhere in the description of a head's duties is it explicitly stated that the head is responsible for the students' emotional well-being. The head is described as an "administrative officer," who is responsible for "the physical well-being and safety of students" and for "shaping the social, cultural, and educational life of the college," by "hosting lectures, study breaks, teas (intimate gatherings during which students have the opportunity to engage with renowned guests from the academy, government, or popular culture), and other events."[38] But the students' perception of the head as a parent responsible for creating a home—not altogether inaccurate, as will become clear—points toward the social utopia envisioned in their protest.

Clearly, their imagined home has little to do with the ideal bourgeois home theorized by Jürgen Habermas, who has argued for the pivotal role of the domestic space in the development of modern societies. In Habermas's theory of the public sphere, that home is the male liberal subject's space of quiet reflection, free from the pressures of public politics and maintained through the invisible labor of his wife and lower-class servants. In contrast, in the student's ideal home, the "father," no less than the "mother," works to create a space of belonging, free from emotional friction, for the 500 racially and ethnically diverse students, rather than for himself. In this space, where the personal is undeniably and unabashedly political, the "parents'" attunement to social difference preempts intrafamilial tensions, and intellectual engagement does not clash with the mandates of cultural sensitivity. ("This is not about creating an intellectual thing," the mixed-race female student says in the viral clip.) In this model, the reflecting white male liberal individual is replaced by *a feeling subject*, and cultural sensitivity—understood as privileging the feeling subjects' needs over liberal rights—structures and delimits intellectual engagement.

In drawing attention to these limits, I am not claiming that the protesting students lacked critical thinking. The open letter they wrote in response to Erika Christakis's email makes a number of salient points that elucidate the blind spots in her defense of free expression. It makes clear, for instance, that the protesting students did not see the email by the Intercultural Affairs Council as a bureaucratic imposition, because, as individuals, they agreed with the letter's stance. The signatories also point out that the Council was not trying to impose Halloween rules, but asked students to consider how their choices, whatever they may be, might be seen by other members of the community.[39] Hence, in their view, the Council's letter proposed, not unlike Christakis's email, that individual students "exercise self-censure." Where they differ is in how each party understands self-censure.

For Christakis, self-censure relies on "social norming"; she trusts that the shared norms of public behavior will guide the students into dressing up appropriately. The protesting students, in contrast, maintain that to be able to exercise self-censure, students should be attuned to cultural sensitivity. And cultural sensitivity, as both the students and Christakis seem to agree, is not yet a shared norm. Perhaps because of this, Christakis is loath to *a priori* define inappropriate costume choices as undeniably (and therefore intentionally) denigrating. Rather, she sees such choices as failing to meet a norm that has yet to be established ("a slippery terrain") and therefore is still negotiable. The students, in contrast, seem to believe that if a choice *could* offend a minoritized subject, it *will* offend a minoritized subject; that such a choice is always already offensive. This belief is summarized in their response to Nicholas Christakis: your right of free expression ends where I (could) start hurting. This radical proposition—which has emerged in this and other similar incidents on college campuses[40]—suggests that the feeling subject at the center of the conflict is, more specifically, a posttraumatic subject: one already traumatized by a history of oppression and likely to be retraumatized by cultural insensitivity, i.e., by subjects who, through their speech and actions, show that they do not understand the hurtful effects of the histories of racism and colonialism. Thus, similar to the *Bezhti* controversy, the Yale controversy exemplifies (what Catherine Chaput has defined as) a transsituational encounter. Though the participants share an institutional and a cultural context, they cannot understand each other's arguments because they uphold two different theories of representation: a semiotic theory according to which an insensitive Halloween costume is "merely" a sign of the cluelessness of the person who wears it, and a mimetic theory, in which an insensitive costume choice is a speech act that retraumatizes a subject who has already been shaped by traumatic history.

To fully understand the gap between the feeling subject and the liberal individual, we also need to understand the specific theory of trauma that informs the feeling subject's stance on representation. For while the notion of the minoritized subject as posttraumatic was already well established in 2015, the Halloween costume controversy represents a new take on it. Briefly, the cultural theorists who turned to trauma at the turn of the century appear to have done so for the same reason that others turned to affect. They were intrigued by how feelings inform political life and public discourse, and they felt that the increasingly abstract poststructuralist theories did not give them tools to address this question.[41] "As a name for experiences of socially situated political violence, trauma forges overt connections between politics and emotion," writes Ann Cvetkovich in *An Archive of Feelings* (2003).[42] "Trauma discourse," she writes further, "has allowed me to ask about the connection between girls like me [i.e., lesbian women] feeling bad and world historical events."[43] Or, as E. Ann Kaplan put it in *Trauma Culture* (2005), "addressing the phenomena of trauma must have seemed one way for critics to begin to link high theory with specific material events that were both personal and which implicated history, memory, and culture generally."[44] The concept of trauma, in other words, offered ways for a minoritized culture to gain insights about itself by thinking through its intellectual and affective relationship to the larger world.

There were also pitfalls. Steeped in 1990s antifoundationalism, these theorists worried that a return to trauma may entail a return to essentialism. They feared that a focus on trauma could lead to undertheorized concepts of the body and the subject and that some critics could downplay the mediating work of fantasy, the unconscious, and the political and cultural context in which the traumatic "event" is being "remembered," i.e., constructed.[45] They worried, too, that theorizing minoritized cultures as produced through trauma could further pathologize them, justifying discrimination against them.[46] Last but not least, they were wary of contributing to the creation of a "hysterical" and "self-righteous" "victim culture."[47] Instead, they hoped that a rigorously theorized concept of trauma would enable them to account for the resilient, creative, and self-reflexive cultures that emerged "in response to the demands of grappling with the psychic consequences of historical events," whether experienced firsthand or vicariously, through art, narrative, and family histories.[48] In retrospect, Du Bois's account of the emergence of double-consciousness (analyzed in chapter 2) exemplifies this exact understanding of trauma.

The new trauma discourse of the 2010s seems a lot less concerned about slipping into essentialism. To put it differently, turn-of-the-century theorists sought to grasp the *truth* of trauma: the cultural effects of a painful but elusive past that could not be fully factually ascertained. In contrast, for the participants in the Halloween costume controversy and other recent controversies around racial and sexual politics, the *truth* of trauma and the *fact* of trauma have become one and the same thing. They have become certainties that require no additional explanation, and questioning them could be interpreted as an act of violence: an abusive negation of the posttraumatic subject's pain.

Thus, for the protesting students at Yale, the history of racist oppression was productive of trauma, rather than trauma *and* resilience; of pain, rather than pain *and* creativity; of transgenerational loss, rather than loss *and* vibrant cultures. In their account, the past is perceived as a well-established fact, rather than fact *and* narrative. In turn, this perception constructs the life of a person of color as unmediated pain that speaks for itself. The resulting lack of nuance is typical of many such incidents on college campuses. For instance, in the controversy that emerged over the then new Title IX policies at Northwestern University in March 2015, film critic Laura Kipnis (whom students accused of hurtful insensitivity to victims of sexual misconduct after she published an essay questioning the reach of those policies) wrote: under the new norms being established on college campuses, "emotional discomfort is regarded as equivalent to material injury, and all injuries have to be remediated."[49]

Indeed, by 2015 these new norms had become so conspicuous that despite the media's avid coverage of the Yale controversy, it was, in a sense, old news. A year earlier, sociologists Bradley Campbell and Jason Manning had assembled enough data to argue that a major shift had been taking place: a rapidly advancing "culture of victimhood" was clashing with a well-established "culture of dignity."[50] In their description, the "culture of dignity" displays all the characteristics of the classic-liberal ideal. Its representatives believe they have an inalienable and inherent worth that does not depend on public opinion. They subscribe to an ethic of self-restraint, and value the ability to ignore offensive behaviors pointed at themselves. (Erika Christakis's suggestion that students ignore costume choices they find offensive to themselves clearly belongs to this ethic.) When conflicts do arise, "dignity cultures" prescribe nonviolent solutions, such as "a negotiated compromise" (which was what Nicholas Christakis was trying to accomplish in the confrontation with his students). "Cultures of dignity," the authors specify, are typical of culturally homogenous societies with strong legal systems.[51] In contrast, "cultures of victimhood" are

> characterized by concern with status and sensitivity to slight combined with a heavy reliance on third parties. [. . .] Domination is the main form of deviance, and victimization a way of attracting sympathy, so rather than emphasize either their strength or inner worth, the aggrieved emphasize their oppression and social marginalization. [. . .] [This culture] emerges in contemporary settings, such as college campuses, that increasingly lack the intimacy and cultural homogeneity that once characterized towns and suburbs, but in which organized authority and public opinion remain as powerful sanctions. Under such conditions complaint to third parties has supplanted both toleration and negotiation. People increasingly demand help from others and advertise their oppression as evidence that they deserve respect and assistance.[52]

While the authors' use of "dignity" and "victimhood" seems inaccurate—the protesters at Yale were concerned with dignity too—I find the main argument of their essay intriguing. Rather than attribute the emergence of the "culture of victimhood" to liberalism's historical failures, they attribute it to liberalism's success. Liberalism, they contend, has succeeded in imposing equality across gender, class, and race as a norm and ideal. This success informs the demands at the core of the new culture.[53]

If Campbell and Manning are right, the feeling subject appears to be the logical offspring of the classic liberal subject, even as they appear radical by comparison. But by using the word "offspring," I am not suggesting, as others have, that this shift is primarily generational.[54] After all, the protesters at Yale included both undergraduates and faculty, and so did the opposing camp: Erika Christakis claimed to represent not just herself but also undergraduates who thought the email of the Intercultural Affairs Council was patronizing. Rather, the protesters are the offspring of classic liberalism in a deeper historical sense. They could be viewed as the heirs of those classic liberal counterpublics that practiced liberalism on its gendered and racially drawn margins.

As literary scholar Joanna Brooks reminds us, neither the physical spaces in which classic liberal publics came together (including coffeeshops and salons, among others) nor the formative texts of classic liberalism were hospitable to racialized subjects (though, by being inhospitable, those spaces became productive of avant-garde communities and practices of rhetorical and institutional disruption). Racialized subjects were often violently chased from public spaces, and major liberal texts, such as the US Constitution, did not extend inalienable rights to them. Hence, Brooks insists that the narratives these counterpublics authored cannot be properly understood without taking into account the affective experiences of their authors: the "literary evidences of anger, grief, resentment, exasperation, embitterment, and irony among African Americans in the early Republic."[55] A historical connection between those counterpublics and the contemporary feeling subject is also implicitly hypothesized by Sara Ahmed in her essay "Against Students," where she proposes that the feeling subject's demands for safe spaces and trigger warnings—some of the most recognizable features of the feeling subject's repertoire—are strategies for "dealing with the consequences of histories that are not over."[56] In an earlier text, *The Promise of Happiness* (2010), she analyzes the link between the liberal perception of such demands as "undignified" and histories of racism and colonialism. Teaching colonized populations Western values and manners, she writes, has been inherent to the colonial project, and those populations' resistance to them has been interpreted as rude, primitive, and childish, and hence proof of the need to reeducate them.[57]

Understanding the feeling subject in this way—as predicated both on liberalism's success in making social equality a norm and an ideal and on its failure to fulfill this promise for all, creating minoritized subjects as a result—gives insight into this subject's perceived sense of entitlement and the utopian "home" toward which their activities are oriented. This utopia is not one to aspire to, in a futurist way, but one that *should have been fulfilled already* had liberalism been true to its own message. The feeling subject's social impact is thus performatively authorized not by a future yet to come (as the historical avant-gardes authorized themselves) or by established institutions (as Austinian performativity does), but by their relationship to a project that they see as having failed to live up to its promise. As a result, the feeling subject perceives liberals as people who owe them; hence, the bitterness, anger, and grief that attach to their encounters with them.

But for a certain kind of liberal, for whom acceptable affects are limited to the pleasures of polite debate and quiet reflection and sympathy for an other who is very much like oneself, the public display of bitterness, anger, and grief is not just indecorous, but pathological. (This is the kind of liberal at whom the historical avant-gardes directed their "merdre," protesting what they saw as that liberal's lack of commitment to genuine social analysis.) Consider the solution proposed to campus controversies by lawyer Gregg Lukianoff and social psychologist Jonathan Haidt.[58] Instead of demanding trigger warnings and safe spaces—demands that, in their view, hinder intellectual growth—students must learn to separate fact from feeling. While such thinking is predictably liberal, the scale of Lukianoff and Haidt's proposed solution makes it every bit as antiliberal as the behaviors it is intended to correct. To learn to separate fact from feeling, millennials, Lukianoff and Haidt suggest, must undergo a generation-wide cognitive therapy that would enable them to overcome the formative mistakes perpetrated by their parents and teachers, whom the authors see as excessively protective. Only such massive intervention will save "the American mind." Stunning in its scope, and taking over the formation of the subject from the family—the arguably "natural" element of the liberal individual—this solution is redolent of social engineering and, hence, antithetical to the liberal principles they espouse. It is also an example of the cruelty with which, according to Berland, the liberal individual clings to liberal social practices even after the social and discursive context that once enabled them—for instance, the cultural homogeneity that, according to Campbell and Manning, informs the "culture of dignity"—has irrevocably changed.

But what factors, in addition to the deadly violence against unarmed Black people, motivated the reckoning with the unfinished history of liberalism, during the second decade of the twenty-first century? According to journalist Tanzina Vega, one important factor was the publication of psychologist Derald W. Sue's book *Microaggressions in Everyday Life* in 2010, which describes the subtle displays of racism, sexism, and homophobia that minoritized subjects grapple with daily. That same year, Sue's study was popularized by two students from Columbia University, where Sue teaches, who created a blog called *The Microaggressions Project*.[59] Sue's concept of microaggressions seems to have given readers a clear picture of how pervasively, yet subtly, racism, sexism, and homophobia shape social interactions. Moreover, his study provided tools for recognizing and calling out microaggressions, giving readers the confidence that now they could do something to make society more equitable. Other factors, discussed by Campbell and Manning, include the growth of university administration, social atomization, and the capacity of the new digital technologies to publicize grievances to unprecedentedly large audiences.[60] (Note that Sue's study became popular after being transformed into a blog.)

But other researchers have contended that the impact of the new social media far exceeds that of circulation. For instance, William R. Stixrud and Ned Johnson have argued, quoting scientific research, that in communication on social media, participants experience less sympathy for one another than they do in in-person communication.[61] If we accept this argument (which is not definitively accepted[62]), it would appear that the social contract facilitated by social media is fundamentally different from the liberal contract based on the ability to picture oneself in the other's shoes. In any case, the feeling subject appears as constitutively dependent on social media, as the classic liberal subject is dependent on print. The social media's streamlined aesthetic—complex emotions reduced to quantifiable emoticons; ethical dilemmas constrained to the Twitter format of 140 signs; algorithms that aggregate similar viewpoints—reinforce the streamlined understanding of trauma inherent to the feeling subject's worldview. While print, accurately or not, is associated with deliberation and reflection (Erika Christakis published her account of the controversy an entire year after the tumultuous events), social media encourage the quick sharing of one's immediate response. The more visceral this response appears to be, the punchier its articulation, the greater its chances to be circulated widely.[63] Similar aesthetic rules shaped the physical encounter between Nicholas Christakis and his students. Any strengths and weaknesses of his apology for free speech were rendered irrelevant by the sheer numbers of racially diverse students visibly displaying their shared anger and pain.

In turn, the quantification of emotion (and the transparency of feeling that such quantification presumes), made normative by social media, has been attributed to the larger cultural influence of neoliberalism.[64] Likewise, at least some thinkers who have puzzled over recent campus controversies (including Kipnis) view the spread of the "culture of victimhood" as in part an effect of the neoliberal push to transform academia: from a place where students and faculty create knowledge together, as citizens involved in a shared pursuit of the public good, to a place where skills are bought and sold by subjects who conceive of themselves and one another as human capital.[65] The obvious motive of this shift is the desire to protect students from the financial precarity, loneliness, and daily humiliation that, according to Berlant, define the lives of the underclass in neoliberal economies.[66] In the name of preempting such a scenario, writes anthropologist Bonnie Urciuoli, students are reimagined as "bundles of self-managed, flexible skills" that can quickly adapt to dynamic markets and work environments.[67] The classic liberal values of autonomy and "the capacity to manage emotions" are important parts of the student's "bundle," and yet students in the elite neoliberal college are given little free choice. Numerous administrators manage their day-to-day lives, including their housing arrangements and their extracurricular activities, aiming to structure both in ways that will guarantee successful post-college futures.[68] In exchange for this all-encompassing care, students are expected to convincingly perform the college's brand to interested stakeholders, including tuition-paying parents, private donors, and future employers.[69]

Both the students' restricted autonomy and their labor of performing the college's brand (which, at Yale, includes the diversity of its student body) are naturalized as a sense of familial belonging. Yale's particular model of housing its students and positioning them vis-à-vis faculty and education seems to be an especially strong case of such naturalization, but according to Urciuoli this model is prevalent across elite private universities. Students, faculty, and administrators, the story goes, work and live together, intimately and with care, for the economic and emotional benefit of each student. As a sense of precarity spreads across social strata, the appeal of this fantasy understandably grows, and even more so for students from racialized and economically disadvantaged backgrounds. For such students, being at a top private college must be a testimony to meritocracy. And the ideal of Western meritocracy, writes Berlant, comes with a promise of intimacy "at home, at work, and in consumer worlds."[70] This promise is writ large across Yale's websites about college life, and the residential colleges are one of the major structures charged with fulfilling it.[71] No wonder, then, that the protesting students demanded that the Christakises give them this ideal home; they were only asking for what they had been promised.

Unwilling to work under such a social contract, the Christakises removed themselves from campus. Erika Christakis resigned from her teaching position, and Nicholas Christakis took a sabbatical. But such palliative measures cannot satisfy avant-garde ambitions. Like any avant-garde, the progressive avant-garde seeks to transform, rather than remove, those who disagree with its utopian vision. And like earlier avant-gardes, this one, too, outlines the process of transformation in efficient manifestos. In the remainder of this chapter, I analyze one such manifesto, a detailed guide to what Streater's character, in the opening monologue of *The Shipment*, calls "walking on eggshells" around people of color. This manifesto is the antiracist manual *White Fragility* (2018) by Robin DiAngelo, a professor of education turned corporate diversity trainer. Her method, based on her radical mistrust of individualism, helps envision a different ending to campus conflicts such as the Halloween costume controversy: an ending whereby a liberal individual may deliver the ideal home to the feeling subject by discarding one's liberal identity for the benefit of all.

COMPELLING CONTRITION

White Fragility scripts the white liberal individual's transformation into an antiracist progressive. In the course of this transformation, the white liberal individual abandons a habitual performance of "white fragility"—the white liberal's unwillingness to account for their complicity with a racially biased social system—and learns the gestures, speech, and thoughts appropriate to white humility. For DiAngelo (who cites as evidence her observations of white people in the diversity seminars she runs), white fragility is most commonly displayed as "emotions such as anger, fear, and guilt and behaviors such as argumentation, silence, and withdrawal from the stress-inducing situation," i.e., a situation in which DiAngelo suggests to a white person that they are probably more racist than they may think.[72] Again, this is a scenario somewhat similar to the one articulated by Streater's character: white people imagining a Black judge as they reflect on their unconscious biases and possible complicity with racism. Only in this case, the judge is not imagined: she is publicly present, and she is white. As will become clear, this sidelining of Black people in DiAngelo's antiracist imaginary is consistent throughout her pedagogy. Unlike critical-race theorists, who center a racially minoritized perspective on a social or philosophical issue, DiAngelo's perspective is that of a white woman with insight into white people's arguably incurable proclivity for racism.

Indeed, for DiAngelo, white fragility is not a "mere" habit that white people can unlearn and still remain white. In her book, whiteness is defined as a repertoire of habitual thoughts and behaviors—including attaching value to individualism, rationalism, and meritocracy—that perpetuates the social dominance of white people.[73] Hence, for a white person, growing aware of these habits and then effortfully shedding them would amount not to a more positive white identity—for according to DiAngelo, a positive white identity is unimaginable—but to becoming "less white."[74] This—becoming less white—is the utopian horizon of DiAngelo's program. To do so, white people must undertake the arduous practice of white humility, which involves continual, public self-examination for implicit racial bias and new protocols of interaction with people of color, including publicly apologizing for speech and actions that a person of color may consider offensive or inappropriate regardless of how they may have been intended.

In the book, DiAngelo models white humility, drawing on her own work with coworkers of color. Once, a team member told her that a remark she had made a few days before about a Black collaborator's locked braids—"The white people were scared of Deborah's hair"—has offended not Deborah, but another team member of color, whom DiAngelo calls "Angela" (not her real name).[75] (Since DiAngelo opposes individualism, it doesn't matter that Deborah has not been offended. If one Black person found the comment inappropriate, it is the white person's job to apologize to that person and to the entire race.) Having learned about Angela's reaction, DiAngelo discusses the incident with a white friend because, in her view, people of color should not be burdened with helping white people sort out their racism. (This reasoning is also her justification for why a white woman like herself, rather than a Black person, should be assuming the role of a judge in white progressives' social reckoning.) Talking to her white friend, DiAngelo comes to understand that her remark was not a tasteless joke, but a full-blown manifestation of the indelible racism that characterizes every white person. Having worked through her feelings of shame, embarrassment, and guilt with the help of her white friend, DiAngelo then calls Angela to apologize. "Would you be willing to grant me the opportunity to repair the racism I perpetrated toward you?" she asks. Angela accepts her apology and asks

DiAngelo about how she would like to be given feedback on her implicit racism in the future: privately or in public. DiAngelo chooses the latter.[76]

It is hard to miss the ceremonial language in which DiAngelo addresses Angela. She could have said, "I apologize for my racist remark; I am sorry I offended you," but such mundane words would diminish the grandness of the occasion. There she stands, a privileged white person, reckoning with America's legacy of racism, with the forgiving Angela pushed to the background. (Noticeably, Deborah, whose hair style provoked DiAngelo's remark, is not even in the picture.) This blocking is at once unfortunate and significant, given DiAngelo's repeated urging that white people abstain from taking center stage in multiracial encounters. To emphasize this point, she dedicates an entire chapter to critiquing white women's tears for victims of racism. Their tears, she argues (much like scholars of sentimentalism), redirect attention from the victims of racism to the sympathizing white woman.

But public confessions do, too. According to Michel Foucault, confession, "since the Middle Ages at least," has been "one of the West's most highly valued techniques for producing truth." Moreover, "the truthful confession was inscribed at the heart of the procedures of individualization by power." Confession, "finally, [is] a ritual in which expression alone, independently of its external consequences, produces intrinsic modifications in the person who articulates it: it exonerates, redeems, and purifies him; it unburdens him of his wrongs, liberates him, and promises him salvation."[77] Likewise, as scripted by DiAngelo, white people's public apologies for their racial insensitivity are performative speech acts, drawing authority from the Western tradition of confession. Such an apology positions the white person as one who has overcome, at least temporarily, their white fragility and so is for the time being a true progressive. As Foucault suggests, the public nature of the apology, performed with ostensible sincerity, draws sympathy and admiration to the apologetic white person, placing them in the center of racial discourse once again.

Curiously, DiAngelo seems unaware of how the aesthetic of confession undermines her attempts to decenter whiteness. She seems to believe that by publicly and genuinely apologizing for their inherent racism, the white liberal literally chips away at white supremacy. According to her script, as they do so, the white liberal undergoes a profound transformation of consciousness, in part through physical work: taking up less space, assuming (one can imagine) a posture and expression that could be read as penitent. It is this embodied performance of white abnegation—working from the outside in, transforming the mind by molding the body in a new shape in relation to other bodies—that, above all, qualifies DiAngelo's approach as avant-garde.

DiAngelo, in other words, seems to believe that representation does what she, the performer, intends: if she wants to remove herself from the spotlight, surely this would be the outcome, as long as she tries to do so in good faith. Hence, she is perpetually astounded when her message does not get across as she expects. Why would white participants in her seminars get enraged as she publicly exposes what she perceives as their racism?[78] For this, she has a ready answer: their rage is the clearest proof of their white fragility. Negative responses from people of color are a more complicated matter. DiAngelo counsels that white people must always strive to receive people of color's views on racism as valuable feedback and learn from them rather than argue against them. This is indeed difficult. When the African American linguist John McWhorter panned *White Fragility* as "a racist track" that portrays Black Americans as people lacking individual agency,[79] she wrote off his critique as "disingenuous." In contrast to DiAngelo, who sees Black people as constantly and relentlessly victimized by racist social systems, McWhorter, a self-described left-leaning liberal, believes that despite persisting racism, opportunities for growth are available to people of color, especially if they were lucky enough to grow up in middle-class families. For DiAngelo, McWhorter's opinion may well reflect his own experience, but it does not reflect the experience of the majority of African Americans, "especially in this moment of racial reckoning."[80] By her own definition, her response should be a manifestation of her white fragility, but why would she take the individual McWhorter seriously, if, as she believes, "the majority of African Americans" think like her? As she sees it, this imagined majority, along with her desire to be antiracist, legitimizes her pedagogy.

Equally important is her language that belies the radical objective of her training: the unmaking of mainstream American identity. For many Americans (perhaps a majority), both white and people of color, to be American is to have the rights and uphold the values of liberal individualism, including meritocracy and rationalism, even though those values were in the past explicitly coded as white. For DiAngelo, however, those values were not just coded as white; they are core white values that prevent Black people from rising to the top of society.[81] She sees those assertions as self-evident truths. Hence, why should white people object? She is *only* asking them to become "less white." She is *only* doing a "training." Such language is a prominent feature of the progressive avant-garde. The protesting students at Yale, too, were *merely* asking that their professors give them a loving family. And if building this loving home or ending racial injustice means giving up on liberal individualism, isn't it worth it? The apparent humbleness of the language presents the speakers' demands as both modest and accomplishable, and their opponent's resistance as unconscionable. If liberals could only see how harmful their values are, the tacit argument goes, they would agree to discard them, and their sense of self, just like they would discard a poorly chosen Halloween costume. For those who are confused, there is training that instructs them in how to do so in some clear steps.

As much as Erika and Nicholas Christakis appeared to be unaware of the extent to which the racial history of liberalism—as it returned in violent events such as the Charleston church shooting in June 2015 and the recurring unrest in Ferguson, Missouri, in August 2015—shaped their confrontation with their students, those students seemed to underestimate what Sara Ahmed might have called the "stickiness" of culture: the liberal public's attachment to some established co-articulations of aesthetics and politics, such as composure and credibility, in a liberal aesthetic regime. While the activists of the Black Lives Matter movement were right, in my view, to openly express their anger at the deaths of unarmed Black people, consciously refusing to have their public presence regulated by the stereotype of the angry Black woman, that stereotype still worked powerfully against the mixed-raced student, stripping her of credibility. At the same time, the well-established association between composure and dignity worked in Nicholas Christakis's favor, drawing sympathy to him and guaranteeing that his perspective on the conflict would be heard across multiple news media.

Likewise, in prescribing that white people publicly admit their "essential" racism, DiAngelo ignores the entrenched co-articulation between the individual's dignity and the classic liberal ritual of *private* self-reflection (whether in one's home or in one's seat in a darkened auditorium), and its connection to a mainstream Protestant habit of *private* contrition.[82] When self-reflection on one's implicit bias is made public, even if the white person engages in it voluntarily, the aesthetic of confession, as I argued, tends to foreground the self-reflecting individual at the expense of the people who suffer from their bias. (In fact, DiAngelo has expressed concern that white people who voluntarily attend her seminars may be doing so to credential themselves as progressive, rather than out of genuine desire to examine themselves for prejudice.[83]) And when such public self-examination is perceived as coerced, as DiAngelo's training has been by some participants in seminars inspired by her method,[84] it is bound to be interpreted as loss of dignity. Because American public culture remains overwhelmingly liberal, forced public contrition marks an abject aberration from American identity. Soviet tribunals, McCarthy's televised anticommunist hearings—for many, these performances are fundamentally un-American.

• • •

But though cultural conventions may be sticky, cultures evolve. Conflicts over the appropriate ways of representing race and gender, such as the conflicts caused by Parks's *Venus* and Kane's *Blasted* in the mid-1990s, made manifest a structure of feeling, an emerging inquiry into better ways of being together with one's others at the turn of the century. As I wrote in chapter 1, the displeasure of the spectators who contested the appropriateness of Parks's and Kane's artistic choices drew on an established, realist aesthetic that those spectators perceived as especially suitable for representing minoritized subjects in a dignified manner. Additionally, they thought of dignity in liberal terms: as a quality deriving from an individual's inalienable rights and as an effect of equitable relations with others, such as the relation of sympathy. When those controversies took place, at the height of the poststructuralist 1990s, critical theorists thought of race and gender as social constructs. But in the reception of *Blasted* and *Venus*, race and gender emerged not just as constructs, but as essential truths produced through violent histories. The proper acknowledgment of those truths as effects of violence, the displeased spectators implied, demanded specific representational choices and invalidated others. Thus, the formalist credo *form is meaning* acquired new moral urgency.

Over the next two decades, with the spread of new digital technologies, the neoliberal empowerment of spectators, who were now more and more conceptualized as consumers, and the recurring outbursts of racism and sexism during the first decades of the new century, the ongoing debate about what multiculturalism means in practice remained critically important. In that context, socially minded artists began experimenting with new ways of sharing space with one's others. Thus, in *The Shipment*, Young Jean Lee and her collaborators proposed that their white spectators try *feeling bad about being white, in public,* as one possible way toward more equitable cross-racial encounters, just as Forced Entertainment had proposed to its own target spectators eight years earlier. The artists' postmodern, occasionally comedic returns to the performance histories that had inspired this proposition at once justified it and made it palatable. Besides, unwilling spectators could always leave.

Some years later, education scholar Robin DiAngelo adopted this same proposition as a central principle of her antiracist training, providing detailed instructions for how to practice feeling bad about being white, in public, more effectively, under the imagined gaze of an ideal antiracist spectator. But her scenario did not leave room for levity, nor did it encourage reflection on the political and aesthetics histories that made this affect a (presumably) good antiracist practice. By that time, the growing number of Black victims of racist violence appeared to make the need for her methods self-explanatory. This same gruesome evidence of racial disparity had also made the playful returns to history, demonstrated by *The Shipment* and *First Night*, appear indulgent. The need for reckoning with racism's effects on minoritized subjects' lives was undeniable, and her program provided appealingly clear guidelines for how such reckoning could be practiced by any willing white individual.

In that practice, the replacement of sympathy, on which some earlier antiracist movements had been based, with the affect of *feeling bad about being white* reflected the presumptions of identity politics, namely that people from different ethnic and racial groups are more different than they are similar, and that even trying to imagine oneself in the shoes of a racial or ethnic other could amount to cultural appropriation. Thinking of race in terms of trauma has similar implications: no one could possibly place themselves in the traumatic circumstances of another; no one can imagine another person's trauma, unless the two share the very same traumatic experience. Consequently, the role of the cross-racial collaborator shifted from that of a sympathetic observer to a person who validates the racial other's perspective without arguing with it. In a cultural moment that conceives of racial and gender disparities as traumatizing, not questioning aspects of the traumatic experience became a new way of conferring dignity on a person socially different from oneself. Indeed, in the progressive discursive context in which DiAngelo's brand of antiracist training took shape, rigorous liberal debate has become socially inappropriate.

Additionally, the redefinition of race as essential trauma informed a mimetic system that is similar to the system operative in the *Behzti* protest in seeing representational choices as capable of effecting material changes on their embodied referents. In that system, insensitive representation can hurt its referents in a way a semiotic system cannot account for. But unlike in the *Behzti* protest, this mimetic understanding of race is not grounded in a non-Western cultural sensibility. Instead, it arose out of the very failures of Western liberalism and the conventions of signification associated with it.

For cultural critics of performance steeped in semiotics, the acceptance of that mimetic system among progressives complicates the notion of critical distance on which criticism depends. As we analyze a performance encounter in which this mimetic system is active, we need to account for the specific factors that make this system operative in this specific encounter, including the tacit historiographies of identity and the affects binding its participants together. Finally, liberally minded critics need to account for our own critical habits and presumptions that adherents of mimetic systems explicitly reject as racially or otherwise socially insensitive, telling us that "we" and "they" do not necessarily share a common sense. Working across that gap stands as a task to be resolved.

Coda

THE LIBERAL INDIVIDUAL'S POSTMODERN RETURN

I have tried to account for a new avant-garde praxis: one that the performances I analyze did not create but helped illuminate, by failing to give spectators what they didn't know they wanted until they went to the theater: the assurance that theatrical performance could confer dignity onto minoritized subjects. In doing so, those spectators have challenged artists' freedom of expression, insisting that it ends where a minoritized subject could be hurt; they have come up with new narratives of gender and race, as identities produced by traumatizing histories of oppression; and they have experimented with new ways of being in public as minoritized subjects or as their white allies, producing new models of political collaboration. For all these reasons, I have described their viewing practices as avant-garde. And as any truly avant-garde praxis tends to do, this one has questioned established views about avant-garde art. Through their determination to hold artists accountable for the possible material effects of their artistic choices, those spectators have contested the understanding of spectatorship as secondary to the artists' creative acts (as Bürger, for instance, has described it). Additionally, by insisting that the traumas of racism and sexism demand careful consideration of representational choices, those spectators have also challenged the applicability of semiotics (as defined by Mahmood) as a critical method when the subject of critique involves the representation of minoritized persons and their cultural practices.

In this book, I have tried to trace the internal contradictions of this spectatorship praxis. But despite those contradictions, this avant-garde praxis has been successful: it has changed our common sense about the proper ways of being together with people different from ourselves, as well as the proper ways of representing minoritized people on stage or in other media. Its success is perhaps most readily apparent in the new manners of engagement in the classrooms and lecture halls of liberal universities, where giving warnings for contentious and potentially disturbing material has now become both common and decorous. It is also apparent in changes to traditional artistic practices, such as blueface replacing the traditional blackface on mummers in England. It doesn't matter whether we practice these new manners in good faith, out of fear of social sanction, or just because students have come to anticipate them and diversity administrators encourage them. In performative terms, all that matters is that these new social rituals are being practiced. As we do so, we affirm an aesthetic of engagement that validates the worldview of the feeling subject, the agent of the turn-of-the-century avant-garde that I have tried to theorize.

Importantly, the progressive avant-garde, as exemplified by Robin DiAngelo antiracist training and the Yale Halloween costume controversy, has successfully attained one of its major objectives: bringing the voices of minoritized subjects to the center of liberal critical discourse. Charged with inherent and possibly incurable racism, the white liberal can no longer occupy the position of impartial reason, and this privileged place can now be finally taken by liberals of color, such as linguist John McWhorter, who has become a prominent opponent to the brand of progressivism practiced by the feeling subject. In a classic liberal fashion, liberals of color continue to insist on the value of individual agency and on a nuanced perspective on oppression (as in McWhorter's comment on how class may compound or attenuate the effects of racism, cited in the fourth chapter). That liberals of color—people who were once denied full humanity in the United States—have come to embody impartial reason is a momentous event, and one for which the feeling subject deserves credit: the Black liberal's reasoned impartiality is at least in part predicated on their disagreement with white antiracist radicals, such as DiAngelo. And yet, the liberal reason that this figure embodies is significantly different from the arguably impartial reason of the white liberal individual theorized by Adam Smith and other classic liberal thinkers. The Black liberal that emerged out of the discursive shift analyzed in this book is a postmodern figure.

In saying so, I am again drawing on Hal Foster's study *The Return of the Real*, which has provided major concepts for my own work. At the end of *The Return of the Real*, Foster asks what became of the death of the humanist subject, proclaimed by poststructuralist thinkers. He argues that by the mid-1990s, the death of the humanist subject was "dead in turn: the subject has returned in the cultural politics of different subjectivities, sexualities, and ethnicities, sometimes in old humanist guise, often in contrary forms—fundamentalist, hybrid, or [. . .] traumatic."[1] But this returning subject, he argues, is not the modern humanist subject. The returning subject is aware of existing within and across multiple splits. Cyberspace promises them that they can transcend their material body, yet their body remains shaped by sexual, racial, and class hierarchies.[2] On the surface, their world appears to have overcome colonialism, but they see the colonial relationship persist in the turn-of-the-century global economy.[3] In their attentiveness to such contradictions, the returning subject becomes postmodern, able to look at themselves and their others with a degree of critical distance.

Likewise, the humanist subject returning in the shape of a Black liberal performs their liberal social critique while grappling with a history that has defined Black liberalism as an intrinsically partial position. Consequently, contemporary Black liberals are forced to continually defend the scope of their own critical and political praxis. This is particularly obvious in the attacks on the "Black Lives Matter" motto as expressive of a partial, biased position. While some philosophers have argued that the Black Lives Matter movement defines the human subject inclusively, and hence the motto "Black Lives Matter" asserts all people's right to protection from police violence,[4] proponents of the slogan "All Lives Matter" are effectively arguing that Black people cannot represent universal humanity. At the same time, on the progressive left, the Black liberal's position may be interpreted as conservative, regardless of the actual content of that position. For instance, in the same interview in which DiAngelo describes McWorther as "disingenuous," the interviewer describes McWorther as conservative, against his own definition as a left-leaning liberal.[5] Thus, recurring attacks from the progressive left, as well as from the right, remind the Black liberal that their critique remains both situated and suspect. While the demotion of the white liberal as immanently biased has pushed liberals of color to the center, they are constantly made aware of the precarity and contingency of their position.

On this complicated terrain, practices akin to sympathy are reemerging, as antiracist activists, whether progressive or more moderately liberal, try to reach across differences. At the 2017 meeting of the Allied Media Conference, Alicia Garcia, a cofounder of the Black Lives Matter movement, urged social justice activists "to set aside our distrust and critique of newer activists and accept that they will hurt and disappoint us. Don't shut them out because their politics are outdated or they don't wield the same language. If we are interested in building the mass movements needed to destroy mass oppression, our movements must include people not like us, people with whom we will never fully agree, and people with whom we have conflict."[6] Garcia encourages her listeners to reach beyond a limiting concept of trauma that inhibits collaboration, to begin thinking of creating a *common sense* with people with whom they seem to have nothing in common, and to take responsibility of their feelings ("accept that they will hurt and disappoint us") in the name of a shared objective.

A similar gesture of reaching across to one's opponent also takes place in the contentious encounter between Nicholas Christakis and his students. At one point, Christakis says he believes that despite their differences, he and the students also share a common humanity and that without believing in that shared humanity, the conversation they are having is meaningless. The tall Black male student who describes himself as a sociology major tells Christakis: "Look at me. Look at me. You understand you and I are not the same person? We are humans. Great. Glad we understand that. But your experiences will never connect to mine. Empathy is not necessary for you to understand you are wrong. Okay? Even if you don't feel what I feel, ever, even if no one's ever been racist to you, cause they can't be racist to you, it doesn't mean that you can just act like you are not being racist." In this brief response, the student summarizes the critical-race critique of appeals to common humanity as a rhetorical move to avoid acknowledging the precarity of Black people's humanity: a precarity that extends from the pre-Emancipation past, through the Civil Rights movement, to recent episodes of racial violence. What could be common about "our common humanity," the student seems to be asking, if Christakis cannot share this sense of precarity? But then Christakis and the student shake hands and briefly hug, patting each other's backs.

This is the kind of moment that feminist theater scholar Jill Dolan might call a "utopian performative": "a small but profound moment, in which performance calls the attention of the audience in a way that lifts everyone slightly above the present, into a hopeful feeling of what the world might be like if every moment of our lives were as emotionally voluminous, generous, aesthetically striking, and intersubjectively intense."[7] Across the breach so poignantly outlined by the student's words, his body and Christakis's body extend toward one another, looking for the common sense that has just been proclaimed impossible, committing to a common ground yet to be called into being.

Notes

INTRODUCTION

1. Paul Gilroy, *Against Race: Imagining Political Culture beyond the Color Line* (Cambridge, MA: Belknap Press of Harvard University Press, 2000).

2. Gillian B. White, "The Recession's Racial Slant," *Atlantic*, June 25, 2015, https://www.theatlantic.com/business/archive/2015/06/black-recession-housing-race/396725/; Danny Dorling, "Race and the Repercussions of Recession," *Runnymede's Quarterly Bulletin*, no. 360 (Dec. 2009): 1–3, https://www.runnymedetrust.org/uploads/publications/pdfs/360-BulletinDecember09.pdf; Institute for Social and Economic Research, "The Impact of the Recession on the UK's Ethnic Minority Groups," May 7, 2015, https://www.iser.essex.ac.uk/2015/05/07/the-impact-of-the-recession-on-the-uk-s-ethnic-minority-groups

3. Francis Fukuyama, *After the End of History: Conversations with Francis Fukuyama*, ed. Mathilde Fasting (Washington, DC: Georgetown University Press, 2021), 168.

4. Gay Gibson Cima, *Performing Anti-Slavery: Activist Women on Antebellum Stages* (Cambridge, UK: Cambridge University Press, 2014), 58.

5. Charles W. Mills, *The Racial Contract* (Ithaca, NY: Cornell University Press, 1999).

6. See Margaret Cohen, *The Sentimental Education of the Novel* (Princeton: Princeton University Press, 1999); and Margaret Cohen, "Sentimental Communities," in *The Literary Channel: The International Invention of the Novel, eds.* Margaret Cohen and Carolyn Dever (Princeton: Princeton University Press, 2002), 106–32.

7. See Cohen, "Sentimental Communities," 106–32; and Cima, *Performing Anti-Slavery*, 52–57.

8. See, for instance, Sandra Kumamoto Stanley, "Teaching the Politics of Identity in a Post-Identity Age: Anna Deavere Smith's Twilight," *Melus* 30, no. 2 (2005): 191–208. I discuss the reception of Kane's *Blasted* in detail in chapter 1.

9. I am referring to Susan Leigh Foster's foundational article, in which she theorized "how bodies make articulate choices based upon their intelligent reading of other bodies" while actively contesting power structures. See Susan Leigh Foster, "Choreographies of Protest," *Theatre Journal* 55, no. 3 (2003): 397.

10. Charles W. Mills, *Black Rights/White Wrongs: The Critique of Racial Liberalism* (New York: Oxford University Press, 2017), 12–15.

11. Jean-Francois Lyotard, "From *Answering the Question: What Is Postmodernism?*" in *Postmodernism: A Reader*, ed. Patricia Waugh (London: Edward Arnold, 1992), 125.

12. "From Answering the Question," 124.

13. "From Answering the Question," 125.

14. See Kimberly Jannarone, ed. *Vanguard Performance Beyond Left and Right* (Ann Arbor: University of Michigan Press, 2015); and Kimberly Jannarone, *Artaud and His Doubles* (Ann Arbor: University of Michigan Press, 2012).

15. Hans Magnus Enzensberger, "The Aporias of the Avant-Garde," in *The Consciousness Industry; on Literature, Politics and the Media*, ed. Michael Roloff (New York: Seabury Press, 1974), 31.

16. Mike Sell, *Avant-Garde Performance and the Limits of Criticism: Approaching the Living Theatre, Happenings/Fluxus and the Black Arts Movement* (Ann Arbor: University of Michigan Press, 2008); and James M. Harding, *Cutting Performances: Collage Events, Feminist Artists, and the American Avant-Garde* (Ann Arbor: University of Michigan Press, 2010), 20–21.

17. Harding, *Cutting Performances*, 32.

18. Paul Mann, *The Theory-Death of the Avant-Garde* (Bloomington: Indiana University Press, 1991), 5, 6.

19. See, for instance, Thomas Postlewait's analysis of the riot that allegedly followed the premiere of Alfred Jarry's *Ubu Roi* in 1896 because, as the story goes, the philistine spectators were deeply offended by Jarry's avant-garde provocation. Based on his analysis of the archive, Postlewait argues that a riot never actually took place. Thomas Postlewait, "Cultural Histories: The Case of Alfred Jarry's *Ubu roi*," in *The Cambridge Introduction to Theatre Historiography*, ed. Thomas Postlewait (Cambridge, UK: Cambridge University Press, 2009), 60–85.

20. For a discussion of those attitudes, see, for instance, Matei Calinescu, *Five Faces of Modernity: Modernism, Avant-Garde, Decadence, Kitsch, Postmodernism* (Durham, NC: Duke University Press, 1987), 136–38, 283.

21. See, for instance, Odai Johnson, "Collision in the Coliseum: Mussolini, Modernism, and the Agon for Antiquity," in *Vanguard Performance Beyond Left and Right*, ed. Kimberly Jannarone (Ann Arbor: University of Michigan Press, 2015), 129–44.

22. Calinescu, *Five Faces*, 276–77, 282.

23. Hal Foster, *The Return of the Real: The Avant-Garde at the End of the Century* (Cambridge, MA: MIT Press, 1996), 1.

24. Foster, *Return of the Real*, 24.

25. Jacques Rancière, *The Politics of Aesthetics: The Distribution of the Sensible*, ed. and trans. Gabriel Rockhill (London: Bloomsbury Academic, 2004), 7.

26. I follow Mills's definition of progressivism here: the attempt to retrieve liberalism for a radical democratic agenda by "endorsing pro-egalitarian structural change to reduce or eliminate unjust hierarchies of domination." Mills, *Black Rights*, 12.

27. Peter Bürger, *Theory of the Avant-Garde*, translated by Michael Shaw (Minneapolis: University of Minnesota Press, 1984), 53.

28. Mann, *Theory-Death*, 7.

29. Bürger, *Theory of the Avant-Garde*, 53.

30. Bürger, *Theory of the Avant-Garde*, 49.

31. Rancière, *Politics of Aesthetics*, 9.

32. Pew Research Center, "Modern Immigration Wave Brings 59 Million to U.S., Driving Population Growth and Change through 2065," *Pew Research Center*, September 28, 2015, https://www.pewresearch.org/hispanic/2015/09/28/modern-immigration-wave-brings-59-million-to-u-s-driving-population-growth-and-change-through-2065/#fn-22980-1

33. Nicholas Watt and Patrick Wintour, "How Immigration Came to Haunt Labour: The Inside Story," *Guardian*, March 24, 2015, https://www.theguardian.com/news/2015/mar/24/how-immigration-came-to-haunt-labour-inside-story

34. Shannon Jackson, *Professing Performance: Theatre in the Academy from Philology to Performativity* (New York: Cambridge University Press, 2004), 191.

35. David Edgar, "Shouting Fire: Race, Religion, and the Right to Be Offended," *Race & Class* 48, no. 2 (2006): 61–76.

36. David Harvey, *A Brief History of Neoliberalism* (Oxford: Oxford University Press, 2005), 2.

37. Wendy Brown, *Undoing the Demos: Neoliberalism's Stealth Revolution* (New York: Zone Books, 2015), 20; Harvey, *Brief History*, 3.

38. Brown, *Undoing the Demos*, 17.

39. See Fukuyama, *After the End*, 12–15; Francis Fukuyama, *Identity: The Demand for Dignity and the Politics of Resentment* (New York: Farrar, Straus, and Giroux, 2018), 6.

40. See Jane Mayer, *Dark Money: The Hidden History of the Billionaires behind the Rise of the Radical Right* (New York: Doubleday, 2016). In the book Mayer, an investigative journalist, explores how conservative foundations and think tanks promoted their ideology in leading US universities, ostensibly in the name of diversity. Mayer also analyzes the racial politics of those foundations allegedly "color-blind" politics.

41. Fukuyama, *Identity*, 10.

42. Stephen Hawkins, Daniel Yudkin, Míriam Juan-Torres, and Tim Dixon, *Hidden Tribes: A Study of America's Polarized Landscape* (New York: More in Common, 2018), 134.

43. See Sell, *Avant-Garde Performance*; Harding, *Cutting Performances*.

44. Mike Sell, *The Avant-Garde: Race, Religion, War* (London: Seagull Books, 2011).

45. "The concept of degeneration was destined to influence the critical terminology of many of the most recent interpreters of avant-garde art, even those not hostile to it," Poggioli wrote in 1962. See Renato Poggioli, *The Theory of the Avant-Garde*, trans. Gerald Fitzgerald (Cambridge, MA: Belknap Press of Harvard University Press, 1968), 165.

46. Sell, *Avant-Garde*, 117; Mike Sell, "Bohemianism, the Cultural Turn of the Avant-Garde, and Forgetting the Roma," *TDR* 51, no. 2 (2007): 41–59.

47. Suzanne Keen, "Introduction: Narrative and Emotions," *Poetics Today* 32, no. 1 (2011): 1–53.

48. Saba Mahmood, "Religious Reason and Secular Affect: An Incommensurable Divide?" in *Is Critique Secular? Blasphemy, Injury, and Free Speech*, by Talal Asad, Wendy Brown, Judith Butler, and Saba Mahmood (Berkeley: Thousand Center for the Humanities, University of California, 2009), 58–94.

CHAPTER 1

1. Susan-Lori Parks, *365 Days/365 Plays* (New York: Theatre Communications Group, 2006), 280–81.

2. In his review of Kane's last play, *4:48 Psychosis*, which was produced posthumously, Michael Billington asserted that the play was Kane's suicide note. Michael Billington, "How Do You Judge a 75-minute Suicide Note?" review of *4:48 Psychosis*, by Sarah Kane, directed by James Macdonald, Royal Court Theatre Upstairs, London, *Guardian*, June 29, 2000; https://www.theguardian.com/stage/2000/jun/30/theatre.artsfeatures. This kind of interpretation, which extended to Kane's entire body of work, was disappointing to her family, friends, and admirers. They were adamant that her work "should be analyzed on its own terms." See John McKie, "Sarah Kane Vindicated by National Theatre Debut," review of *Cleansed*, by Sarah Kane, directed by Katie Mitchell, Dorfman, National Theatre, London, *BBC News*, Feb. 24, 2016, https://www.bbc.com/news/entertainment-arts-35613160. See also Andrew Dickson, "'The Strange Thing Is We Howled with Laughter': Sarah Kane's Enigmatic Last Play," review of *4:48 Psychosis*, by Sarah Kane, music score by Philip Venables, directed by Ted Huffman, Lyric Hammersmith, London, *Guardian*, May 21, 2016, https://www.theguardian.com/stage/2016/may/11/448-psychosis-sarah-kane-new-opera-philip-venables-royal-opera-house

3. Foster, *Return of the Real*, 214.

4. "'Hottentot Venus' Goes Home," *BBC News*, April 29, 2002, http://news.bbc.co.uk/2/hi/europe/1957240.stm

5. See Karen O'Kane, "Before the New Criticism: Modernism and the Nashville Group," *Mississippi Quarterly* 51, no. 4 (1998): 683–97; Anthony G. Medici, "The Restless Ghost of the New Criticism," review of *The New Criticism and Contemporary Literary Theory: Connections and Continuities*, eds. William J. Spurlin and Michael Fisher, *Style* 31, no. 4 (1997): 760–73.

6. Hortense Spillers discusses the debates about formalism in African American literary critical circles. Spillers argues that there is nothing inherently ahistorical or racist in formalism and that formalist analysis may help uncover the richness of African American writers' symbolic language. See Hortense Spiller, "Formalism Comes to Harlem," *African American Review* 50, no. 4 (2017): 694.

7. This question resurfaces through the history of American theater: from W. E. B. Du Bois and Alain Locke's argument about the definition of "Negro drama" early

in the twentieth century, through Amiri Baraka and Lorraine Hansberry's disagreement over the proper aesthetic of African American theater in the mid-twentieth century, to August Wilson and Robert Brustein's confrontation over funding and production politics in the 1990s, and to present-day discussions about the racial and gender politics of casting practices.

8. *Venus*, by Suzan-Lori Parks, directed by Richard Foreman, performed by Adina Porter, Mel Johnson Jr., Peter Francis James, and Sandra Shipley, Joseph Papp Public Theater, New York, May 9, 1996, videocassette (VHS), Billy Rose Theatre Collection, New York Public Library.

9. See, for instance, Harry J. Elam Jr. and Alice Rayner, "Body Parts: Between Story and Spectacle in *Venus* by Suzan-Lori Parks," in *Staging Resistance: Essays on Political Theater*, eds. Jeanne Colleran and Jenny S. Spencer (Ann Arbor: University of Michigan Press, 2001), 265–82.

10. Jackson says, "If there is ever a time when the tolerance for ambiguous address is low and the quest for literal representation high, it is in instances of explicitly racialized performance. In anti-racist performance, audience members often forget whatever they once knew about theatrical irony." Jackson, *Professing Performance*, 191.

11. Abiola Sinclair, "Notes on 'Venus,'" review of *Venus*, by Suzan-Lori Parks, the Joseph Papp Public Theater, New York, *New York Amsterdam News*, May 4, 1996: 22.

12. Alain Locke, "The Negro and the American Stage," in *The Works of Alain Locke*, ed. Charles Molesworth (Oxford: Oxford University Press, 2012), 119.

13. See Fionnghuala Sweeney and Kate Marsh, eds., *Afromodernisms: Paris, Harlem, and the Avant-Garde* (Edinburgh: Edinburgh University Press, 2013).

14. See LaDonna L. Forsgren, *In Search of Our Warrior Mothers: Women Dramatists of the Black Arts Movement* (Evanston, IL: Northwestern University Press, 2018), 78.

15. Sinclair, "Notes on 'Venus,'" 22.

16. Alexis Greene, *Theater Week*, May 20, 1996: 54; See also Michael Feingold, "Carnival Knowledge," review of *Venus*, by Suzan-Lori Parks, *Village Voice*, May 14, 1996: 81; and Irene Backalenick, "'Venus' Plays Yale Rep before Going Public," review of *Venus*, by Suzan-Lori Parks, *Westport News*, March 27, 1996: 31.

17. Jean Young, "The Re-Objectification and Re-Commodification of Saartjie Baartman in Suzan-Lori Parks's 'Venus,'" *African American Review* 31, no. 4 (1997): 703.

18. Carl Weber, "Brecht's 'Street Scene'—On Broadway of All Places? A Conversation with Anna Deavere Smith," in *Brecht Then and Now. The Brecht Yearbook*, vol. 20, ed. John Wilett (Madison: International Brecht Society, 1995), 50–64.

19. Jonathan Kalb, "Remarks on Parks I: A Hunter College Symposium on the Work of Suzan-Lori Parks," in *Suzan-Lori Parks in Person: Interviews and Commentaries*, eds. Philip C. Kolin and Harvey Young (New York: Routledge, 2014), 157.

20. Greene, *Theater Week*, May 20, 1996: 54.

21. Elam and Rayner, "Body Parts," 271.

22. See, for instance, Tom Sellar, "Making History, Suzan-Lori Parks, The Shape of the Past," interview with Suzan-Lori Parks, in *Suzan-Lori Parks in Person*, eds. Phillip C. Kolin and Harvey Young (New York: Routledge, 2013), 52.

23. Here is the phrase again, in its original paragraph:

> A machine which does not serve the purposes of labor is useless. In addition, it falls a prey to the destructive influence of natural forces. Iron rusts, and wood rots. Yarn with which we neither weave nor knit, is cotton wasted. ***Living labor must seize upon these things and rouse them from their death-sleep***, change them from mere possible use-values into real and effective ones. Bathed in the fire of labor, appropriated as part and parcel of labor's organism, and, as it were, made alive for the performance of their functions in the process, they are in truth consumed, but consumed with a purpose, as elementary constituents of new use-values, of new products, ever ready as means of subsistence for individual consumption, or as means of production for some new labor-process.

Karl Marx, *Capital: A Critique of Political Economy*, Vol. 1, trans. Samuel Moore and Edward Aveling, ed. Frederick Engels, 1st English ed. (Moscow: Progress Publishers, 1887), 130, https://www.marxists.org/archive/marx/works/download/pdf/Capital-Volume-I.pdf. I have highlighted and italicized the phrase adapted by Godard.

24. Sadia Qureshi, "Displaying Sara Baartman, the Hottentot Venus," *History of Science* 42, no. 2 (June 2004): 233.

25. See C. Riley Snorton, *Black on Both Sides* (Minneapolis: University of Minnesota Press, 2017), 55–57.

26. See Elizabeth Maddock Dillon, *The Gender of Freedom* (Stanford: Stanford University Press, 2004), 32, 40–41.

27. Adam Smith, *The Theory of Moral Sentiments*, edited by Knud Haakonssen (Cambridge, UK: Cambridge University Press, 2004); 128–29 and elsewhere; and Dillon, *Gender of Freedom*, 39–40.

28. Cohen, "Sentimental Communities," 109, 112.

29. In the 1927 film, Mrs. Shelby points out that Eliza has received the same education they would have given her if she were their own daughter, and George is shown designing a machine, presumably for mechanizing the processing of cotton or another plantation product.

30. Scholars of Smith's theory of sympathy have also debated the nature of that imagined judge. Some read this figure as a generalized and impersonal "juridical self." Others point out that it may also be read as a stand-in for the sympathizing individual's actual community. In an often-quoted passage, Smith describes this judge as a "fair and impartial spectator." See Smith, *Theory of Moral Sentiments*, 161–62, quoted in Dillon, *Gender of Freedom*, 39. See also Dillon, *Gender of Freedom*, 39–41.

31. Additionally, in the nineteenth century, when Beecher Stowe wrote *Uncle Tom's Cabin* while working as an abolitionist activist, women were believed (as they are now) to be naturally more sympathetic than men, which explains why Mrs.

Shelby, rather than her husband, is so central to that scene. See Cima, *Performing Anti-Slavery*, 45, 39.

32. Bertold Brecht, *Brecht on Theatre* (New York: Hill and Wang, 1964), 71.

33. Suzan-Lori Parks, "An Equation for Black People on Stage," in *The America Play and Other Works* (New York: Theater Communications Group, 1995), 21.

34. Kristine Stiles, "Never Enough Is *Something Else*," in *Contours of the Theatrical Avant-Garde*, ed. James M. Harding (Ann Arbor: University of Michigan Press, 2000), 270–71.

35. Sell, "Bohemianism," 46.

36. On the connection between the Roma's alleged dishonesty and their talent for performance, see Sell, *Avant-Garde*, 116–17.

37. Parks, "Possessions," *The America Play and Other Works*, 3.

38. Parks, "From Elements of Style," *The America Play and Other Works*, 12.

39. Parks, "From Elements of Style," 12.

40. See Paul Gilroy, *The Black Atlantic: Modernity and Double Consciousness* (Cambridge, MA: Harvard University Press, 1993), 6–7, 10, 15.

41. Parks, "Possessions," 4. In this essay, she specifies that she doesn't write for herself or for the audience. Instead, she writes *for*, rather than *about*, the figures who inhabit her plays. My italics.

42. Suzan-Lori Parks, *Venus* (New York: Theatre Communications Group, 1997), 76.

43. Parks, *Venus*, ix.

44. Shklovsky, "Art as Technique," *Russian Formalist Criticism*, eds. and trans. Lee T. Lemon and Marion J. Reis (Lincoln: University of Nebraska Press, 1965), 9.

45. Bürger, *Theory of the Avant-Garde*, 4.

46. Parks, "Elements of Style," 7.

47. Parks, "Elements of Style," 6.

48. Parks, "Elements of Style," 13.

49. Ed Bullins, *The Theme Is Blackness*, in *The Theme Is Blackness: "The Corner" and Other Plays* (New York: William Morrow and Company, 1973), 84.

50. On the spells, as an imperative to stage absence as absence, meaning the absence of Black people from Western histories, see Jennifer Johung, "Figuring the 'Spells'/Spelling the Figures: Suzan-Lori Parks's 'Scene of Love (?),'" *Theatre Journal*, no. 58 (2006): 39–52.

51. Parks, *The America Play*, in *The America Play and Other Works*, 175.

52. See, for instance, Richard Dyer's analysis of the qualities most commonly associated with whiteness: "What is absent from white is any *thing*; in other words, material reality. Cleanliness is the absence of dirt, spirituality the absence of flesh, virtue the absence of sin, chastity the absence of sex and so on." Richard Dyer, *White* (New York: Routledge, 1997), 75.

53. John Locke, *Two Treatises of Government*, ed. Peter Laslett (Cambridge, UK: Cambridge University Press, 1960), 301.

54. Scott Venters, "The (Im)mediate Animal: Interspecies Entanglements in

Early Enlightenment Transactions," PhD dissertation, University of Washington, 2021, 17. See also Locke, *Two Treatises*, 297.

55. The essays of the first series were published between 1841 and 1844, and include "History," "Self-reliance," "Compensation," "Spiritual Laws," "Love," "Friendship," "Prudence," "Heroism," "The Over-Soul," "Circles," "Intellect," and "Art." See Ralph Waldo Emerson, *Essays* (Boston: Munroe, 1844).

56. Charles E. Mitchell, *Individualism and Its Discontents: Appropriations of Emerson, 1880–1950* (Amherst: University of Massachusetts Press, 1997), 8.

57. Ralph Waldo Emerson, "Self-Reliance," in *Nature and Selected Essays*, ed. Larzer Ziff (New York: Penguin Books, 2003), 180, 189. See also Emerson, "Circles," in *Nature and Selected Essays*, 225.

58. Emerson, "Circles," 236.

59. Robert Weisbusch, "Postcolonial Emerson and the Erasure of Europe," *The Cambridge Companion to Ralph Waldo Emerson*, eds. Joel Porte and Sandra Morris (Cambridge, UK: Cambridge University Press, 1999), 194, 208.

60. Virginia Woolf, *Between the Acts* (London: Harcourt, 1970), 175.

61. Woolf, *Between the Acts*, 115.

62. Woolf, *Between the Acts*, 19.

63. Woolf, *Between the Acts*, 19, 20.

64. Parks, *Venus*, 80.

65. *Venus*, by Suzan-Lori Parks, dir. By Richard Foreman.

66. See Aleks Sierz, "Sarah Kane," in *In-Yer-Face Theatre: British Drama Today* (London: Faber and Faber, 2001), 100–101; and Graham Saunders, *"Love Me or Kill Me": Sarah Kane and the Theatre of Extremes* (Manchester: Manchester University Press, 2002), 38–39.

67. Cima, *Performing Anti-Slavery*, 56–57.

68. Kane, interview, in *Rage and Reason*, eds. Heidi Stephenson and Natasha Langridge (London: Bloomsbury Publishing, 2017), 131. My italics.

69. Mike Ellison and Alex Bellos, "*Blasted*: A Deeply Moral and Compassionate Piece of Theatre or Simply a Disgusting Feast of Filth?" review of *Blasted*, by Sarah Kane, directed by James Macdonald, Royal Court Theatre Upstairs, London, *Guardian*, January 22, 1995: 22; Charles Spencer, "Awful Shock," review of *Blasted*, by Sarah Kane, *Daily Telegraph*, January 20, 1995: n. pag.; Paul Taylor, "Courting Disaster," review of *Blasted*, by Sarah Kane, *Independent*, January 20, 1995: 27; and Jack Tinker, "Killer Thriller Shows *Blasted* How to Do It," *Daily Mail*, January 27, 1995: 47.

70. Sarah Kane, *Blasted*, in Sarah Kane, *Complete Plays* (London: Methuen Drama, 2001), 3.

71. Saunders, *"Love Me or Kill Me,"* 26.

72. Kane, *Blasted*, 3.

73. Quoted in Saunders, *"Love Me or Kill Me,"* 53.

74. Saunders, "*Love Me or Kill Me*," 134.

75. Kane, *Blasted*, 48.

76. Dyer, *White*, 30.

77. See Stacy Wolf, "Disability's Invisibility in Joan Schenkar's *Signs of Life* and Heather McDonald's *An Almost Holy Picture*," in *Bodies in Commotion: Disability and Performance*, eds. Carrie Sandahl and Philip Auslander (Ann Arbor: University of Michigan Press, 2005), 304–5.

78. Kane, *Blasted*, 7–8.

79. Like Parks, who felt that her blackness created expectations about the way she should write, Kane found a feminist label limiting. See David Savran, "Suzan-Lori Parks," in *Suzan-Lori Parks in Person*, 93; and "Sarah Kane," in *Rage and Reason*, 134–35.

80. The gender politics of Kane's drama has attracted much feminist analysis. Two essays that inform my own reading of Kane include Elaine Aston, "Feeling the Loss of Feminism: Sarah Kane's *Blasted* and an Experiential Genealogy of Contemporary Women's Playwriting," *Theatre Journal* 62, no. 4 (2010): 575–91; and Janelle Reinelt, "Navigating Postfeminism: Writing Out of the Box," in *Feminist Futures? Theatre, Performance, Theory*, eds. Geraldine Harris and Elaine Aston (London: Palgrave Macmillan, 2006), 24–29.

81. See Elin Diamond, *Unmaking Mimesis: Essays on Feminism and Theatre* (New York: Routledge, 1997), xiv: "A feminist mimesis, if there is such a thing, would take the relation to the real as productive, not referential, geared to change, not to reproducing the same."

82. See Carole Woddis, "Taking a Blasting," review of *Blasted*, by Sarah Kane, *Herald (Glasgow)*, January 24, 1995: 20.

83. Dragan Klaić, *The Plot of the Future: Utopia and Dystopia in Modern Drama* (Ann Arbor: University of Michigan Press, 1991), 3–4.

84. Kane, *Blasted*, 10.

85. This notion has been especially rigorously examined by feminist disability scholars, as in Rosemarie Garland-Thomson's foundational essay "Integrating Disability, Transforming Feminist Theory," in *Feminist Disability Theory*, ed. Kim Q. Hall (Bloomington: Indiana University Press, 2011), 34.

86. Kane, *Blasted*, 55.

87. Kane, *Blasted*, 23.

88. James Macdonald, conversation with Graham Saunders, in Saunders, *"Love Me or Kill Me,"* 126.

89. Macdonald, conversation with Graham Saunders, 122.

90. Tabert, conversation with Graham Saunders, in *"Love Me or Kill Me,"* 138.

91. Sarah Hemming, "Blasted by Violence," review of *Blasted*, by Sarah Kane, *Financial Times*, January 23, 1995, art section, p. 15.

92. Fukuyama, *After the End*, 110.

93. Fukuyama, *Identity*, 7.

94. Fukuyama, *Identity*, 115.

95. Fukuyama, *After the End*, 101.

96. Sierz, *In-Yer-Face Theatre*.

97. See Saunders, *"Love Me or Kill Me,"* 123.

98. Martin Puchner, *Poetry of the Revolution: Marx, Manifestos, and the Avant-Gardes* (Princeton: Princeton University Press, 2005), 201.

99. Puchner, *Poetry of the Revolution*, 198; 201–2.

100. Quoted in Saunders, *"Love Me or Kill Me,"* 87.

CHAPTER 2

1. *First Night*, by Forced Entertainment, perf. Robin Arthur, Jerry Killick, Richard Lowdon, Claire Marshall, Cathy Nadan, Terry O'Conner, John Rowley, and K. Michael Weaver, dir. Tim Etchells, The Place, London, 5 Dec. 2001, videotape.

2. See, for instance, Peggy Phelan, "Performing Questions, Producing Witnesses," foreword to *Certain Fragments: Contemporary Performance and Forced Entertainment*, by Tim Etchells (London: Routledge, 1999), 10; Lynn Gardner, "The Crazy Gang," *Guardian*, October 25, 2004, https://www.theguardian.com/stage/2004/oct/25/theatre. In this article Gardner quotes Marie-Hélène Falcon, director of Montreal's Festival de Théatre des Amériques, who praises Forced Entertainment's piece *Speak Bitterness* (1997) as uniquely and radically "political, provocative, and poetic."

3. See, for instance, Liz Tomlin, "Transgressing Boundaries: Postmodern Performance and the Tourist Trap," *TDR* 43, no. 2 (1999): 136–49.

4. Tim Etchells, *Certain Fragments: Contemporary Performance and Forced Entertainment* (New York: Routledge, 1999), 19.

5. Etchells, *Certain Fragments*, 17.

6. Etchells, *Certain Fragments*, 17.

7. Tim Etchells, "By Means of the Future," *Theater* 46, no. 3 (2016): 16.

8. See Sara Ahmed, *The Cultural Politics of Emotion* (Edinburgh: Edinburgh University Press, 2014), 133. "[M]ulticulturalism becomes an imperative to love difference."

9. I adapt here Hortense Spiller's concept of the stigmatized subject from her essay about modern Black subjecthood, "'All the Things You Could Be by Now, If Sigmund Freud's Wife Was Your Mother': Psychoanalysis and Race," *Boundary 2* 23, no. 3 (1996): 425.

10. See Oldham Independent Review, panel report, December 11, 2001, especially p. 77, https://web.archive.org/web/20140315105508/http://resources.cohesioninstitute.org.uk/Publications/Documents/Document/DownloadDocumentsFile.aspx?recordId=97&file=PDFversion. The report was named "the Ritchie Report" by the press, after David Ritchie, the chairperson of the panel tasked with studying the reasons for the riot. See also Paul Harris, "Exposed: Secret Plans to Start Race Riots," *Guardian*, September 2, 2001, https://www.theguardian.com/uk/2001/sep/02/race.world

11. Ahmed, *Cultural Politics*, 20.

12. Ahmed, *Cultural Politics*, 21.

13. Ahmed, *Cultural Politics*, 13.

14. Etchells, *Certain Fragments*, 18.

15. Smith, *Theory of Moral Sentiments*, 29–30.

16. Bürger, *Theory of the Avant-Garde*, 64–65.

17. Bürger, *Theory of the Avant-Garde*, 66.

18. Artur Joseph and E. B. Ashton, "Nauseated by Language: From an Interview with Peter Handke," *TDR* 15, no.1 (1970): 58.

19. Joseph and Ashton, "Nauseated," 57.

20. Joseph and Ashton, "Nauseated," 58.

21. Susan Sontag, "Happenings: An Art of Radical Juxtaposition" (1962), in *Against Interpretation and Other Essays* (New York: Octagon Books, 1982), 265, quoted in Judith F. Rodenbeck, *Radical Prototypes: Allan Kaprow and the Invention of Happenings* (Cambridge, MA: MIT Press, 2011), 165.

22. Rodenbeck, *Radical Prototypes*, 164.

23. Rodenbeck, *Radical Prototypes*, 77.

24. Bürger, *Theory of the Avant-Garde*, 64.

25. See Rodenbeck, *Radical Prototypes*, 44–45, 76–78, 165.

26. Rodenbeck, *Radical Prototypes*, 77.

27. The Milgram experiment refers to the social psychology experiments conducted by the Yale scientist Stanley Milgram in the 1960s and 1970s. Milgram tested participants' willingness to inflict pain on another person if an authority figure (such as a scientist) told them that they were not really hurting that person, despite visual evidence suggesting that this may not have been true.

28. Michelle McGuire, "Forced Entertainment on Politics and Pleasure," *Variant* 2, no. 5 (1998): 12.

29. Liz Tomlin was extremely critical of the unacknowledged class dynamic of *Nights in This City*. See Tomlin, "Transgressing Boundaries," 141.

30. Etchells, *Certain Fragments*, 95; and Rancière, *Politics of Aesthetics*, 3.

31. Etchells, *Certain Fragments*, 95.

32. See Harvey, *Brief History*. As I noted in the introduction, Harvey considers Margaret Thatcher's economic reforms the turning point in Britain's transition from economic liberalism to neoliberalism. See also Brown, *Undoing the Demos*, 203.

33. Tracy C. Davis, "Theatricality and Civil Society." In *Theatricality*, eds. Tracy C. Davis and Thomas Postlewait (Cambridge, UK: Cambridge University Press, 2003), 153–54.

34. Smith, *Theory of Moral Sentiments*, 61; quoted in Davis, "Theatricality," 144.

35. Davis, "Theatricality," 153–54.

36. Rodenbeck, *Radical Prototypes*, 80–82.

37. Brown, *Undoing the Demos*, 202–3.

38. See, for instance, Hazel Waters, *Racism on the Victorian Stage* (Cambridge, UK: Cambridge University Press, 2007), 89–90.

39. See Patricia Bater, "'Blacking Up': English Folk Traditions and Changing Per-

ceptions about Black People in England," MPhil thesis, National Center for Cultural Tradition, March 2013, 145–98. http://etheses.whiterose.ac.uk/4181/1/MPhil_upload.pdf

40. See BBC News, "'Blacking Up' Ban for Actors," December 13, 2000, http://news.bbc.co.uk/2/hi/entertainment/1068743.stm, quoted in Bater, "'Blacking Up,'" 143; Equity, 'Equity's Policy Statement on Integrated Casting,' April 6, 2011, http://www.equity.org.uk/documents/integrated-casting-race/

41. Rancière, *Politics of Aesthetics*, 7.

42. Tracy C. Davis, *The Economics of the British Stage, 1800–1914* (Cambridge, UK: Cambridge University Press, 2000), 104–10. Kimberly Jannarone describes a similar relationship between bourgeois ideology and theater decorum in the context of late-nineteenth-century French theater. See Jannarone, *Artaud and His Doubles*, 76–77.

43. See, for instance, Robert R. Weyeneth, "The Architecture of Social Segregation: The Challenges of Preserving a Problematical Past," *Public Historian* 27, no. 4 (2005): 19–20.

44. Jacqueline Stewart, "Negroes Laughing at Themselves?" *Critical Inquiry*, 29, no. 4 (2003): 670.

45. Dorothy Chansky, *Composing Ourselves: The Little Theatre Movement and the American Audience* (Carbondale: Southern Illinois University Press, 2005), 113–31.

46. Ahmed, *Cultural Politics*, 88, 95.

47. Stewart, "Negroes Laughing," 663–64.

48. W. E. B. Du Bois, "The Colored Audience," in *The Seventh Son: The Thought and Writings of W. E. B. Du Bois*, ed. Julius Lester (New York: Random House, 1971), 52.

49. Etchells, *Certain Fragments*, 18.

50. Michèle Barret, ed., *Bobby Baker: Redeeming Features of Daily Life* (London: Routledge, 2008), 4.

51. Virginia Woolf, *A Room of One's Own* (New York: John Wiley & Sons, 2014), 70–71. My italics.

52. Woolf, *A Room of One's Own*, 70.

53. Ahmed, *Cultural Politics*, 146–49.

54. Ahmed, *Cultural Politics*, 146.

55. W. E. B. Du Bois, *The Souls of Black Folk*, with an introduction by Arnold Rampersad (Oxford: Oxford University Press, 2007), 3.

56. Du Bois, *The Souls of Black Folk*, 3.

57. W. E. B. DuBois, "The Souls of White Folk," in *The Seventh Son*, 486–87. According to the literary historian James Edward Smethurst, this move—from a history of suffering to a mythic African past where the Black man was and can be whole again—is well established in twentieth-century Black political and artistic imagination. James Edward Smethurst, *The Black Arts Movement: Literary Nationalism in the 1960s and 1970s* (Chapel Hill: University of North Carolina Press, 2005), 79.

58. According to Emmanuel C. Eze, in using the term "double-consciousness" to describe post-emancipation Black personhood, Du Bois radically rearticulated

the already-existing psychiatric term, "double-consciousness," which described as pathological the desire of southern US plantation slaves to run away. See Emmanuel C. Eze, "On Double Consciousness," *Callaloo* 34, no. 3 (2011): 890.

59. This romantic thinking also informs his pageant *The Star of Ethiopia* (1911), which scripts the transformation of post-emancipation Black Americans into free, whole persons, New Negroes, by revisiting mythic and historical moments of their past.

60. Du Bois's reference to the slave/master dynamic and to the opposition between capitalist and artisan signals his rethinking of both Hegelian dialectics and Marxism in racial terms. See Lisa Lowe, *The Intimacies of Four Continents* (Durham, NC: Duke University Press, 2015), 148–53.

61. Eve Kosofsky Sedgwick, *Tendencies* (Durham, NC: Duke University Press, 1993), xii.

62. By 1907, when the International Psychoanalytic Association was founded, Freud's ideas had become popular in scientific circles across Europe and in the United States. At Harvard, Du Bois had studied with the American psychologist William James, who considered himself a Freudian. Virginia Woolf's husband, Leonard Woolf, published an English translation of Freud's book *The Ego and the Id* in 1927. See Peter Coviello, "Intimacy and Affliction: DuBois, Race, and Psychoanalysis," *MLQ* 64, no. 1 (2003): 1–32; George Makari, *Revolution in Mind: The Creation of Psychoanalysis* (New York: Harper Collins Publishers, 2008), 269, 464.

63. Rodenbeck, *Radical Prototypes*, 173 and 170–71.

64. Konstantin Stanislavski, *An Actor Prepares*, translated by Elizabeth Reynolds Hapgood (New York: Theatre Arts Books, 1948), 191–92. My italics. The word "analogous" is italicized in the English translation, but not in the Russian text.

65. „Можно понять, почувстовать роли, поставить себя на ее место и начать действовать так же, как изображаемое лицо. Это творческое действие вызовет и в самом артисте аналогичные с ролю переживания. Но эти чувства принадлежат не изображаемому лицу, созданному поэтом, а самому артисту." К. С. Станиславский, *Работа актера над собой: части I и II* (Москва; Государственое издательство „Изкуство," 1951), 242. My translation. My italics.

66. In *Creating a Role*, Stanislavski makes this point again: "Analysis is a means of coming to know, that is, to feel a play." Constantin Stanislavski, *Creating a Role*, trans. Elizabeth Reynolds Hapgood (New York: Taylor and Francis Group, 1987), 153.

67. Cima, *Performing Anti-Slavery*, 45, 39.

68. Elise Marks, "Othello/me: Racial Drag and the Pleasures of Boundary-Crossing with *Othello*," *Comparative Drama* 35, no. 1 (2001): 117.

69. Constantin Stanislavski, *My Life in Art* (London: Taylor and Francis Group, 1987), 144. The Italian actor Tomaso Salvini had performed as Othello in Moscow in 1822, leaving a strong impression on Stanislavski and inspiring him to produce the play with his company.

70. Stanislavski, *My Life in Art*, 144.

71. Stanislavski, *Creating a Role*, 158, 172.

72. Stanislavski, *Creating a Role*, 181.

73. Ahmed, *Cultural Politics*, 65–66, 72. According to the Ritchie Report, one factor that strongly influenced white people's involvement in the Oldham riots was their unfounded belief that because of their supposedly higher birth rates, the ethnic Bangladeshi and Pakistani would soon become a majority in Oldham. See Oldham Independent Review, panel report, 77.

74. Ahmed, *Cultural Politics*, 71.

75. Ahmed, *Cultural Politics*, 72, 80.

76. Ahmed, *Cultural Politics*, 75, 78.

77. McGuire, "Forced Entertainment," 13.

78. McGuire, "Forced Entertainment," 13.

CHAPTER 3

1. See Neutral Singh, "Statement by Sikh Groups on *Behzti*," December 17, 2004, https://www.sikhphilosophy.net/threads/statement-by-sikh-groups-on-behzti.1260/

2. Commission for Racial Equality, "Resolving Tensions around Behzti," archived on February 4, 2007, http://webarchive.nationalarchives.gov.uk/20070204212330/http://www.cre.gov.uk/about/sci/casestudy6_behzti.html#achieve

3. The "Rushdie affair" refers to the clash between Salman Rushdie and fundamentalist Muslims on the publication of his novel *Satanic Verses* in 1988. On August 12, 2022, Rushdie endured another (failed) assassination attack while preparing to give a lecture in Chautauqua, New York state. This second attempt on his life revived discussions about artistic freedom.

4. Janet Steele, "Shame in Birmingham," *Index on Censorship* 2 (2005): 123.

5. Sell, *Avant-Garde*, 156, 158.

6. The Muhammed cartoon controversy includes the protests by Muslims around the world against the *Jyllands-Posten*'s publication of caricatures of the prophet Muhammed in 2005. The controversy was analyzed by Talal Asad, Wendy Brown, Judith Butler, and Saba Mahmood in their book *Is Critique Secular?* (2005).

7. Fiona Mactaggart, quoted in Salil Tripathi, "Drawing a Line," *Index on Censorship* 2 (2005): 166.

8. Salman Rushdie, quoted in Tripathi, "Drawing a Line": 166.

9. Dominic Dromgoole, "Theatre's Role Is to Challenge Religion," *Guardian*, December 20, 2004, http://arts.guardian.co.uk/features/story/0,,1377489,00.html

10. Edgar, "Shouting Fire," 63.

11. Helen Freshwater, *Theatre Censorship in Britain: Silencing, Censure, and Suppression* (Houndmills, UK: Palgrave Macmillan, 2009), 151.

12. Jasdev Singh Rai, "Behind *Behzti*," *Guardian*, January 17, 2005, https://www.theguardian.com/stage/2005/jan/17/theatre.religion

13. Sarita Malik, letter to the editor, *Guardian*, January 17, 2005, https://www.theguardian.com/world/2005/jan/18/religion.uk

14. Gurharpal Singh, "British Multiculturalism and Sikhs," *Sikh Formations* 2 (2005): 171.

15. Monica Mookherdjee, "Permitting Dishonour: Culture, Gender, and Freedom of Expression," *Res Publica* 13 (2007): 29–52.

16. Priyamvada Gopal, "Speaking with Difficulty: Feminism and Racism in Britain after 9/11," *Feminist Studies* 1 (2013): 107.

17. Brian Crow, "The *Behzti* Affair Revisited: British Multiculturalism, Audiences, and Strategy," *Studies in Theatre and Performance* 27, no. 3 (2007): 215–16. Italics in the original.

18. Crow, "The *Behzti* Affair Revisited," 216. See also See Roshan Doug, "Outrage Is Hypocritical," *Birmingham Post*, December 22, 2004: 2; Nirpal Singh Dhaliwal, "The Great Sikh Divide," *Evening Standard* (London), December 22, 2004: 23; and Pervaiz Khan, "Perspective: Do I Now Have to Worry about Offending?" *Birmingham Post*, December 23, 2004: 8.

19. Crow, "The *Behzti* Affair," 18.

20. See Elin Diamond, "Feminism, Assemblage, and Performance: Karen Walker in Neoliberal Times," in *Performance, Feminism, and Affect in Neoliberal Times*, eds. Elin Diamond, Denise Varney, and Candice Amich (London: Palgrave Macmillan, 2017), 259.

21. Gurpreet Kaur Bhatti, foreword to *Behzti (Dishonour)* (London: Oberon Books, 2004), 17.

22. See Nikky-Guninder Kaur Singh, "Why Did I Not Light the Fire? The Refeminization of Ritual in Sikhism," in *Sikhism and Women: History, Texts, and Experience*, ed. Doris R. Jakobsh (New Delhi: Oxford University Press, 2010), 212–3; Gurharpal Singh and Darshan Singh Tatla, *Sikhs in Britain: The Making of a Community* (Phagwara: Ajanta, 2008), 13; and Nikky-Guninder Kaur Singh, *Sikhism: An Introduction* (London: I. B. Tauris, 2011), 66–68.

23. Doris R. Jakobsh and Eleanor Nesbitt, "Sikhism and Women: Contextualizing the Issue," introduction to Jakobsh, ed., *Sikhism and Women*, 20.

24. Kaur Singh, "Why Did I Not Light the Fire?" 228.

25. Kamala Elizabeth Nayar, "Sikh Women in Vancouver: An Analysis of Their Psychosocial Issues," in Jakobsh, ed., *Sikhism and Women*, 269.

26. Saba Mahmood, *Politics of Piety: The Islamic Revival and the Feminist Subject* (Princeton: Princeton University Press, 2004).

27. Kaur Singh, *Sikhism*, 70–73.

28. Gurpreet Kaur Bhatti, *Behzti (Dishonour)* (London: Oberon Books, 2004), 38.

29. Bhatti, *Behzti*, 65.

30. Bhatti, *Behzti*, 48.

31. Bhatti, *Behzti*, 100–101.

32. Bhatti, *Behzti*, 21.

33. Bhatti, *Behzti*, 139.

34. Eric Weitz, *The Cambridge Introduction to Comedy* (New York: Cambridge University Press, 2009), 192.

35. See, for instance, Maggie Hennefeld, "Editor's Introduction: Toward a Feminist Politics of Comedy and History," *Feminist Media Histories* 2 (2017): 1–14; Lisa Merrill, "Feminist Humor: Rebellious and Self-Affirming," *Women's Studies* 15 (1988): 271–80; and Martha Lauzen, "The Funny Business of Being Tina Fey: Constructing a (Feminist) Comedy Icon," *Feminist Media Studies* 11 (2014): 106–17.

36. Weitz, *Cambridge Introduction*, 192.

37. In the production, Shelly King, who played Balbir, stood behind a curtain. Freshwater, *Theatre Censorship*, 150.

38. Bhatti, *Behzti*, 21.

39. Kaur Singh, *Sikhism*, 66, 69.

40. Kaur Singh, *Sikhism*, 75.

41. Jo Ind, "Perspective: A Little Understanding; Gopinder Kaur, Manpreet Kaur, Ranjit Kaur, Amarjit Kaur and Gursharan Kaur Feel that the Rep's Decision to Close *Behzti* Should Not Be Seen as a Victory for Anybody," *Birmingham Post*, December 22, 2004: 8.

42. Sewa Singh Mandha, quoted in Sarah Left, "Play Axed after Sikh Protest," *Guardian*, December 20, 2004, https://www.theguardian.com/uk/2004/dec/20/arts.religion1

43. J. L. Austin, *How to Do Things with Words: The William James Lectures Delivered at Harvard University in 1955* (London: Oxford University Press, 1962), 22.

44. Judith Butler, *Bodies That Matter: On the Discursive Limits of Sex* (New York: Routledge, 1993), 12–13.

45. See Shannon Jackson's discussion of theater scholars' critique of Butler in Jackson, *Professing Performance*, 188–91.

46. Baz Kershaw, *The Radical in Performance: Between Brecht and Baudrillard* (London: Routledge, 1999), 5.

47. Kershaw, *The Radical in Performance*, 7.

48. See, for instance, D. Keith Peacock, *Thatcher's Theatre: British Theatre and Drama in the Eighties* (Westport, CT: Greenwood Press, 1999).

49. Kershaw, *Radical in Performance*, 15.

50. Edgar, *Shouting Fire*, 61.

51. Slavoj Žižek, "Holding the Place," in *Contingency, Hegemony, Universality: Contemporary Dialogues on the Left*, by Judith Butler, Ernesto Laclau, and Slavoj Žižek, (London: Verso, 2000), 322–23.

52. Singh and Tatla, *Sikhs in Britain*, 94–95, 124–25.

53. Singh and Tatla, *Sikhs in Britain*, 126.

54. See Neutral Singh, "Statement."

55. Andrew Sinclair, *Arts and Cultures: The History of the 50 Years of the Arts Council of Great Britain* (London: Sinclair-Stevenson, 1995), 353, quoted in Peacock, *Thatcher's Theatre*, 60.

56. See Brown, *Undoing the Demos*, 39; and Catherine Chaput, "Rhetorical Circulation in Late Capitalism: Neoliberalism and the Overdetermination of Affective Energy," *Philosophy and Rhetoric* 43, no. 1 (2010): 3.

57. Neutral Singh, "Statement."

58. Anthony Frost, "Drama in the Age of *Kalyug*: *Behzti* and Sikh Self-Censorship," in *Alternatives Within the Mainstream: British Black and Asian Theatres*, ed. Dimple Godiwala (Newcastle, UK: Cambridge Scholars Press, 2006), 213. Italics in the original.

59. Frost, "Drama in the Age of *Kalyug*," 213.

60. Wendy Brown, Judith Butler, and Saba Mahmood, "Preface, 2013," in Talal Asad, Wendy Brown, Judith Butler, and Saba Mahmood, *Is Critique Secular? Blasphemy, Injury, and Free Speech* (New York: Fordham University Press, 2013), xi.

61. Brown, Butler, and Mahmood, "Preface, 2013," xiii.

62. Brown, Butler, and Mahmood, "Preface, 2013," xiii.

63. Mahmood, "Religious Reason," 64.

64. Mahmood, "Religious Reason," 69. My italics.

65. Mahmood, "Religious Reason," 72. My italics.

66. Mahmood, "Religious Reason," 72.

67. Mahmood, "Religious Reason," 82.

68. Mahmood, "Religious Reason," 146–47.

69. Rai, "Behind *Behzti*."

70. See "Holy Offensive," *Dispatches*, Channel 4, February 28, 2005, DVD.

71. Kaur Singh, *Sikhism*, 74.

72. Jeremy Gilbert, *Common Ground: Democracy and Collectivity in an Age of Individualism* (London: Pluto Press, 2014), 147.

73. "ECE-5/8: *Behzti (Dishonour)*," Channel 4, news report, YouTube video, https://www.youtube.com/watch?v=xnxCfgYTD3g

74. Michael Rowe, *The Racialization of Disorder in Twentieth-Century Britain* (Aldershot, UK: Ashgate, 1998), 5.

75. Talal Asad, "Free Speech, Blasphemy, and Secular Criticism," in *Is Critique Secular?*, 32–33.

76. Singh and Tatla, *Sikhs in Britain*, 9.

77. Singh, "British Multiculturalism," 159.

78. Singh and Tatla, *Sikhs in Britain*, 127–38.

79. Singh, "British Multiculturalism," 163.

80. Singh, "British Multiculturalism," 158.

81. "There is over 250,000 Sikhs in the West Midlands and East Midlands together, and it's only a forty-minute drive [to Birmingham] from wherever you are," declared Mohan Singh from the Guru Nanak Gurdwara in South Birmingham. See "Holy Offensive."

82. Singh, "British Multiculturalism," 162.

83. Singh, "British Multiculturalism," 162.

84. "ECE-5/8: *Behzti (Dishonour)*." My italics.

85. Mahmood, "Religious Reason," 67.

86. Mahmood, "Religious Reason," 67, 72.

87. See Brown, *Undoing the Demos*, 39.

88. Kimberly Jannarone, "Confederation and Control: Mass Gymnastics and the Czech and German Bodies Politic," *Theatre Journal* 71, no. 1 (2019): 1–27.

89. Tom Sellar, "Up Front," *Theater* 35, no. 2 (2005): 3.

90. Randhir Singh Baines, letter to the editor, *Guardian*, January 17, 2005, https://www.theguardian.com/world/2005/jan/18/religion.uk

91. See Freshwater, *Theatre Censorship*, 151.

92. Rai, "Behind *Behzti*."

93. Jasdev Singh Rai, "The Monologue of Western Liberalism and Its Imagination of the Sacred in Minority Cultures," in *Negotiating the Sacred II: Blasphemy and Sacrilege in the Arts*, eds. Elizabeth Burns Coleman and Maria Suzette Fernandes-Dias (Canberra: Australian National University Press, 2008), 120.

94. Puchner, *Poetry of the Revolution*, 24.

95. Rai, "Behind Behzti."

96. Rai, "Monologue of Liberalism," 116.

97. Rai, "Monologue of Liberalism,"114.

98. Rai, "Monologue of Liberalism," 115.

99. Rai, "Monologue of Liberalism," 111.

100. Rai, "Monologue of Liberalism," 119.

101. Rai, "Monologue of Liberalism," 120.

102. Rai, "Monologue of Liberalism," 42.

103. Gunjeet Aurora, "Punjabi Theatre: Spaces, Icons, and Culture," *Sikh Formations* 2 (2014): 271.

104. Aurora, "Punjabi Theatre," 272.

105. Aurora, "Punjabi Theatre," 276.

106. Rai, "Monologue of Liberalism," 114.

107. Singh and Tatla, *Sikhs in Britain*, 15.

108. See, for instance, Hardeep Singh, "Sikh Lives Matter in Britain Too—Whether Sikh or Muslim, Racists Don't Discriminate," *Telegraph*, October 19, 2015, http://www.telegraph.co.uk/news/religion/11410809/Sikh-lives-matter-in-Britain-too-whether-Sikh-or-Muslim-racists-dont-discriminate.html; Emma Green, "The Trouble with Wearing Turbans in America," *Atlantic*, January 27, 2015, https://www.theatlantic.com/politics/archive/2015/01/the-trouble-with-wearing-turbans-in-america/384832/

109. Sell, *The Avant-Garde*, 94–95.

110. Sell, *The Avant-Garde*, 61.

111. Sell, *The Avant-Garde*, 106–18.

112. Gohar Homayounpour, *Doing Psychoanalysis in Tehran* (Cambridge, MA: MIT Press, 2012), xvii.

113. The Black Panthers' unapologetic assertion of blackness as a superior aesthetic ("Black is beautiful") provides one strong example, precisely because it actively

reflects on white avant-gardes' uses of the racial other as a source, but not an agent, of their own "authenticity."

114. Homayounpour, *Doing Psychoanalysis*, xix.

115. Smith, *Theory of Moral Sentiments*, 130–31.

116. Smith, *Theory of Moral Sentiments*, 233.

117. Smith, *Theory of Moral Sentiments*, 233.

118. Smith, *Theory of Moral Sentiments*, 231.

119. Rai, "Behind *Behzti*."

120. Ian Prior, "TV Pundit Ron Atkinson Sacked for Racist Remark," *Guardian*, April 22, 2004, https://www.theguardian.com/media/2004/apr/22/football.raceintheuk

121. Judith Butler, "The Sensibility of Critique: Response to Asad and Mahmood," in *Is Critique Secular?*, 116–17. My italics.

122. Wendy Brown, introduction to *Is Critique Secular?*, 10–11.

123. Brown, introduction to *Is Critique Secular?*, 11.

124. Harding, *Cutting Performances*, 30. Italics in the original.

125. Harding illustrates this argument with his analysis of Carolee Schneemann's performance at the leftist Dialectics of Liberation Congress that convened in London in July 1967. Harding, *Cutting Performances*, 121–49.

126. See also Sell, *Avant-Garde Performance*, 30.

127. Sell, *Avant-Garde*, 35, 37.

128. See, for instance, Stanley Fish's canonical essay, "Is There a Text in This Class?" (1982) in *Critical Theory Since Plato*, eds. Hazard Adams and Leroy Searle. 3rd ed. (Belmont, CA: Wadsworth Publishing, 2004), 1396–402. See also Susan Bennett's discussion of the differing reception, in Los Angeles and New York, of the Center Theatre Group's 1978 production of *Zoot Suit*, by Luis Valdez, in Susan Bennet, *Theatre Audiences: A Theory of Production and Reception* (New York: Routledge, 1997), 156–60.

129. See Chaput, "Rhetorical Circulation."

130. Chaput, "Rhetorical Circulation," 6.

131. Chaput, "Rhetorical Circulation," 20–22.

CHAPTER 4

1. Harry Elam, "Black Theatre in the Age of Obama," in *The Cambridge Companion to African American Theatre*, ed. Harvey Young (Cambridge, UK: Cambridge University Press, 2013), 257; Ryan Anthony Hatch, "First as Minstrelsy, Then as Farce: On the Spectacle of Race in the Theater of Young Jean Lee," *CR: The New Centennial Review*, no. 13 (2013): 90.

2. See, for instance, Young Jean Lee, "Young Jean Lee, Playwright," interview by John Del Signore, *Gothamist*, January 22, 2009, https://gothamist.com/arts-entertainment/young-jean-lee-playwright

3. Lee has said that she created *The Shipment* as a response to "the backlash to

political correctness" following Obama's election as president. According to Lee, many saw Obama as the ultimate proof that American society had reached a postracial state. In this postracial state, jokes and comments that were previously perceived as racist had arguably lost their potential to hurt; hence, political correctness was now irrelevant. See Signore, "Young Jean Lee."

4. Hilton Als, "By the Skin of Our Teeth: Young Jean Lee's Irreverent Take on Racial Politics," *New Yorker*, January 26, 2009, https://www.newyorker.com/magazine/2009/01/26/by-the-skin-of-our-teeth

5. "Young Jean Lee Gets into the Minds of Straight White Men," interview by Larissa FastHorse, *American Theatre*, March 24, 2015, https://www.americantheatre.org/2015/03/24/young-jean-lee-gets-into-the-minds-of-straight-white-men/

6. Signore, "Young Jean Lee."

7. Jesse Green, "*Straight White Men* Is Impressive (Not Oppressive)," review of *Straight White Men*, by Young Jean Lee, *Vulture*, November 17, 2014, https://www.vulture.com/2014/11/theater-review-straight-white-men.html

8. Lauren Berlant, *Cruel Optimism* (Durham, NC: Duke University Press, 2011), 1–3.

9. *The Shipment*, written and directed by Young Jean Lee, performed by Prentice Onayemi, Mikéah Ernest Jennings, Okieriete Onodawan, Douglas Scott Streater, and Amelia Workman, set design by Davis Evans Morris, lighting design by Mark Barton, costumes by Roxana Ramseur, sound by Mathew Theirny, and choreography by Faye Driscoll. Performed and recorded at On the Boards, Seattle, October 2009, https://youngjeanlee.org/work/the-shipment/

10. Young Jean Lee, *The Shipment*, in *The Shipment; LEAR* (New York: Theatre Communications Group, 2010), 7.

11. *The Shipment*, On the Boards, Seattle.

12. *The Shipment*, On the Boards, Seattle. Laurelhurst is an upper-middle-class neighborhood in Seattle.

13. Lee, *The Shipment*, 12.

14. Lee, *The Shipment*, 15.

15. Dillon, *Gender of Freedom*, 40. My italics.

16. Hatch, "First as Minstrelsy," 101.

17. Ralina Joseph, *Postracial Resistance: Black Women, Media, and the Uses of Strategic Ambiguity* (New York: New York University Press, 2018), xi.

18. Joseph, *Postracial Resistance*, 28.

19. Lee, *Shipment*, 5.

20. Lee, *Shipment*, 25, 67–71.

21. I am referring to "Get the Guests," one of the games that Albee's characters play in act 2 of his play.

22. Lee, *The Shipment*, 53.

23. Harvey, *Brief History*, 50.

24. Signore, "Young Jean Lee."

25. Signore, "Young Jean Lee."

26. Lee, *The Shipment*, 28.

27. The binary between wisdom and reason is particularly conspicuous in Aunt Nancy's character. Though she can heal serious illnesses with traditional medicine, she is unable to count the money people pay her for her services.

28. See Emily Bernard, "The Renaissance and the Vogue," in *The Cambridge Companion to the Harlem Renaissance*, ed. George Hutchinson (Cambridge, UK: Cambridge University Press, 2007), 28.

29. "Open Letter to Associate Master Christakis," October 31, 2015, https://downatyale.com/open-letter-to-associate-master-christakis/. The position was later renamed from "master" to "head," because for many members of the Yale community "master" spurred associations with slavery. See Peter Salovey, "Decisions on Residential College Names and 'Master' Title," April 27, 2016, https://president.yale.edu/speeches-writings/statements/decisions-residential-college-names-and-master-title

30. *Washington Post*, "Yale Students Confront Administrator over Halloween Email," video, in Erika Christakis, "My Halloween Email Led to a Campus Storm—and a Troubling Lesson about Self-Censorship," *Washington Post*, October 28, 2016, https://www.washingtonpost.com/opinions/my-halloween-email-led-to-a-campus-firestorm--and-a-troubling-lesson-about-self-censorship/2016/10/28/70e55732-9b97-11e6-a0ed-ab0774c1eaa5_story.html

31. While internet hounds were able to identify the student's name and her family's home, the Christakises never mentioned her by name in their statements about the controversy in order to protect her anonymity. I will not be including her name either.

32. "Yale University—Full Version—New Videos of the Halloween Email Protest, uploaded on September 20, 2016," https://www.youtube.com/watch?v=hiMVx2C5_Wg, 2020.

33. Erika Christakis, email to the students of Silliman College, Yale, Oct 30, 2015, https://www.thefire.org/email-from-erika-christakis-dressing-yourselves-email-to-silliman-college-yale-students-on-halloween-costumes/

34. Dillon, *The Gender of Freedom*, 47.

35. Christakis, "My Halloween Email."

36. See Joseph, *Postracial Resistance*, 70–1.

37. See Khadija White, "Black Lives on Campuses Matter: The Rise of the New Black Student Movement," *Soundings* 63 (2016): 89.

38. Head of College's Office, https://pierson.yalecollege.yale.edu/people/head-colleges-office.

39. "Open Letter to Associate Master Christakis."

40. For instance, the conflict at Northwestern University, in 2015, over whether faculty and students should be allowed to date. See Michelle Goldberg, "The Laura Kipnis Melodrama," *Nation*, March 16, 2015, https://www.thenation.com/article/archive/laura-kipnis-melodrama/

41. E. Ann Kaplan, *Trauma Culture: The Politics of Terror and Loss in Media and Literature* (New Brunswick, NJ: Rutgers University Press, 2005), 35.

42. Ann Cvetkovich, *An Archive of Feelings: Trauma, Sexuality, and Lesbian Public Cultures* (Durham, NC: Duke University Press, 2003), 3.

43. Cvetkovich, *Archive of Feelings*, 3.

44. Kaplan, *Trauma Culture*, 35. See also Foster, *Return of the Real*, 180, 209.

45. Kaplan, *Trauma Culture*, 35.

46. Cvetkovich, *Archive of Feelings*, 44.

47. Cvetkovich, *Archive of Feelings*, 4; and Kaplan, *Trauma Culture*, 35.

48. Cvetkovich, *Archive of Feelings*, 18; Kaplan, *Trauma Culture*, 87, 91. For instance, Cvetkovich explores how the AIDS crisis of the 1980s inspired a new aesthetic of public mourning, defying the notion that gay people, because of their "shameful" and "abnormal" ways, should grieve in private. Cvetkovich, *Archive of Feelings*, 5.

49. Laura Kipnis, "My Title IX Inquisition," *Chronicle of Higher Education*, May 2015, https://www.chronicle.com/article/my-title-ix-inquisition/

50. Bradley Campbell and Jason Manning, "Microaggressions and Public Culture," *Comparative Sociology* 13 (2014): 692–726.

51. Campbell and Manning, "Microaggressions," 713–14.

52. Campbell and Manning, "Microaggressions," 715.

53. Campbell and Manning, "Microaggressions," 707.

54. See, for instance, Gregg Lukianoff and Jonathan Haidt, "The Coddling of the American Mind," *The Atlantic*, September 2015, https://www.theatlantic.com/magazine/archive/2015/09/the-coddling-of-the-american-mind/399356/

55. Joanna Brooks, "The Early American Public Sphere and the Emergence of a Black Print Counterpublic," *William and Mary Quarterly* 62, no. 1 (2005): 88.

56. Sara Ahmed, "Against Students," *New Inquiry*, June 29, 2015, https://thenewinquiry.com/against-students/

57. Sara Ahmed, *The Promise of Happiness* (Durham, NC: Duke University Press, 2010), 126–27.

58. Lukianoff and Haidt, "Coddling of the American."

59. Tanzina Vega, "Students See Many Slights as Racial 'Microaggressions,'" *New York Times*, March 21, 2014, https://www.nytimes.com/2014/03/22/us/as-diversity-increases-slights-get-subtler-but-still-sting.html

60. Campbell and Manning, "Microaggressions," 710, 718.

61. William R. Stixrud and Ned Johnson, *The Self-Driven Child: The Science and Sense of Giving Your Kids More Control over Their Lives* (New York: Viking, 2018). Page numbers?

62. See, for instance, Helen G. M. Vossen and Patti M. Valkenburg, "Do Social Media Foster or Curtail Adolescents' Empathy? A Longitudinal Study," *Computers in Human Behavior* 63 (October 2016): 118–24. This study distinguishes between *empathy* (as feeling with someone) and *sympathy* (feeling [sorrow] for someone), and finds no evidence that social media use, on its own, decreases the capacity for either feeling.

63. Jonathan Haidt discusses the technological features that Facebook and Twitter introduced to emphasize emotion-laden content in "Why the Past 10 Years of American Life Have Been Uniquely Stupid," *Atlantic*, April 11, 2022, https://www.theatlantic.com/magazine/archive/2022/05/social-media-democracy-trust-babel/629369/

64. Ahmed, *Promise of Happiness*, 3–5.

65. See Brown, *Undoing the Demos*, 175–200.

66. Berlant, *Cruel Optimism*, 167.

67. Bonnie Urciuoli, "The Experience Experts," in *The Experience of Neoliberal Education*, ed. Bonnie Urciuoli (New York: Berghahn Books, 2018), 156.

68. Urciuoli, "The Experience Experts," 150, 145. See also Yale's "Goals of Spring-term First-year Advising," https://advising.yalecollege.yale.edu/advisers/spring-term-first-year-advisers/goals-spring-term-first-year-advising. One major question that advisors are expected to ask is how students' extracurricular activities "fit in with their academic or post-Yale-related plans."

69. Bonnie Urciuoli, ed. "Introduction: Neoliberalizing Undergraduate Experience," in *The Experience of Neoliberal Education* (New York: Berghahn Books, 2018), 9.

70. Berlant, *Cruel Optimism*, 167.

71. See, for instance, Katherine, "Finding a First-Year Family," https://admissions.yale.edu/bulldogs-blogs/katherine/2018/11/13/finding-first-year-family

72. Robin DiAngelo, *White Fragility: Why It's So Hard for White People to Talk about Racism* (Boston: Beacon Press, 2018), 2.

73. DiAngelo, *White Fragility*, 8.

74. DiAngelo, *White Fragility*, 149–50.

75. DiAngelo, *White Fragility*, 139.

76. DiAngelo, *White Fragility*, 140.

77. Michel Foucault, *The History of Sexuality*, Vol. 1: *An Introduction*, trans. Robert Hurley (New York: Pantheon Books, 1978), 58–62.

78. For negative responses to DiAngelo's antiracist training by white participants, see Daniel Bergner, "'White Fragility' Is Everywhere. But Does Antiracism Training Work?" *New York Times Magazine*, July 15, 2020, https://www.nytimes.com/2020/07/15/magazine/white-fragility-robin-diangelo.html

79. In his review of *White Fragility*, McWhorter critiques DiAngelo for infantilizing Black people by denying them individual agency, even as he is aware that this is an inevitable effect of DiAngelo's denouncement of individualism as a white-supremacist value. McWorter cites DiAngelo's contention that Jackie Robinson, the first African American to play in major-league baseball, and hence for many an icon of Black resilience, was in fact "the first Black man whites *allowed* to play major-league baseball." (See DiAngelo, *White Fragility*, 149, my italics.) McWorter is also critical of DiAngelo's admonition that white people should not demand that people of color educate them about how they perceive the world, lest the demand trigger traumatic memories. In his view, this admonition renders people of color, rather than white people, fragile. See John McWhorter, "The Dehumanizing Con-

descension of White Fragility," *The Atlantic*, July 15, 2020, https://www.theatlantic.com/ideas/archive/2020/07/dehumanizing-condescension-white-fragility/614146/. For another negative critique from an intellectual of color, see Kelefa Sanneh, "The Fight to Redefine Racism," *New Yorker*, August 12, 2019, https://www.newyorker.com/magazine/2019/08/19/the-fight-to-redefine-racism

80. Robin DiAngelo, "Q & A: Author Robin DiAngelo Talks White Fragility, Race, and Privilege," interview by Joyce Taylor, October 8, 2020, https://www.king5.com/article/news/community/facing-race/talking-about-white-fragility-with-seattle-author-robin-diangelo/281-3a619ded-3384-4997-b07d-885571c83d67

81. In a conversation with Daniel Bergner, she argues that the entire capitalist system must be abandoned to achieve racial equity, for instance, by making corporate law firms hire people with "resiliency and compassion" rather than with the arguably white qualification of rationalism. See Bergner, "White Fragility Is Everywhere."

82. Dillon discusses the genealogical connection between Protestant practices and classic liberalism in *The Gender of Freedom*, especially in chapter 2, "Puritan Bodies and Transatlantic Texts."

83. Bergner, "White Fragility Is Everywhere."

84. Bergner, "White Fragility Is Everywhere."

CODA

1. Foster, *Return of the Real*, 209.

2. Foster, *Return of the Real*, 221.

3. Foster, *Return of the Real*, 216.

4. Andrew J. Pierce, "Whose Lives Matter? The Black Lives Matter Movement and the Contested Legacy of Philosophical Humanism," *Journal of Social Philosophy* 51, no. 2 (2020): 262.

5. DiAngelo, "Q & A."

6. Quoted in Frances Lee, "Excommunicate Me from the Church of Social Justice," *Autostraddle*, July 13, 2017, https://www.autostraddle.com/kin-aesthetics-excommunicate-me-from-the-church-of-social-justice-386640/

7. Jill Dolan, *Utopia in Performance: Finding Hope at the Theater* (Ann Arbor: University of Michigan Press, 2005), 5.

Bibliography

Ahmed, Sara. "Against Students." *New Inquiry*, June 29, 2015, https://thenewinquiry.com/against-students/

Ahmed, Sara. *The Cultural Politics of Emotion*. Edinburgh: Edinburgh University Press, 2014.

Ahmed, Sara. *The Promise of Happiness*. Durham, NC: Duke University Press, 2010.

Als, Hilton. "By the Skin of Our Teeth: Young Jean Lee's Irreverent Take on Racial Politics." *New Yorker*, January 26, 2009, https://www.newyorker.com/magazine/2009/01/26/by-the-skin-of-our-teeth

Asad, Talal. "Free Speech, Blasphemy, and Secular Criticism." In *Is Critique Secular? Blasphemy, Injury, and Free Speech*, by Talal Asad, Wendy Brown, Judith P. Butler, and Saba Mahmood, 14–57. New York: Fordham University Press, 2013.

Aston, Elaine. "Feeling the Loss of Feminism: Sarah Kane's *Blasted* and an Experiential Genealogy of Contemporary Women's Playwriting." *Theatre Journal* 62, no. 4 (2010): 575–91.

Aurora, Gunjeet. "Punjabi Theatre: Spaces, Icons, and Culture." *Sikh Formations* 2 (2014): 271–83.

Austin, J. L. *How to Do Things with Words: The William James Lectures Delivered at Harvard University in 1955*. London: Oxford University Press, 1962.

Backalenick, Irene. "'Venus' Plays Yale Rep before Going Public." Review of *Venus*, by Suzan-Lori Parks. *Westport News*, March 27, 1996: 31.

Baines, Randhir Singh. Letter to the editor. *Guardian*, January 17, 2005, https://www.theguardian.com/world/2005/jan/18/religion.uk

Barret, Michèle, ed. *Bobby Baker: Redeeming Features of Daily Life*. London: Routledge, 2008.

Bater, Patricia. "'Blacking Up': English Folk Traditions and Changing Perceptions about Black People in England." MPhil thesis. National Center for Cultural Tradition, March 2013, 145–98, http://etheses.whiterose.ac.uk/4181/1/MPhil_upload.pdf

BBC News. "'Blacking Up' Ban for Actors," December 13, 2000, http://news.bbc.co.uk/2/hi/entertainment/1068743.stm

Bennet, Susan. *Theatre Audiences: A Theory of Production and Reception*. New York: Routledge, 1997.

Bergner, Daniel. "'White Fragility' Is Everywhere. But Does Antiracism Training Work?" *New York Times Magazine*, July 15, 2020, https://www.nytimes.com/2020/07/15/magazine/white-fragility-robin-diangelo.html

Berlant, Lauren. *Cruel Optimism*. Durham, NC: Duke University Press, 2011.

Bernard, Emily. "The Renaissance and the Vogue." In *The Cambridge Companion to the Harlem Renaissance*, ed. George Hutchinson. Cambridge, UK: Cambridge University Press, 2007.

Bhatti, Gurpreet Kaur. Foreword to *Behzti (Dishonour)*, 17–18. London: Oberon Books, 2004.

Bhatti, Gurpreet Kaur. *Behzti (Dishonour)*. London: Oberon Books, 2004.

Billington, Michael. "How Do You Judge a 75-minute Suicide Note?" Review of *4:48 Psychosis*, by Sarah Kane, directed by James Macdonald, Royal Court Theatre Upstairs, London. *Guardian*, June 29, 2000, https://www.theguardian.com/stage/2000/jun/30/theatre.artsfeatures

Brecht, Bertolt. *Brecht on Theatre*. New York: Hill and Wang, 1964.

Brooks, Joanna. "The Early American Public Sphere and the Emergence of a Black Print Counterpublic." *William and Mary Quarterly* 62, no. 1 (2005): 67–92.

Brown, Wendy. Introduction to *Is Critique Secular? Blasphemy, Injury, and Free Speech*, by Talal Asad, Wendy Brown, Judith P. Butler, and Saba Mahmood, 1–13. New York: Fordham University Press, 2013.

Brown, Wendy. *Undoing the Demos: Neoliberalism's Stealth Revolution*. New York: Zone Books, 2015.

Brown, Wendy, Judith Butler, and Saba Mahmood, "Preface, 2013." In *Is Critique Secular? Blasphemy, Injury, and Free Speech*, by Talal Asad, Wendy Brown, Judith Butler, and Saba Mahmood, vii–xx. New York: Fordham University Press, 2013.

Bürger, Peter. *Theory of the Avant-Garde*, translated by Michael Shaw. Minneapolis: University of Minnesota Press, 1984.

Bullins, Ed. *The Theme Is Blackness*. In *The Theme Is Blackness: "The Corner" and Other Plays*. New York: William Morrow and Company, 1973.

Butler, Judith. *Bodies That Matter: On the Discursive Limits of Sex*. New York: Routledge, 1993.

Butler, Judith. "The Sensibility of Critique: Response to Asad and Mahmood." In *Is Critique Secular? Blasphemy, Injury, and Free Speech*, by Talal Asad, Wendy Brown, Judith Butler, and Saba Mahmood, 95–130. New York: Fordham University Press, 2013.

Calinescu, Matei. *Five Faces of Modernity: Modernism, Avant-Garde, Decadence, Kitsch, Postmodernism*. Durham, NC: Duke University Press, 1987.

Campbell, Bradley, and Jason Manning. "Microaggressions and Public Culture." *Comparative Sociology* 13 (2014): 692–726.

Chansky, Dorothy. *Composing Ourselves: The Little Theatre Movement and the American Audience*. Carbondale: Southern Illinois University Press, 2005.

Chaput, Catherine. "Rhetorical Circulation in Late Capitalism: Neoliberalism and the Overdetermination of Affective Energy." *Philosophy and Rhetoric* 43, no.1 (2010): 1–25.

Christakis, Erika. Email to the students of Silliman College. Yale, Oct 30, 2015, https://www.thefire.org/email-from-erika-christakis-dressing-yourselves-email-to-silliman-college-yale-students-on-halloween-costumes/

Christakis, Erika. "My Halloween Email Led to a Campus Storm—and a Troubling Lesson about Self-Censorship." *Washington Post*, October 28, 2016, https://www.washingtonpost.com/opinions/my-halloween-email-led-to-a-campus-firestorm--and-a-troubling-lesson-about-self-censorship/2016/10/28/70e55732-9b97-11e6-a0ed-ab0774c1eaa5_story.html

Cima, Gay Gibson. *Performing Anti-Slavery: Activist Women on Antebellum Stages*. New York: Cambridge University Press, 2014.

Cohen, Margaret. "Sentimental Communities." In *The Literary Channel: The International Invention of the Novel*, eds. Margaret Cohen and Carolyn Dever, 106–32. Princeton: Princeton University Press, 2002.

Cohen, Margaret. *The Sentimental Education of the Novel*. Princeton: Princeton University Press, 1999.

Commission for Racial Equality. "Resolving Tensions around Behzti." Archived on February 4, 2007, http://webarchive.nationalarchives.gov.uk/20070204212330/http://www.cre.gov.uk/about/sci/casestudy6_behzti.html#achieve

Coviello, Peter. "Intimacy and Affliction: DuBois, Race, and Psychoanalysis." *MLQ* 64, no. 1 (2003): 1–32.

Crow, Brian. "The *Behzti* Affair Revisited: British Multiculturalism, Audiences, and Strategy." *Studies in Theatre and Performance* 27, no. 3 (2007): 211–22.

Станиславский, К. С. *Работа актера над собой: части I и II*. Москва: Государственое издательство „Изкуство," 1951.

Cvetkovich, Ann. *An Archive of Feelings: Trauma, Sexuality, and Lesbian Public Cultures*. Durham, NC: Duke University Press, 2003.

Davis, Tracy C. *The Economics of the British Stage, 1800–1914*. Cambridge, UK: Cambridge University Press, 2000.

Davis, Tracy C. "Theatricality and Civil Society." In *Theatricality*, eds. Tracy C. Davis and Thomas Postlewait, 127–55. Cambridge, UK: Cambridge University Press, 2003.

Dhaliwal, Nirpal Singh. "The Great Sikh Divide." *Evening Standard* (London), December 22, 2004: 23.

Diamond, Elin. "Feminism, Assemblage, and Performance: Karen Walker in Neoliberal Times." In *Performance, Feminism, and Affect in Neoliberal Times*, eds. Elin Diamond, Denise Varney, and Candice Amich, 255–68. London: Palgrave Macmillan, 2017.

Diamond, Elin. *Unmaking Mimesis: Essays on Feminism and Theatre*. New York: Routledge, 1997.

DiAngelo, Robin. "Q & A: Author Robin DiAngelo Talks White Fragility, Race, and

Privilege."; Interview with Joyce Taylor. October 8, 2020, https://www.king5.com/article/news/community/facing-race/talking-about-white-fragility-with-seattle-author-robin-diangelo/281-3a619ded-3384-4997-b07d-885571c83d67

DiAngelo, Robin. *White Fragility: Why It's So Hard for White People to Talk about Racism*. Boston: Beacon Press, 2018.

Dickson, Andrew. "'The Strange Thing Is We Howled with Laughter': Sarah Kane's Enigmatic Last Play." Review of *4:48 Psychosis*, by Sarah Kane. Music score by Philip Venables. Directed by Ted Huffman. Lyric Hammersmith, London. *Guardian*, May 21, 2016, https://www.theguardian.com/stage/2016/may/11/448-psychosis-sarah-kane-new-opera-philip-venables-royal-opera-house

Dillon, Elizabeth Maddock. *The Gender of Freedom*. Stanford: Stanford University Press, 2004.

Dolan, Jill. *Utopia in Performance: Finding Hope at the Theater*. Ann Arbor: University of Michigan Press, 2005.

Dorling, Danny. "Race and the Repercussions of Recession." *Runnymede's Quarterly Bulletin*, no. 360 (Dec. 2009): 1–3, https://www.runnymedetrust.org/uploads/publications/pdfs/360-BulletinDecember09.pdf

Doug, Roshan. "Outrage Is Hypocritical." *Birmingham Post*, December 22, 2004: 2.

Dromgoole, Dominic. "Theatre's Role Is to Challenge Religion." *Guardian*, December 20, 2004, http://arts.guardian.co.uk/features/story/0,,1377489,00.html

Du Bois, W. E. B. "The Colored Audience." In *The Seventh Son: The Thought and Writings of W. E. B. Du Bois*, ed. Julius Lester. New York: Random House, 1971.

Du Bois, W. E. B. *The Souls of Black Folk*. Introduction by Arnold Rampersad. Oxford: Oxford University Press, 2007.

Du Bois, W. E. B. "The Souls of White Folk." In *The Seventh Son: The Thought and Writings of W. E. B. DuBois*, Vol. 1, ed. Julius Lester. New York: Random House, 1971.

Dyer, Richard. *White*. New York: Routledge, 1997.

"ECE-5/8: Bezhti (Dishonour)." Channel 4, news report. YouTube video, https://www.youtube.com/watch?v=xnxCfgYTD3g

Edgar, David. "Shouting Fire." *Race & Class* 48, no. 2 (2006): 61–76.

Elam, Harry. "Black Theatre in the Age of Obama." In *The Cambridge Companion to African American Theatre*, ed. Harvey Young, 255–78. Cambridge: Cambridge University Press, 2013.

Elam, Harry J., Jr., and Alice Rayner. "Body Parts: Between Story and Spectacle in *Venus* by Suzan-Lori Parks." In *Staging Resistance: Essays on Political Theater*, eds. Jeanne Colleran and Jenny S. Spencer, 265–82. Ann Arbor: University of Michigan Press, 2001.

Ellison, Mike, and Alex Bellos. "*Blasted*: A Deeply Moral and Compassionate Piece of Theatre or Simply a Disgusting Feast of Filth?" Review of *Blasted*, by Sarah Kane. Directed by James Macdonald, Royal Court Theatre Upstairs, London, *Guardian*, January 22, 1995: 22.

Emerson, Ralph Waldo. "Circles." In *Nature and Selected Essays*, ed. Larzer Ziff, 225–38. New York: Penguin Books, 2003.

Emerson, Ralph Waldo. *Essays*. Boston: Munroe, 1844.

Emerson, Ralph Waldo. "Self-Reliance." In *Nature and Selected Essays*, ed. Larzer Ziff, 175–203. New York: Penguin Books, 2003.

Enzensberger, Hans Magnus. "The Aporias of the Avant-Garde." In *The Consciousness Industry: On Literature, Politics and the Media*, ed. Michael Roloff, 16–41. New York: Seabury Press, 1974.

Equity, "Equity's Policy Statement on Integrated Casting," April 6, 2011, http://www.equity.org.uk/documents/integrated-casting-race/

Etchells, Tim. "By Means of the Future: Forced Entertainment, Prediction, and the Community of Audience." *Theater* 46, no. 3 (2016): 15–29.

Etchells, Tim. *Certain Fragments: Contemporary Performance and Forced Entertainment*. New York: Routledge, 1999.

Eze, Emmanuel C. "On Double Consciousness." *Callaloo* 34, no. 3 (2011): 877–98.

Feingold, Michael. "Carnival Knowledge." Review of *Venus*, by Suzan-Lori Parks. *Village Voice*, May 14, 1996: 81.

First Night, by Forced Entertainment. Perf. Robin Arthur, Jerry Killick, Richard Lowdon, Claire Marshall, Cathy Nadan, Terry O'Conner, John Rowley, and K. Michael Weaver. Directed by Tim Etchells. The Place, London, Dec. 5, 2001. Videotape.

Fish, Stanley. "Is There a Text in This Class?" In *Critical Theory Since Plato*, eds. Hazard Adams and Leroy Searle. 3rd ed., 1396–1402. Belmont, CA: Wadsworth Publishing, 2004.

Forsgren, LaDonna L. *In Search of Our Warrior Mothers: Women Dramatists of the Black Arts Movement*. Evanston, IL: Northwestern University Press, 2018.

Foster, Hal. *The Return of the Real: The Avant-Garde at the End of the Century*. Cambridge, MA: MIT Press, 1996.

Foster, Susan Leigh. "Choreographies of Protest." *Theatre Journal* 55, no. 3 (2003): 395–412.

Foucault, Michel. *The History of Sexuality*, Vol. 1, *An Introduction*, translated by Robert Hurley. New York: Pantheon Books, 1978.

Freshwater, Helen. *Theatre Censorship in Britain: Silencing, Censure, and Suppression*. Houndmills, UK: Palgrave Macmillan, 2009.

Frost, Anthony. "Drama in the Age of *Kalyug*: *Behzti* and Sikh Self-Censorship." In *Alternatives Within the Mainstream: British Black and Asian Theatres*, ed. Dimple Godiwala, 203–25. Newcastle, UK: Cambridge Scholars Press, 2006.

Fukuyama, Francis. *After the End of History: Conversations with Francis Fukuyama*, ed. Mathilde Fasting. Washington, DC: Georgetown University Press, 2021.

Fukuyama, Francis. *Identity: The Demand for Dignity and the Politics of Resentment*. New York: Farrar, Straus, and Giroux, 2018.

Gardner, Lyn. "The Crazy Gang." *Guardian*, October 25, 2004, https://www.theguardian.com/stage/2004/oct/25/theatre

Garland-Thomson, Rosemarie. "Integrating Disability, Transforming Feminist Theory." In *Feminist Disability Theory*, ed. Kim Q. Hall, 13–47. Bloomington: Indiana University Press, 2011.

Gilbert, Jeremy. *Common Ground: Democracy and Collectivity in an Age of Individualism.* London: Pluto Press, 2014.

Gilroy, Paul. *Against Race: Imagining Political Culture beyond the Color Line.* Cambridge, MA: Belknap Press of Harvard University Press, 2000.

Gilroy, Paul. *The Black Atlantic: Modernity and Double Consciousness.* Cambridge, MA: Harvard University Press, 1993.

Goldberg, Michelle. "The Laura Kipnis Melodrama." *Nation*, March 16, 2015, https://www.thenation.com/article/archive/laura-kipnis-melodrama/

Gopal, Priyamvada. "Speaking with Difficulty: Feminism and Racism in Britain after 9/11." *Feminist Studies* 1 (2013): 98–118.

Greene, Alexis. *Theatre Week*, May 20, 1996: 54.

Green, Emma. "The Trouble with Wearing Turbans in America." *Atlantic*, January 27, 2015, https://www.theatlantic.com/politics/archive/2015/01/the-trouble-with-wearing-turbans-in-america/384832/

Green, Jesse. "*Straight White Men* Is Impressive (Not Oppressive)." Review of *Straight White Men*, by Young Jean Lee. *Vulture*, November 17, 2014, https://www.vulture.com/2014/11/theater-review-straight-white-men.html

Haidt, Jonathan. "Why the Past 10 Years of American Life Have Been Uniquely Stupid." *Atlantic*, April 11, 2022, https://www.theatlantic.com/magazine/archive/2022/05/social-media-democracy-trust-babel/629369/

Harding, James M. *Cutting Performances: Collage Events, Feminist Artists, and the American Avant-Garde.* Ann Arbor: University of Michigan Press, 2012.

Harris, Paul. "Exposed: Secret Plans to Start Race Riots." *Guardian*, September 2, 2001, https://www.theguardian.com/uk/2001/sep/02/race.world

Harvey, David. *A Brief History of Neoliberalism.* Oxford: Oxford University Press, 2005.

Hatch, Ryan Anthony. "First as Minstrelsy, Then as Farce: On the Spectacle of Race in the Theater of Young Jean Lee." *CR: The New Centennial Review* 13, no. 3 (2013): 89–114.

Hawkins, Stephen, Daniel Yudkin, Míriam Juan-Torres, and Tim Dixon. *Hidden Tribes: A Study of America's Polarized Landscape.* New York: More in Common, 2018.

Head of College's Office, https://pierson.yalecollege.yale.edu/people/head-colleges-office

Hemming, Sarah. "Blasted by Violence." Review of *Blasted*, by Sarah Kane. *Financial Times*, January 23, 1995, art section: 15.

Hennefeld, Maggie. "Editor's Introduction: Toward a Feminist Politics of Comedy and History." *Feminist Media Histories* 2 (2017): 1–14.

"Holy Offensive." *Dispatches*, Channel 4, February 28, 2005. DVD.

Homayounpour, Gohar. *Doing Psychoanalysis in Tehran.* Cambridge, MA: MIT Press, 2012.

"'Hottentot Venus' Goes Home." *BBC News*, April 29, 2002, http://news.bbc.co.uk/2/hi/europe/1957240.stm

Ind, Jo. "Perspective: A Little Understanding; Gopinder Kaur, Manpreet Kaur, Ranjit Kaur, Amarjit Kaur and Gursharan Kaur Feel that the Rep's Decision to Close *Behzti* Should Not be Seen as a Victory for Anybody." *Birmingham Post*, December 22, 2004: 8.

Institute for Social and Economic Research. "The Impact of the Recession on the UK's Ethnic Minority Groups." May 7, 2015, https://www.iser.essex.ac.uk/2015/05/07/the-impact-of-the-recession-on-the-uk-s-ethnic-minority-groups

Jackson, Shannon. *Professing Performance: Theatre in the Academy from Philology to Performativity*. Cambridge: Cambridge University Press, 2004.

Jakobsh, Doris R., and Eleanor Nesbitt. "Sikhism and Women: Contextualizing the Issue." Introduction to *Sikhism and Women: History, Texts, and Experience*, ed. Doris R. Jakobsh, 1–39. New Delhi: Oxford University Press, 2010.

Jannarone, Kimberly. *Artaud and His Doubles*. Ann Arbor: University of Michigan Press, 2012.

Jannarone, Kimberly. "Confederation and Control: Mass Gymnastics and the Czech and German Bodies Politic." *Theatre Journal* 71, no. 1 (2019): 1–27.

Jannarone, Kimberly, ed. *Vanguard Performance Beyond Left and Right*. Ann Arbor: University of Michigan Press, 2015.

Johnson, Odai. "Collision in the Coliseum: Mussolini, Modernism, and the Agon for Antiquity." In *Vanguard Performance Beyond Left and Right*, ed. Kimberly Jannarone, 129–44. Ann Arbor: University of Michigan Press, 2015.

Johung, Jennifer. "Figuring the 'Spells'/Spelling the Figures: Suzan-Lori Parks's 'Scene of Love (?).'" *Theatre Journal* 58, no. 1 (2006): 39–52.

Joseph, Artur, and E. B. Ashton. "Nauseated by Language: From an Interview with Peter Handke." *TDR* 15, no. 1 (1970): 56–61.

Joseph, Ralina. *Postracial Resistance: Black Women, Media, and the Uses of Strategic Ambiguity*. New York: New York University Press, 2018.

Kalb, Jonathan. "Remarks on Parks I: A Hunter College Symposium on the Work of Suzan-Lori Parks." In *Suzan-Lori Parks in Person: Interviews and Commentaries*, eds. Philip C. Kolin and Harvey Young, 151–74. New York: Routledge, 2014.

Kane, Sarah. *Blasted*. In *Sarah Kane: Complete Plays*, ed. David Greig, 1–61. London: Methuen Drama, 2001.

Kaplan, E. Ann. *Trauma Culture: The Politics of Terror and Loss in Media and Literature*. New Brunswick, NJ: Rutgers University Press, 2005.

Katherine, "Finding a First-Year Family," https://admissions.yale.edu/bulldogs-blogs/katherine/2018/11/13/finding-first-year-family

Keen, Suzanne. "Introduction: Narrative and Emotions." *Poetics Today* 32, no. 1 (2011): 1–53.

Kershaw, Baz. *The Radical in Performance: Between Brecht and Baudrillard*. London: Routledge, 1999.

Khan, Pervaiz. "Perspective: Do I Now Have to Worry about Offending?" *Birmingham Post*, December 23, 2004: 8.

Kipnis, Laura. "My Title IX Inquisition." *Chronicle of Higher Education*, May 2015, https://www.chronicle.com/article/my-title-ix-inquisition/

Klaić, Dragan. *The Plot of the Future: Utopia and Dystopia in Modern Drama*. Ann Arbor: University of Michigan Press, 1991.

Lauzen, Martha. "The Funny Business of Being Tina Fey: Constructing a (Feminist) Comedy Icon." *Feminist Media Studies* 11 (2014): 106–17.

Lee, Frances. "Excommunicate Me from the Church of Social Justice." *Autostraddle*, July 13, 2017, https://www.autostraddle.com/kin-aesthetics-excommunicate-me-from-the-church-of-social-justice-386640/

Left, Sarah. "Play Axed after Sikh Protest." *Guardian*, December 20, 2004, https://www.theguardian.com/uk/2004/dec/20/arts.religion1

Locke, Alain. "The Negro and the American Stage." In *The Works of Alain Locke*, ed. Charles Molesworth, 117–21. Oxford: Oxford University Press, 2012.

Locke, John. *Two Treatises of Government*, ed. Peter Laslett. Cambridge, UK: Cambridge University Press, 1960.

Lowe, Lisa. *The Intimacies of Four Continents*. Durham, NC: Duke University Press, 2015.

Lukianoff, Gregg, and Jonathan Haidt. "The Coddling of the American Mind." *Atlantic*, September 2015, https://www.theatlantic.com/magazine/archive/2015/09/the-coddling-of-the-american-mind/399356/

Lyotard, Jean-Francois. "From *Answering the Question: What Is Postmodernism?*" In *Postmodernism: A Reader*, ed. Patricia Waugh, 117–25. London: Edward Arnold, 1992.

Mahmood, Saba. *Politics of Piety: The Islamic Revival and the Feminist Subject*. Princeton: Princeton University Press, 2004.

Mahmood, Saba. "Religious Reason and Secular Affect: An Incommensurable Divide?" In *Is Critique Secular? Blasphemy, Injury, and Free Speech*, by Talal Asad, Wendy Brown, Judith P. Butler, and Saba Mahmood, 58–94. New York: Fordham University Press, 2013.

Makari, George. *Revolution in Mind: The Creation of Psychoanalysis*. New York: Harper Collins Publishers, 2008.

Malik, Sarita. Letter to the editor. *Guardian*, January 17, 2005, https://www.theguardian.com/world/2005/jan/18/religion.uk

Mann, Paul. *The Theory-Death of the Avant-Garde*. Bloomington: Indiana University Press, 1991.

Marks, Elise. "Othello/me: Racial Drag and the Pleasures of Boundary Crossing with *Othello*." *Comparative Drama* 35, no. 1 (2001): 101–23.

Marx, Karl. *Capital: A Critique of Political Economy*. Vol. 1, ed. Frederick Engels, translated by Samuel Moore and Edward Aveling. 1st English ed. Moscow: Progress Publishers, 1887. https://www.marxists.org/archive/marx/works/download/pdf/Capital-Volume-I.pdf

Mayer, Jane. *Dark Money: The Hidden History of the Billionaires Behind the Rise of the Radical Right*. New York: Doubleday, 2016.

McGuire, Michelle. "Forced Entertainment on Politics and Pleasure." *Variant* 2, no. 5 (1998): 11–13.

McKie, John. "Sarah Kane Vindicated by National Theatre Debut." Review of *Cleansed*, by Sarah Kane, directed by Katie Mitchell, Dorfman, National Theatre, London. *BBC News*, Feb. 24, 2016, https://www.bbc.com/news/entertainment-arts-35613160

McWhorther, John. "The Dehumanizing Condescension of White Fragility." *Atlantic*, July 15, 2020, https://www.theatlantic.com/ideas/archive/2020/07/dehumanizing-condescension-white-fragility/614146/

Medici, Anthony G. "The Restless Ghost of the New Criticism." Review of *The New Criticism and Contemporary Literary Theory: Connections and Continuities*, eds. William J. Spurlin and Michael Fisher. *Style* 31, no. 4 (1997): 760–73.

Merrill, Lisa. "Feminist Humor: Rebellious and Self-Affirming." *Women's Studies* 15 (1988): 271–80.

Mills, Charles W. *Black Rights/White Wrongs: The Critique of Racial Liberalism*. New York: Oxford University Press, 2017.

Mills, Charles W. *The Racial Contract* (Ithaca, NY: Cornell University Press, 1999).

Mitchell, Charles E. *Individualism and Its Discontents: Appropriations of Emerson, 1880–1950*. Amherst: University of Massachusetts Press, 1997.

Mookherdjee, Monica. "Permitting Dishonour: Culture, Gender, and Freedom of Expression." *Res Publica* 13 (2007): 29–52.

Nayar, Kamala Elizabeth. "Sikh Women in Vancouver: An Analysis of Their Psychosocial Issues." In *Sikhism and Women: History, Texts, and Experience*, ed. Doris R. Jakobsh, 252–75. New Delhi: Oxford University Press, 2010.

O'Kane, Karen. "Before the New Criticism: Modernism and the Nashville Group." *Mississippi Quarterly* 51, no. 4 (1998): 683–97.

Oldham Independent Review. Panel report. December 11, 2001, https://web.archive.org/web/20140315105508/http://resources.cohesioninstitute.org.uk/Publications/Documents/Document/DownloadDocumentsFile.aspx?recordId=97&file=PDFversion

"Open Letter to Associate Master Christakis," October 31, 2015, https://downatyale.com/open-letter-to-associate-master-christakis/

Parks, Suzan-Lori. *365 Days/365 Plays*. New York: Theatre Communications Group, 2006.

Parks, Suzan-Lori. *The America Play and Other Works*. New York: Theater Communications Group, 1995.

Parks, Suzan-Lori. "An Equation for Black People on Stage." In *The America Play and Other Works*, 19–22. New York: Theater Communications Group, 1995.

Parks, Suzan-Lori. "From Elements of Style." In *The America Play and Other Works*, 6–18. New York: Theater Communications Group, 1995.

Parks, Suzan-Lori. "Possession." In *The America Play and Other Works*, 3–5. New York: Theater Communications Group, 1995.

Parks, Suzan-Lori. *Venus*. New York: Theatre Communications Group, 1997.

Peacock, D. Keith. *Thatcher's Theatre: British Theatre and Drama in the Eighties*. Westport, CT: Greenwood Press, 1999.

Pew Research Center. "Modern Immigration Wave Brings 59 Million to U.S., Driving Population Growth and Change through 2065." *Pew Research Center*, September 28, 2015, https://www.pewresearch.org/hispanic/2015/09/28/modern-immigration-wave-brings-59-million-to-u-s-driving-population-growth-and-change-through-2065/#fn-22980-1

Phelan, Peggy. "Performing Questions, Producing Witnesses." Foreword to *Certain Fragments: Contemporary Performance and Forced Entertainment*, by Tim Etchells, 9–14. London: Routledge, 1999.

Pierce, Andrew J. "Whose Lives Matter? The Black Lives Matter Movement and the Contested Legacy of Philosophical Humanism." *Journal of Social Philosophy* 51, no. 2 (2020): 261–82.

Poggioli, Renato. *The Theory of the Avant-Garde*, translated by Gerald Fitzgerald. Cambridge, MA: Belknap Press of Harvard University Press, 1968.

Postlewait, Thomas. "Cultural Histories: The Case of Alfred Jarry's *Ubu roi*." In *The Cambridge Introduction to Theatre Historiography*, 60–85. Cambridge: Cambridge University Press, 2009.

Prior, Ian. "TV Pundit Ron Atkinson Sacked for Racist Remark." *Guardian*, April 22, 2004, https://www.theguardian.com/media/2004/apr/22/football.raceintheuk

Puchner, Martin. *Poetry of the Revolution: Marx, Manifestos, and the Avant-Gardes*. Princeton: Princeton University Press, 2005.

Qureshi, Sadia. "Displaying Sara Baartman, the Hottentot Venus." *History of Science* 42, no. 2 (June 2004): 233–57.

Rai, Jasdev Sing. "Behind *Behzti*." *Guardian*, January 17, 2005, February 20, 2007, https://www.theguardian.com/stage/2005/jan/17/theatre.religion

Rai, Jasdev Sing. "The Monologue of Western Liberalism and Its Imagination of the Sacred in Minority Cultures." In *Negotiating the Sacred II: Blasphemy and Sacrilege in the Arts*, eds. Elizabeth Burns Coleman and Maria Suzatte Fernandes-Dias, 105–26. Canberra: Australian National University Press, 2008.

Rancière, Jacques. *The Politics of Aesthetics: The Distribution of the Sensible*, ed. and translated by Gabriel Rockhill. London: Continuum, 2004.

Reinelt, Janelle. "Navigating Postfeminism: Writing Out of the Box." In *Feminist Futures? Theatre, Performance, Theory*, eds. Geraldine Harris and Elaine Aston, 17–33. London: Palgrave Macmillan, 2006.

Rodenbeck, Judith F. *Radical Prototypes: Allan Kaprow and the Invention of Happenings*. Cambridge, MA: MIT Press, 2011.

Rowe, Michael. *The Racialization of Disorder in Twentieth-Century Britain*. Aldershot, UK: Ashgate, 1998.

Salovey, Peter. "Decisions on Residential College Names and 'Master' Title." April 27, 2016, https://president.yale.edu/speeches-writings/statements/decisions-residential-college-names-and-master-title

Sanneh, Kelefa. "The Fight to Redefine Racism." *New Yorker*, August 12, 2019, https://www.newyorker.com/magazine/2019/08/19/the-fight-to-redefine-racism

"Sarah Kane." In *Rage and Reason: Women Playwrights on Playwriting*, eds. Heidi Stephenson and Natasha Langridge, 129–35. London: Bloomsbury, 2017.

Saunders, Graham. *"Love Me or Kill Me": Sarah Kane and the Theatre of Extremes*. Manchester, UK: Manchester University Press, 2002.

Savran, David. "Suzan-Lori Parks." In *Suzan-Lori Parks in Person*, eds. Philip Kolin and Harvey Young, 78–98. New York: Routledge, 2013.

Sedgwick, Eve Kosofsky. *Tendencies*. Durham, NC: Duke University Press, 1993.

Sell, Mike. *Avant-Garde Performance and the Limits of Criticism: Approaching the Living Theatre, Happenings/Fluxus, and the Black Arts Movement*. Ann Arbor: University of Michigan Press, 2005.

Sell, Mike. *The Avant-Garde: Race, Religion, War*. Calcutta, India: Seagull Books, 2011.

Sell, Mike. "Bohemianism, the Cultural Turn of the Avant-Garde, and Forgetting the Roma." *TDR* 51, no. 2 (2007): 41–59.

Sellar, Tom. "Making History, Suzan-Lori Parks, The Shape of the Past," interview with Suzan-Lori Parks, in *Suzan-Lori Parks in Person*, eds. Phillip C. Kolin and Harvey Young, 49–54. New York: Routledge, 2013.

Sellar, Tom. "Up Front." *Theater* 35, no. 2 (2005): 1–3.

The Shipment. Written and directed by Young Jean Lee. Performed by Prentice Onayemi, Mikéah Ernest Jennings, Okieriete Onodawan, Douglas Scott Streater, and Amelia Workman. Set design by Davis Evans Morris. Lighting design by Mark Barton. Costumes by Roxana Ramseur. Sound by Mathew Theirny. Choreography by Faye Driscoll. Performed and recorded at On The Boards Theatre, Seattle, October 2009, https://youngjeanlee.org/work/the-shipment/

Shklovsky, Viktor. "Art as Technique." In *Russian Formalist Criticism: Four Essays*, eds. and translated by Lee T. Lemon and Marion J. Reis, 3–24. Lincoln: University of Nebraska Press, 1965.

Sierz, Aleks. *In-Yer-Face Theatre: British Drama Today*. London: Faber and Faber, 2001.

Sinclair, Abiola. "Notes on 'Venus.'" Review of *Venus*, by Suzan-Lori Parks. *New York Amsterdam News*, May 4, 1996: 22.

Sinclair, Andrew. *Arts and Cultures: The History of the 50 Years of the Arts Council of Great Britain*. London: Sinclair-Stevenson, 1995.

Singh, Gurharpal. "British Multiculturalism and Sikhs." *Sikh Formations* 2 (2005): 157–73.

Singh, Gurharpal, and Darshan Singh Tatla. *Sikhs in Britain: The Making of a Community*. Phagwara, India: Ajanta, 2008.

Singh, Hardeep. "Sikh Lives Matter in Britain Too—Whether Sikh or Muslim, Racists Don't Discriminate." *Telegraph*, October 19, 2015, http://www.telegraph.co.uk/news/religion/11410809/Sikh-lives-matter-in-Britain-too-whether-Sikh-or-Muslim-racists-dont-discriminate.html

Singh, Neutral. "Statement by Sikh Groups on *Behzti*." December 17, 2004, https://www.sikhphilosophy.net/threads/statement-by-sikh-groups-on-behzti.1260/

Singh, Nikky-Guninder Kaur. *Sikhism: An Introduction*. London: I. B. Tauris, 2011.

Singh, Nikky-Guninder Kaur. "Why Did I Not Light the Fire? The Refeminization of Ritual in Sikhism." In *Sikhism and Women: History, Texts, and Experience*, ed. Doris R. Jakobsh, 205–33. New Delhi: Oxford University Press, 2010.

Smethurst, James Edward. *The Black Arts Movement: Literary Nationalism in the 1960s and 1970s*. Chapel Hill: University of North Carolina Press, 2005.

Smith, Adam. *The Theory of Moral Sentiments*, ed. Knut Haakonssen. Cambridge, UK: Cambridge University Press, 2004.

Snorton, C. Riley. *Black on Both Sides*. Minneapolis: University of Minnesota Press, 2017.

Sontag, Susan. "Happenings: An Art of Radical Juxtaposition" (1962), in *Against Interpretation and Other Essays*, 263–74. New York: Octagon Books, 1982.

Spencer, Charles. "Awful Shock." Review of *Blasted*, by Sarah Kane. *Daily Telegraph*, January 20, 1995.

Spillers, Hortense. "'All the Things You Could Be by Now, If Sigmund Freud's Wife Was Your Mother': Psychoanalysis and Race." *Boundary 2* 23, no. 3 (1996): 75–141.

Spillers, Hortense. "Formalism Comes to Harlem." *African American Review* 50, no. 4 (2017): 692–97.

[Stanislavsky] Станиславский, К. С. *Работа актера над собой: части I и II*. Москва: Государственое издательство „Изкуство," 1951.

Stanislavsky, Konstantin. *An Actor Prepares*, translated by Elizabeth Reynolds Hapgood. New York: Theatre Arts Books, 1948.

Stanislavsky, Konstantin. *Creating a Role*, translated by Elizabeth Reynolds Hapgood. New York: Theatre Arts Books, 1961.

Stanislavsky, Konstantin. *My Life in Art*. London: Taylor and Francis Group, 1987.

Stanley, Sandra Kumamoto. "Teaching the Politics of Identity in a Post-Identity Age: Anna Deavere Smith's Twilight." *Melus* 30, no. 2 (2005): 191–208.

Steele, Janet. "Shame in Birmingham." *Index on Censorship* 2 (2005): 121–23.

Stewart, Jacqueline. "Negroes Laughing at Themselves?" *Critical Inquiry* 29, no. 4 (2003): 650–77.

Stiles, Kristine. "Never Enough Is *Something Else*: Feminist Performance Art, Avant-Gardes, and Probity." In *Contours of the Theatrical Avant-Garde*, ed. James M. Harding, 239–89. Ann Arbor: University of Michigan Press, 2000.

Stixrud, William R., and Ned Johnson. *The Self-Driven Child: The Science and Sense of Giving Your Kids More Control over Their Lives*. New York: Viking, 2018.

Sweeney, Fionnghuala, and Kate Marsh, eds. *Afromodernisms: Paris, Harlem, and the Avant-Garde*. Edinburgh: Edinburgh University Press, 2013.

Taylor, Paul. "Courting Disaster." Review of *Blasted*, by Sarah Kane. *Independent*, January 20, 1995: 27.

Tinker, Jack. "Killer Thriller Shows *Blasted* How to Do It." *Daily Mail*, January 27, 1995: 47.

Tomlin, Liz. "Transgressing Boundaries: Postmodern Performance and the Tourist Trap." *TDR* 43, no. 2 (1999): 136–49.

Tripathi, Salil. "Drawing a Line." *Index on Censorship* 2 (2005): 162–66.

Urciuoli, Bonnie. "The Experience Experts." In *The Experience of Neoliberal Education*, ed. Bonnie Urciuoli, 144–70. New York: Berghahn Books, 2018.

Urciuoli, Bonnie, ed. "Introduction: Neoliberalizing Undergraduate Experience." In *The Experience of Neoliberal Education*, 1–16. New York: Berghahn Books, 2018.

Vega, Tanzina. "Students See Many Slights as Racial 'Microaggressions.'" *New York Times*, March 21, 2014, https://www.nytimes.com/2014/03/22/us/as-diversity-increases-slights-get-subtler-but-still-sting.html

Venters, Scott. "The (Im)mediate Animal: Interspecies Entanglements in Early Enlightenment Transactions." PhD dissertation. Seattle: University of Washington, 2021.

Venus, by Suzan-Lori Parks. Directed by Richard Foreman. Performed by Adina Porter, Mel Johnson Jr., Peter Francis James, and Sandra Shipley. Joseph Papp Public Theater. New York, May 9, 1996. Videocassette (VHS). Billy Rose Theatre collection. New York Public Library.

Vossen, Helen G. M., and Patti M. Valkenburg. "Do Social Media Foster or Curtail Adolescents' Empathy? A Longitudinal Study." *Computers in Human Behavior* 63 (October 2016): 118–24.

Washington Post. "Yale Students Confront Administrator over Halloween Email." Video. In "My Halloween Email Led to a Campus Storm—and a Troubling Lesson about Self-Censorship," by Erika Christakis. *Washington Post*, October 28, 2016, https://www.washingtonpost.com/opinions/my-halloween-email-led-to-a-campus-firestorm--and-a-troubling-lesson-about-self-censorship/2016/10/28/70e55732-9b97-11e6-a0ed-ab0774c1eaa5_story.html

Waters, Hazel. *Racism on the Victorian Stage*. Cambridge, UK: Cambridge University Press, 2007.

Watt, Nicholas, and Patrick Wintour. "How Immigration Came to Haunt Labour: The Inside Story." *Guardian*, March 24, 2015, https://www.theguardian.com/news/2015/mar/24/how-immigration-came-to-haunt-labour-inside-story

Weber, Carl. "Brecht's 'Street Scene'—On Broadway of All Places? A Conversation with Anna Deavere Smith." In *Brecht Then and Now. The Brecht Yearbook*. Vol. 20, ed. John Wilett, 50–64. Madison, WI: International Brecht Society, 1995.

Weisbusch, Robert. "Postcolonial Emerson and the Erasure of Europe." In *The Cambridge Companion to Ralph Waldo Emerson*, eds. Joel Porte and Sandra Morris, 192–217. Cambridge, UK: Cambridge University Press, 1999.

Weitz, Eric. *The Cambridge Introduction to Comedy*. New York: Cambridge University Press, 2009.

Weyeneth, Robert R. "The Architecture of Social Segregation: The Challenges of Preserving a Problematical Past." *Public Historian* 27, no. 4 (2005): 11–44.

White, Gillian B. "The Recession's Racial Slant." *Atlantic*, June 25, 2015, https://www.theatlantic.com/business/archive/2015/06/black-recession-housing-race/396725/

White, Khadija. "Black Lives on Campuses Matter: The Rise of the New Black Student Movement," *Soundings* 63 (2016): 86–97.

Woddis, Carole. "Taking a Blasting." Review of *Blasted*, by Sarah Kane. *Herald (Glasgow)*, January 24, 1995: 20.

Wolf, Stacy. "Disability's Invisibility in Joan Schenkar's *Signs of Life* and Heather McDonald's *An Almost Holy Picture*." In *Bodies in Commotion: Disability and Performance*, eds. Carrie Sandahl and Philip Auslander, 302–18. Ann Arbor: University of Michigan Press, 2005.

Woolf, Virginia. *Between the Acts*. London: Harcourt, 1970.

Woolf, Virginia. *A Room of One's Own*. New York: John Wiley & Sons, 2014.

Yale's "Goals of Spring-term First-year Advising," https://advising.yalecollege.yale.edu/advisers/spring-term-first-year-advisers/goals-spring-term-first-year-advising

"Yale University—Full Version—New Videos of the Halloween Email Protest, uploaded on September 20, 2016," https://www.youtube.com/watch?v=hiMVx2C5_Wg

Young, Jean. "The Re-Objectification and Re-Commodification of Saartjie Baartman in Suzan-Lori Parks's 'Venus.'" *African American Review* 31, no. 4 (1997): 699–708.

Young Jean Lee. *The Shipment*. In *The Shipment; LEAR*, 1–53. New York: Theatre Communications Group, 2010.

"Young Jean Lee Gets into the Minds of Straight White Men." Interview by Larissa FastHorse. *American Theatre*, March 24, 2015, https://www.americantheatre.org/2015/03/24/young-jean-lee-gets-into-the-minds-of-straight-white-men/

"Young Jean Lee, Playwright." Interview by John Del Signore, *Gothamist*, January 22, 2009, https://gothamist.com/arts-entertainment/young-jean-lee-playwright

Žižek, Slavoj. "Holding the Place." In *Contingency, Hegemony, Universality: Contemporary Dialogues on the Left*, by Judith Butler, Ernesto Laclau, and Slavoj Žižek, 308–29. London: Verso, 2000.

Index